Group Counseling

A Developmental Approach

George M. Gazda

Professor of Education
University of Georgia
and
Consulting Professor of Psychiatry
Medical College of Georgia

Allyn and Bacon, Inc.
Boston

To
My wife, Barbara, and my son, David

Printed in the United States of America
Library of Congress Catalog Card No. 73–141676

Contents

Preface

My purpose in writing this book is to provide the student of group counseling, the practitioner of group counseling, and the group counseling practicum supervisor a comprehensive guide for *group counseling* with *all* age levels. My experience as a practitioner, teacher, supervisor, and student of group counseling has convinced me that we must have a theory and a method of group counseling that is relevant to the identifiable age groups with which we work: the young child, the preadolescent, the adolescent, and the adult. Although there are theories and methods of group psychotherapy that have been developed for the treatment of all age groups, (and I have been influenced considerably by them) no one has heretofore made more than a cursory attempt to develop a theoretical rationale and methods for group counseling that are applicable to all age groups.

Even more important to me than my attempt through this text to fill the theoretical and methodological void in the field of group counseling, is my firm conviction that we in the helping professions must alert all those within the helping professions and those tangential to them, especially teachers and parents, to the fact that our most potent forms of treatment for serious personality and behavioral problems at best are minimally effective. We must, nevertheless, continue to do what we can through psychotherapy and related practices to alleviate human suffering, but henceforth *we must prevent* individuals, especially children, from becoming mental and emotional cripples.

To do this we must provide a form of *group guidance* that is applicable to the classroom setting and that focuses on the *prevention of problems*. I have defined group guidance as a cognitively oriented method of helping, applicable to large, classroom-size groups, in which information relative to a person's physical, emotional, social, educational, and vocational needs is provided. In this text I have indicated the relationship of

group guidance to group counseling and to group psychotherapy in the overall continuum of helping, and I have briefly outlined group guidance procedures which are prevention-oriented and which are applicable to young children, preadolescents, adolescents, and adults. However, it stands to reason, that we can be most preventive if we apply guidance procedures to the young child.

The needs of a child, preadolescent, adolescent, and adult can be related to his developmental stages of growth and the developmental tasks that confront him. How he copes with or fulfills the tasks is related directly to his level of adjustment and well-being. The developmental tasks with their appropriate coping behaviors serve as excellent guideposts or signals for all those who are responsible for facilitating growth and development. These tasks and the appropriate coping behaviors are summarized for each identifiable age group so that those who use this text can apply it in the course of prevention.

Group counseling is described as a preventive-remedial process. It is *preventive* if it is implemented at the first sign of inappropriate coping behaviors for given developmental tasks, and *remedial* to the extent that it is applied before a person has become debilitated to the extent that he has extreme difficulty functioning in society.

The developmental model provides a *comprehensive* approach for the application of group counseling and guidance. A rationale and methods for working with the child from age five through nine, the preadolescent from age nine through thirteen, and the adolescent and adult from thirteen through old age have been developed in Chapters three, four, and five respectively. Each of these chapters contains tables summarizing the developmental tasks and appropriate coping behaviors for the specific age group and appropriate group guidance procedures. The focus, however, for each of these three chapters is on group counseling with its rationale and methodology. In each chapter, also, I have used examples or protocols of group sessions to illustrate the elements which are interacting to produce change, my thesis being that all change must be explained through various principles of learning which are facilitated through the intervention of healthy human relationships. Essential to the success of the group counseling intervention are appropriate selection procedures and group composition, group size, media utilized, group setting, frequency and length of sessions, and duration of treatment. Each of these areas is treated extensively in each of these three chapters.

Chapter two is related to Chapters three, four, and five insofar as it provides an *overview* of the theoretical rationale and methodology. The conditions essential for a group counselor to facilitate growth in his counselees are developed around the core conditions of a helping relationship *a la* Carkhuff. The dynamics operative in a group, which must be understood and controlled are detailed in Chapter two under the topics of group leadership, structuring, ground rules, goal setting, norm setting, and stages of group development.

Chapter six which presents a model for Systematic Human Relations Training through small groups was written especially for this text by Dr.

Robert R. Carkhuff. This chapter was solicited and included in this text for two reasons. First, it appropriately serves my emphasis on prevention, because it is a method which can be used by group specialists to train people as helpers or facilitators. Parents, teachers, school administrators, and pupil personnel specialists, especially, could be converted from persons who may be harmful in their relationships, to persons who function effectively as helpers and facilitators as a result of systematic training in human relations. I highly recommend this model for use with groups where counseling is less acceptable such as with schoolteachers, groups of school administrators, and parent groups.

The second reason for including the Carkhuff chapter is that it provides the group counselor with a very useful method for a continuous evaluation of his level of functioning. It also gives the group counselor a system for building a relationship (facilitative base) and a means for appraising the counselee and/or group's readiness for more direct counselor intervention such as through confrontation.

The three remaining chapters of this text are included to complete the Gestalt. Chapter one traces the history and development of group counseling and guidance and shows the interrelationship among the contributing disciplines. In addition, definitions are given for group guidance, group counseling, and group psychotherapy.

Chapter seven includes a rather thorough survey of group counseling research from 1938 to 1970. The studies were critically analyzed and, based on this analysis, a summary of the research status of group counseling was given with recommendations for expanding and improving research in this speciality.

The final chapter on ethics and professional issues is built around a national survey of professionals practicing group work. It includes a summary of reported unethical practices/behavior and recommendations, gleaned from the survey and from my own experiences, for developing standards and a code of ethics for group practitioners to alleviate the problems.

I have delayed writing this book until through my own practice, participation in groups led by others, and through my study of the research and related professional literature, I felt that I had formulated a rationale and methodology that would be useful to others. To this end I have labored. Although I expect to change and to improve upon these efforts, I offer them for practice and evaluation.

G. M. Gazda

Acknowledgments

Innumerable persons and experiences have influenced me in what I have tried to present in this volume—too many to recall and recognize adequately. But to my teachers, my students and the many professionals whose writings have influenced me, I express my appreciation. To my wife and my son, my parents and my brothers who provided me the warmth of human nourishment, to my teachers who shared their knowledge with me and stimulated me, to my students who challenged me and supported me, and to the many professionals who shared their knowledge and experiences with me through their writing, I am deeply grateful.

The immediate details that directly involve the production of a book are prodigious and without the direct assistance of others I would not have been able to produce this manuscript. First, I wish to thank Dr. Carkhuff for the contribution of Chapter six and Appendix C to this text and for the other influences that his works have had on my professional development. My thanks goes to Dr. Richard Jones for his contribution of Appendix B, an action maze. I thank Dr. Joe Sisson for his efforts in tracing references for me. To my graduate students who, during the fall and winter quarters of 1969–70 served as my critics, I express my appreciation. Dr. Jack Duncan has once more provided me with yeoman's service by editing the manuscript for which I am deeply grateful.

With all the help that I have already cited, the manuscript could not have materialized had not my wife, Barbara, typed and assembled it managing all the while to support me in my writing efforts. And then there is David my son, who patiently endured his father's need to attend to the manuscript and yet by his very existence served as an inspiration to begin the manuscript and to complete it. To my wife, Barbara, and to my son, David, I dedicate this book.

Group Counseling

A Developmental Approach

1 | Group Counseling and Group Guidance

Origins, Definitions, and Significant Contributors

Origins

Group Guidance

Group guidance is probably as old as the guidance movement itself. The guidance movement began essentially as *vocational guidance* when Frank Parsons founded the Vocations Bureau of Boston in 1908 (Brewer, 1942). Just when, where, and by whom the word *group* was added to the word *guidance* is not known; however, according to Brewer (1942), Charles L. Jacobs of San Jose, California was one of the first to suggest a wider use of the term guidance when, in the October, 1915 issue of *Manual Training and Vocational Education* he stated that his work included three departments—educational guidance, vocational guidance, and avocational guidance.

Vocational Guidance

According to Glanz and Hayes, "As early as 1907, Jesse B. Davis, principal of the Cedar Rapids High School in Iowa, devoted weekly periods in English classes to 'Vocational and Moral Guidance,' and George Boyden in 1912 introduced a course in vocations at the Beauport, Connecticut, high school. So 'group guidance' was "born" (1967, p. 3). Glanz and Hayes caution that these first "group guidance" courses were instructional groups and the techniques

used were instructional and devoid, for the most part, of systematic use of group dynamics principles and techniques.

Classes in Occupational Information

As early as 1908, William A. Wheatley was instrumental in introducing a course in occupational information for freshman boys at the Westport, Connecticut high school. Similar courses were offered in Boston and New York City soon after Wheatley's course (Brewer, 1942). The movement continued to grow until, according to Glanz and Hayes, "The 1930's became the era of the group guidance class, where units on character, vocation, and citizenship were prominent. Hardly a city junior high or high school was without such a program, and the guidance literature of the era was saturated with texts on 'group guidance' " (1967, p. 3).

Homeroom

In 1934 McKown authored a text, *Home Room Guidance.* The content of the text and the fact that McKown proposed the director of guidance as the director of homeroom guidance suggest its close association to group guidance and counseling. In fact, some schools referred to the homeroom as "the 'guidance hour' or 'guidance room' " (McKown, 1934, p. 53). R. Strang (1935) cited the contribution of the homeroom teacher as being fourfold: "to establish friendly relationships, to discover the abilities and needs, and to develop right attitudes toward school, home, and community" (p. 116). Here again the group guidance and counseling "flavor" was evident in the work of the homeroom teacher.

Extracurricular Activities

C. R. Foster authored a book, *Extra-Curricular Activities,* in 1925 in which he recognized guidance as an extracurricular activity. In the same text, Foster also urged the counselor to "hold many group conferences with the students on the subject of future educational or vocational plans" (p. 182). Pittsburgh schools were cited by Foster as including instructional guidance taking "the form of tenth grade group conferences which were held for the purpose of discussing Pittsburgh's industrial life and the opportunities it affords the young people" (1925, p. 183).

Group Dynamics

The group dynamics movement, under the leadership of Kurt Lewin, began to influence education in the 1930's and early 1940's.

At this time the group or vocational guidance movement was affected by the application of group dynamics principles to the group guidance classes. At this point also group guidance was heavily vocational and students were "taught" how to make career or vocational decisions. Those teachers and the few school counselors available in the 1930's and 1940's who were responsible for group guidance tried to instruct the group guidance classes as they would any other academic class. Some students were even given grades in group guidance. Where these procedures were employed, group guidance failed. However, where teachers and school counselors were influenced by the group dynamics movement and applied the principles and techniques to group guidance classes, the classes were more successful. Unfortunately for group guidance, too few teachers and counselors were acquainted with group dynamics, and consequently the 1950's saw a decline in the enthusiasm of school administrators toward group guidance.

CONCLUSIONS. Group guidance is almost synonymous with "guidance" in general. Guidance got its start with Parson's Vocations Bureau of Boston in 1908, although one can point to isolated guidance practices which antedate 1908. When "group" was added to "guidance" is not precisely known, but it is likely that it occurred on several fronts at the same time—probably before 1915. Glanz and Hayes (1967) suggest that it was during the period 1907–1912.

Vocational guidance, homeroom guidance, classes in occupational information, certain extracurricular activities, and the group dynamics movement all influenced group guidance. In turn, the group guidance movement, along with several other related movements, contributed significantly to the evolution and emergence of group counseling.

Group Counseling

The origin of the term *group counseling* is also somewhat obscured. Its historical antecedent was most likely group guidance or case conference. In other words, much like its counterpart, group psychotherapy, group counseling in its inception was very likely a class method similar to what is referred to today as group guidance. One of the earliest appearances in print in the United States of the term *group counseling* appears to have been in 1931. Dr. Richard D. Allen (1931), in an article titled "A Group Guidance Curriculum in the Senior High School" published in *Education,* used group counseling in the following context:

> Group thinking and the case-conference method *usually take the place of the recitation. . . . Problems of educational and vocational guidance require teachers who are specially selected and trained for the work, who understand problems of individual differences and are continually studying them. These teachers require continuous contacts with the same pupils for several years, a knowledge of occupations and occupational problems, and special training in methods of individual and group counseling.*
>
> *All of these considerations draw attention to the class counselor as the logical teacher of the new unit. There is much similarity between the techniques of individual guidance and group guidance. When the counselor finds by individual interviews that certain problems are common to most of the pupils, such problems become units in the group guidance courses. The class discussions of these problems should reduce the length and number of individual interviews with a saving of considerable time and expense. In fact, the separation of group counseling from individual counseling would seem very short-sighted.*
>
> *If the above principle prevails, the next serious problem concerns its practical application in the time schedule of the school. Ideally, such a course should be extensive rather than* intensive *in its nature, in order to accomplish its objectives effectively. Its purpose is to arouse interests in current educational, vocational and social problems, to develop social attitudes, and to build up a back-ground of occupational information. Such objectives require considerable* time extended *over several years (p. 190).*[1]

This lengthy quotation demonstrates that what Allen described as group counseling in 1931 is today generally referred to as group guidance. Also, it should be noted that Allen used the terms *case-conference, group guidance,* and *group counseling* interchangeably.

Although Allen's use of *group counseling* appeared in print in 1931, it is quite possible that he had used the expression before 1931. For example, Brewer (1937), writing the Introduction to Allen's *Organization and Supervision of Guidance in Public Education,* published in 1937, wrote, "For more than a decade his colleagues in the Harvard Summer School have urged Dr. Allen to put his ideas into permanent form" (p. xxi).

---

[1] From Allen, R. D. A group guidance curriculum in the senior high school. *Education,* 1931, *52,* 189–194. Reprinted from the October, 1931, issue of *Education,* by permission of the publishers, the Bobbs-Merrill Company, Inc.

Jones, in 1934, in his second edition of *Principles of Guidance,* stated, "It [group guidance] is a term that has come into use chiefly through the excellent work of Richard T. [D.] Allen in Providence, R.I. It includes all those forms of guidance activities that are undertaken in groups or in classes" (1934, p. 284). Jones (1934, p. 291) also refers to the "Boston Plan for Group Counseling in Intermediate Schools" and cites the source as two circulars developed by the Committee on Guidance of the Boston Public Schools: Boston Public Schools, Guidance-Educational and Vocational, A Tentative Plan for Group Counseling, Board of Superintendents' Circular No. 2, 1928–1929 and Board of Superintendents' Circular No. 17, 1928–1929, First Supplement to Board of Superintendents' Circular No. 2 Boston: Printing Department, 1929. Although group counseling is used in the title of the Boston publication, the description of the nature of the process described by Jones places it squarely in the realm of group guidance and not group counseling as it is defined today.

In his fifth edition of *Principles of Guidance,* published in 1963, Jones had this to say about Allen's case conference procedures: "A technique that combined the techniques of counseling in groups and group counseling was used by Allen and practiced in the public schools of Providence, Rhode Island more than twenty-five years ago" (1963, pp. 218–219). Jones believed that the purpose of the case conference was to provide the counselor with a means for students to discuss their personal and social relationships. The general approach was to use common problems of group members as the basis for discussion. A case was presented to the group to illustrate the problem, and each student was expected to compare his own experiences with those revealed through the case. The leader encouraged the group to seek the "more permanent values" exposed rather than the more "immediate temporary" ones, and he also encouraged the participants to consider the effect upon others of their proposed action. Conclusions were summarized to formulate generalizations for other situations. Jones stated that Allen believed his method worked best when "each case represented a common, usual, or typical situation that concerned most of the group. The case should in-involve persons and personal or social relations" (Jones, 1963, p. 219).

According to Jones, Allen characterized the case conference leader as one who never expressed approval or disapproval of any opinion or attitude and never stated opinions of his own. In addition, the leader was impartial and open-minded and encouraged

the expression of all points of view; he would occasionally restate and summarize the group thinking, and organize the group so that it was large enough to guarantee a diversity of opinions, but not so large as to prevent each member the opportunity to enter into discussion.

The goals and procedures of Allen's case conference approach are similar to those of contemporary group counselors. However, most contemporary group counselors do not structure their groups around specific cases.

Although Allen may have been the first person to introduce the term group counseling, he is not recognized by contemporary group counselors as having significantly influenced the group guidance or counseling movement. It was not until about ten years after World War II that group counseling, per se, received much of an impetus. It was during this era that group guidance, group dynamics and group therapy had begun their rapid rise in popularity and group counseling seemed to be an outgrowth of these disciplines.

There were few if any textbooks devoted primarily to group counseling as such before Driver's (1958) *Counseling and Learning through Small Group Discussion.* The group guidance specialists such as Bennett, Warters, Ohlsen, and Froehlich had written chapters on group counseling which were part of their texts in group guidance and general guidance in the mid-fifties and early sixties. In 1961 Lifton's *Working with Groups* was the most comprehensive effort to apply client-centered counseling to group work and at the same time Mahler and Caldwell (1961) produced a booklet *Group Counseling in Secondary Schools.*

Historically, as group guidance seemed to lose its impetus in the late 50's and early 60's, group counseling took its place, especially within educational institutions, as a potential source for bringing about behavioral change. Whereas in the 1950's there were no popular complete texts on group counseling, the late 1960's saw the emergence of several, e.g., Lifton's (1966) second edition of *Working With Groups,* Muro and Freeman's (1968) *Readings in Group Counseling,* MacLennan and Felsenfeld's (1968) *Group Counseling and Psychotherapy with Adolescents,* Mahler's (1969) *Group Counseling in the Schools,* and Gazda's (1969) *Theories and Methods of Group Counseling in the Schools.* In the first year of the 1970's two group counseling texts were published: Ohlsen's (1970) *Group Counseling,* and Kemp's (1970) *Foundations of Group Counseling.* With the current keen interest in group counseling, a considerable expansion of practice, research, and writing can be

predicted. Instead of group guidance influencing group counseling as it once did, the direction has been reversed and the rampant group counseling movement seems to be effecting a rebirth of interest and activity in group guidance, especially at the elementary school level.

Definitions| Group Guidance, Group Counseling, and Group Psychotherapy

Group Guidance

Group guidance is organized to prevent the development of problems (see Figure 1.1). The content includes educational–vocational–personal–social information which is not otherwise systematically taught in academic courses. The typical setting is the classroom which ranges in size from approximately 20 to 35. Providing accurate information for use in improved understanding of self and others is the direct emphasis in group guidance, whereas attitude-change frequently is an indirect outcome or goal. The leadership is provided by a classroom teacher or a counselor who utilizes a variety of instructional media and group dynamics concepts in motivating students and in obtaining group interaction. Instructional media include unfinished stories, puppet plays, movies, films, filmstrips, guest speakers, audio and video-taped interviews, student reports, and the like. Group dynamics concepts refer to the process employed in group guidance, such as sociodramas, buzz groups, panels, and other related techniques. (A more complete description of group guidance can be found in Gazda and Folds (1968), *Group Guidance: A Critical Incidents Approach*.)

Group Counseling

Whereas the goal of group guidance is to provide students with accurate information which will help them make more appropriate plans and life decisions and, in this sense is prevention-oriented, group counseling is both prevention- and remediation-oriented (see Figure 1.1). Group counseling is prevention-oriented in the sense that the counselee or client is capable of functioning in society, but may be experiencing some 'rough spots' in his life. If counseling is successful, the rough spots may be resolved successfully with no serious personality defects incurred.

Group counseling is remedial for those individuals who have entered into a spiral of self-defeating behavior but who are, never-

theless, capable of reversing the spiral without counseling intervention. However, with counseling intervention, the counselee is likely to recover more quickly and with fewer emotional scars.

Group counseling is defined as follows:

> *Group counseling is a dynamic interpersonal process focusing on conscious thought and behavior and involving the therapy functions of permissiveness, orientation to reality, catharsis, and mutual trust, caring, understanding, acceptance, and support. The therapy functions are created and nurtured in a small group through the sharing of personal concerns with one's peers and the counselor(s). The group counselees are basically normal individuals with various concerns which are not debilitating to the extent requiring extensive personality change. The group counselees may utilize the group interaction to increase understanding and acceptance of values and goals and to learn and/ or unlearn certain attitudes and behaviors (Gazda, Duncan, & Meadows, 1967, p. 305).*

Although the content of group counseling is very similar to group guidance—including educational, vocational, personal, and social concerns—a number of other factors are quite different. First, *group guidance* is recommended for *all* school students on a regularly scheduled basis; *group counseling* is recommended only for those who are experiencing continuing or temporary problems that information alone will not resolve. Secondly, group guidance makes an *indirect* attempt to change attitudes and behaviors through accurate information or an emphasis on cognitive or intellective functioning; group counseling makes a *direct* attempt to modify attitudes and behaviors by emphasizing affective involvement. Finally, group guidance is applicable to classroom-size groups, whereas group counseling is dependent upon the development of strong group cohesiveness and the sharing of personal concerns which are most applicable to small, intimate groups.

Group Psychotherapy

Group psychotherapy, the third part of the guidance, counseling, therapy continuum, was coined by J. L. Moreno in 1936 (Corsini, 1957). Moreno's definition is a general definition: "Group psychotherapy means simply to treat people in groups" (Moreno, 1962, p. 263). It is generally accepted that there is a difference in group counseling and group psychotherapy although there is overlap between them. Brammer and Shostrom have characterized these

differences by the following series of adjectives in which counseling is described as

> *educational, supportive, situational, problem-solving, conscious awareness, emphasis on "normals," and short-term. Psychotherapy is characterized by supportive (in a more particular sense), reconstructive, depth analysis, analytical, focus on the unconscious, emphasis on 'neurotics' or other severe emotional problems, and long-term (1960, p. 6).*

Although these differentiations were applied to individual counseling and psychotherapy, they are equally applicable to group counseling and group psychotherapy.

Figure 1.1 shows the relationships among group guidance, group counseling, and group psychotherapy.

FIGURE 1.1

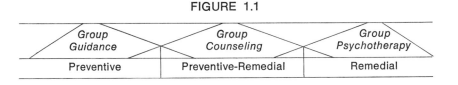

Group Guidance	Group Counseling	Group Psychotherapy
Preventive	Preventive-Remedial	Remedial

Disciplines Contributing to Group Counseling

The previous reference to R. D. Allen's use of the term group counseling suggests that Allen may have coined the expression; however, I do not contend that I have discovered the missing link. More likely than not, other individuals were also using the term in Allen's era.

Other related movements which have contributed to the group counseling movement must also be considered in attempting to trace its historical development. The most significant of these contributing movements were group guidance (previously described), group psychotherapy, child guidance, social casework, group work, group dynamics, and human potential.

Group Psychotherapy

Corsini (1957) has referred to group psychotherapy as "a conglomerate of methods and theories having diverse multiple origins in the past, resulting inevitably from social demands, and developed in various forms by many persons" (p. 9). On the other hand, J. L.

Moreno (1966) contends that group psychotherapy has its roots in medicine, sociology, and religion. However, if we accept July 1, 1905 (Hadden, 1955), the date that J. H. Pratt introduced his "class method," as the beginning of group psychotherapy, rather than some ancient ritual such as Mesmer's group treatment through suggestion, the history of group psychotherapy covers a mere 65 years.

The term *group therapy* was introduced by J. L. Moreno in 1931 (Z. Moreno, 1966), and *group psychotherapy* was introduced, also by J. L. Moreno, in 1932 (Corsini, 1957). For the most part, group therapy and group psychotherapy are used synonymously in current discourse. Specifically group therapy has become the shortened or colloquial version of group psychotherapy.

Even though the term group psychotherapy was not coined until 1932 by J. L. Moreno, an emigrant to America, there is considerable evidence that group psychotherapy is an American invention and that various forms were being practiced in the United States, mostly by psychiatrists and ministers, long before Moreno coined the term. Group therapy was coined by Moreno about the same time as the expression *group counseling* was used in the literature by R. D. Allen; however, there is every reason to believe that Allen's use of group counseling was more closely related to group *instruction* than was the meaning that Moreno intended when he coined group therapy and group psychotherapy.

Numerous systems of group psychotherapy were described in the professional literature well in advance of the appearance of group counseling professional literature, which is still quite meager. It is recognized, therefore, that group psychotherapy, as practiced and as described in the literature, provided much of the theoretical rationale for the emergence of group counseling. Just how much credit the group psychotherapy movement should receive for the emergence and development of group counseling is uncertain, but I believe it to be considerable, probably the most significant of the several disciplines or movements contributing to its emergence and growth.

Child Guidance

The possibility exists that group counseling originated in Europe. Dreikurs and Corsini (1954) contend that between 1900 and 1930 major steps were being made in Europe toward a systematic use of the group method called "collective counceling" (sic). They be-

lieve that Alfred Adler, in his child guidance clinic in Vienna, was likely the first psychiatrist to use *collective counseling* formally and systematically.

Ansbacher and Ansbacher (1956) translated many of Adler's works, and in their commentary on his writing, they stated, "Although Adler himself never practiced group therapy, he suggested its use for the treatment of criminals" (p. 347). It is not because of his suggestion for using group therapy with criminals that Adler is considered by some to be the father of the movement, but rather because of his application of group techniques in his child guidance clinics. According to the Ansbachers, Adler was conducting group procedures—perhaps collective counseling—as early as 1922.

The rationale and methods employed by Adler and his followers are described by Ansbacher and Ansbacher (1956). However, the Ansbachers, because they were unable to find "more than a mere mention" of Adler's rationale and methods in his own writings, were forced to turn to secondary sources, i.e., the writings of Seidler and Zilat, and Rayner and Holub. Seidler and Zilat described the "public" character of Adlerian child guidance clinics in which the child was interviewed in the presence of an adult audience. Doris Rayner defends this form of treatment by stating that the child benefits because he comes to view his difficulty as a "community problem," and his audience (parents) receive an education in parent-child behavior.

In 1942 Brewer described the child guidance movement "as yet largely dissociated from the work of the schools . . ." (p. 263). Nevertheless, because of its many similarities, the child guidance movement *may* have influenced, directly or indirectly, and/or have been somewhat akin to the group counseling movement.

Social Casework

In reviewing the history of the Marriage Council of Philadelphia, Gaskill and Mudd (1950) stated that group counseling and family life education had been part of the "Marriage Council's service from the agency's inception in 1932" (p. 194). Whether or not the term *group counseling* itself was actually used by the Council as early as 1932 and whether or not the treatment was similar to current group counseling is not indicated. However, Gaskill and Mudd (1950) gave the following definition of group counseling which they attributed to Hazel Froscher, Margery Klein, and Helen Phillips:

> ... a dynamic relationship between a counselor and the members of a group, involving presentation and discussion of subjects about which the counselor has special knowledge, which is of general or specific concern to the group, and around which emotions may be brought out and attitudes developed or changed. The relationship between the group members themselves and the counselor's use of this is essentially important in the total process (1950, p. 195).[2]

The definition implies that the counselor gives a presentation and encourages discussion of it. Gaskill and Mudd (1950), in their description of the group counseling session, indicated that the group ranged between 35 and 50 persons in size, and they further described the group session as a *course* including speakers other than the group counselor. This approach to group counseling seems more closely related to group guidance or a family living class rather than the typical small, eight- to ten-member counseling groups where leader-imposed content is absent or minimal.

Group Work

Sullivan (1952) described a group in the following manner:

> ... The group must be a small stable one which feels itself as an entity and which the individual can feel close identification. Membership ... is voluntary. There is a group leader, who is consciously making constructive use of the process of personality interaction among the members. The leader utilizes the desire of a normal person to be accepted by his fellows. He establishes the dignity of the individual and teaches acceptance of differences in race, creed, and nationality. Group work stresses programs evolved by the group itself, in consultation with the leader who guides toward socially desirable ends. Creative activities are encouraged to provide legitimate channels of self-expressions and to relieve emotional stress. Competition for its own sake is minimized and group members learn from situations where cooperation brings rich satisfaction. The trained leader arranges for leadership practice by group members; individual responsibility and group responsibility grow as the group takes on new functions. The atmosphere is friendly, informal, and democratic (p. 189).[3]

[2]From Gaskill, E., & Mudd, E. A decade of group counseling. *Social Casework*, 1950, *31*, 194–201. Reproduced with permission of Family Service Association of America.
[3]From Sullivan, D. F. Let X = Group Work. *The Group*, 1944, 2 (2). Reprinted with permission of the National Association of Social Workers.

Since this description of group work contains many of the ingredients that are present in definitions of group counseling, the possible influence on group counseling of the group work specialists becomes readily apparent.

Group Dynamics

Bonner (1959) has outlined the development of the group dynamics movement as beginning in the late 1800's, notably in Europe, and including contributions from sociology, psychology, philosophy, and education—but primarily contributions came from sociology and psychology. Bonner is cautious not to credit a single individual or a single discipline for the origin of group dynamics; however, Kurt Lewin and J. L. Moreno are cited for making significant, yet differing contributions to the discipline during its contemporary phase of development—the 1930's to the present.

Although the National Training Laboratory (NTL) was established in Bethel, Maine in 1946, "it was not until the middle to late 1950's before the tools and techniques of group dynamics really found their way into education and more specifically, into guidance" (Glanz & Hayes, 1967, p. 4). As late as 1964, Durkin, after a careful survey of group dynamicists and group therapists, wrote:

> *In spite of the general impression to the contrary, there was almost no therapy actually being conducted on solely group dynamic principles by group dynamicists. From private correspondence with some of the leading social scientists, I learned that they did not acknowledge group dynamics therapy as an identifiable approach and that they were meticulous in distinguishing between their work and group therapy (p. 4).*

The statement by Glanz and Hayes suggests that group dynamics principles and concepts only very recently have begun to affect the field of group *guidance*. And Durkin stressed the point that, although group dynamics had begun to affect the field of group therapy as late as 1964, there was still no complete theory of group dynamics being applied to group therapy.

In 1966, I began to assemble a book, *Innovations to Group Psychotherapy,* and was able to secure a contribution from some group dynamicists, Jack and Lorraine Gibb, of a theory of group dynamics applied to group therapy. They referred to their theory as Emergence Therapy: The TORI Process in an Emergent Group. This theory really represents a leaderless approach to group therapy as well as to small and large groups in general.

The application of group dynamics principles to group *counseling* has a very recent history. The formulations can be found in the writings of Bonney (1969), Fullmer (1969), Mahler (1969), Ohlsen (1966), and in this text.

Human Potential Movement

The Human Potential Movement is a very recent (middle and early 1960's) movement. It has multiple and diverse origins, but is probably most closely related to the efforts of Humanistic psychologists, e.g., Carl Rogers, Abraham Maslow, Jack Gibb, and William Schutz. In its more practical emphasis, features of the Movement are being adapted to classroom instruction and, in that sense, are group guidance-oriented; in the highly experimental and perhaps even ethically questionable forms of group application, it is affecting group counseling by introducing more body contact and more structured game playing.

Conclusions

The tracing of the development of group counseling suggests that it is a hybrid. Perhaps that is why it has always been difficult to arrive at a definition for it that is satisfactory to group counseling theorists and practitioners. Those who were most influenced by group guidance also reflect a vocational guidance orientation and prefer a leader-centered and topic-centered approach with an emphasis on educational and vocational counseling. They also prefer a definition which reflects these elements.

Those group counseling theorists and practitioners, on the other hand, who have been significantly influenced by the discipline of group psychotherapy, tend to emphasize the rehabilitative or adjustive (personal-social) qualities of the process. In addition, they tend to utilize less structure as leader and focus on the uniqueness of the individual problems brought to the group rather than "group" problems, per se.

There are those group counseling theorists and practitioners who have come from a background of study and/or practice in the group dynamics movement. For these practitioners the group themes or goals are developed, emphasized, and dealt with. The process which the group follows and the nature of leadership are of considerable interest to this type of practitioner. Often he prac-

tices leaderless, i.e., defaulted leadership and also, of late, literally leaderless groups or instrumented group procedures.

The group counselors who have evolved from the group work and social casework disciplines frequently bring to their groups a combination of group dynamics emphasis with a psychoanalytic orientation. The psychoanalytic orientation reflects their social work training.

Child guidance-oriented group counselors reflect an Adlerian theoretical influence. As such, they tend to concentrate on family counseling, working especially with elementary school children, their parents, and their teachers. They also tend to be leader-centered and, as such, oriented toward advisement.

The Human Potential Movement is the most recent movement to affect group counseling and it may prove to have the most profound effect on the group counseling movement. The heavy emphasis on body contact and non-verbal "games" introduces experimental processes that have high potential for helping or harming. They have not been experimentally validated and the theoretical underpinnings are all but absent at the moment. Nevertheless, there are those practitioners of this very broad and inclusive movement who emphasize positive verbal-reinforcement techniques and de-emphasize responding to or recognizing negative behavior. This subgroup of the Human Potential Movement seems to be the most theoretically sound subgroup and may offer means for improving group counseling techniques as well as extend the practices to other settings such as the classroom. The current emphasis on body contact in small group work, including group counseling, seems to offer the greatest threat to the professional respectability of group counseling.

Significant Contributors

For one to attempt to cite some of the most significant contributors to the speciality of group counseling while living in the era of the beginning of the movement is to court professional suicide; nevertheless, an attempt will be made to sketch briefly my perception of those who have been and, in most instances, are still making significant contributions to the group counseling movement. Included also are citations of some of the more significant contributions to the field of group guidance. I concluded that the leaders of the group counseling movement are residing in the United States, and this assumption seems supported by Brewer (1942). If this

conclusion is erroneous, it might at least stimulate others to investigate and challenge it.

The credit for coining the term group counseling may be attributed to Richard D. Allen, although there is no absolute proof of this. (The term group guidance has no single originator, at least, none that I could locate.) Others who were among the first to publish and teach in the field of group counseling *and* group guidance were Margaret Bennett, Ruth Strang, and Jane Warters. More recent contributors to the *group guidance* literature are Gilbert Wrenn, Edward Glanz, Donald Peters, Jonell Folds Kirby and G. M. Gazda.

Evelyn Gaskill and Emily Mudd should be cited for their early use of group counseling in social casework; Hanna Grunwald for the current application of group counseling in casework agencies; Gisela Konopka for her many years of training group workers in the field of social work; and Joseph Knowles for his successful application of the group approach to pastoral counseling.

Clifford Froehlich and Helen Driver influenced the group counseling movement with their introduction of multiple counseling, and E. Wayne Wright, upon the death of Froehlich, has become one of the leading proponents for the multiple counseling emphasis of the movement.

Merle Ohlsen, Fred Proff, and several of their colleagues and students at the University of Illinois, the author among them, are known for their early attempts to research group counseling. Ben Cohn, who was influenced by Ohlsen, and his associates of the Board of Cooperative Educational Services of Bedford Hills, New York, researched the effects of group counseling on acting-out adolescents. Stanley Caplan did research with similar groups.

Norman Kagan is also adding new information to the field through his recent research efforts, as is Charles Truax, Robert Carkhuff and associates. Clarence Mahler and Edson Caldwell co-authored one of the first texts on group counseling in the schools, and Mahler has since authored a second group counseling book.

Among those representing the various schools of group counseling are Walter Lifton, Thomas Gordon, and Nicholas Hobbs—three of the most prominent proponents of the client-centered approach to group counseling. Rudolf Dreikurs, Manford Sonstegard, Donald Dinkmeyer, Oscar Christensen and G. Edward Stormer are among the most significant Adlerian-oriented contributors to the field of group counseling, while John Krumboltz, Barbara Varenhorst, and Carl E. Thoresen are making their place with a behavior-oriented application of group counseling. Warren

Bonney and his students have pioneered in the application of group dynamics principles and concepts to group counseling, and Betty Berzon has championed self-directed and instrumented or programmed counseling groups and studied group process and climate.

Dan Fullmer and Harold Bernard have introduced to the field Family Group Consultation. Jack Blakeman and Sherman Day have described an activity group counseling approach for use with preadolescents and adolescents.

Dwight Arnold, G. Edward Stormer, C. G. Kemp, and I have developed an "interest group" among the American Personnel and Guidance Association members for the purpose of defining the field, sharing information on training programs, and establishing communication among practitioners to provide some form of organization to the loose-knit movement.

Douglas Abbott has spearheaded a similar interest group within the American School Counselor's Association. In an attempt to establish the present status of the movement and to arrive at a definition of group counseling, my former students Jack Duncan and Eugene Meadows and I surveyed recent contributors to the field of group counseling. The results have been published in *Counselor Education and Supervision,* Summer, 1967.

Even as this chapter is being written, significant contributions are being made by persons unknown to me and because of the explosion of interest in the field of group procedures and group counseling and as a result of the publication lag, many persons will be well-established in this speciality whose names will not appear in this chapter on its publication date.

Summary

This chapter traces the history of the development of group counseling and guidance by attempting to establish the persons who were responsible for coining the terms and the related disciplines contributing to their growth and development.

The related disciplines found to have contributed to the evolution and development of group counseling include group guidance, group psychotherapy, child guidance, social casework, group work, group dynamics, and the Human Potential Movement. These disciplines and the manner in which they have most likely influenced group counseling are systematically described. The disciplines contributing to group guidance also are cited.

Group counseling and group guidance are defined as well as contrasted with other related group procedures. In addition a paradigm for group guidance, group counseling, and group psychotherapy is outlined.

This chapter closes with an enumeration of some of the more prominent contributors to group counseling and group guidance. Included is a brief description of the nature of their contribution.

References

ALLEN, R. D. A group guidance curriculum in the senior high school. *Education,* 1931, *52,* 189–194.

ANSBACHER, H. L. & ANSBACHER, R. R. (Eds.) *The individual psychology of Alfred Adler.* New York: Basic Books, 1956.

BONNER, H. *Group dynamics.* New York: Ronald Press, 1959.

BONNEY, W. C. Group counseling and developmental processes. In G. M. Gazda (Ed.), *Theories and methods of group counseling in the schools.* Springfield, Ill.: Charles C. Thomas, 1969. Pp. 157–180.

BRAMMER, L. M. & SHOSTROM, E. L. *Therapeutic psychology.* Englewood Cliffs, New Jersey: Prentice-Hall, 1960.

BREWER, J. M. Introduction. In R. D. Allen (Ed.), *Organization and supervision of guidance in public education.* New York: Inor, 1937. Pp. xxi–xxii.

BREWER, J. M. *History of vocational guidance.* New York: Harper, 1942.

CORSINI, R. J. *Methods of group psychotherapy.* Chicago: William James Press, 1957.

DREIKURS, R., & CORSINI, R. J. Twenty years of group psychotherapy. *American Journal of Psychiatry,* 1954, *110,* 567–575.

DRIVER, H. I. *Counseling and learning through small-group discussion.* Madison, Wisc.: Monona Publications, 1958.

DURKIN, H. E. *The group in depth.* New York: International Universities Press, 1964.

FOSTER, C. R. *Extra-curricular activities in high school.* Richmond, Va.: Johnson, 1925.

FULLMER, D. W. Family group consultation. In G. M. Gazda (Ed.), *Theories and methods of group counseling in the schools.* Springfield, Ill.: Charles C. Thomas, 1969. Pp. 181–208.

GASKILL, E. R., & MUDD, E. H. A decade of group counseling. *Social Casework,* 1950, *31,* 194–201.

GAZDA, G. M. (Ed.) *Innovations to group psychotherapy.* Springfield, Ill.: Charles C. Thomas, 1968.

GAZDA, G. M. (Ed.) *Theories and methods of group counseling in the schools.* Springfield, Ill.: Charles C. Thomas, 1969.

GAZDA, G. M., DUNCAN, J. A., & MEADOWS, M. E. Group counseling and group procedures—Report of a survey. *Counselor Education and Supervision,* 1967, *6,* 305–310.

GAZDA, G. M., & FOLDS, J. H. *Group guidance: A critical incidents approach.* Chicago: Parkinson Div., Follett Educational Corporation, 1968.

GLANZ, E. C., & HAYES. *Groups in guidance.* (2nd ed.) Boston: Allyn & Bacon, 1967.

HADDEN, S. B. Historic background of group psychotherapy. *International Journal of Group Psychotherapy,* 1955, *5,* 162–168.

JONES, A. J. *Principles of guidance.* (2nd ed.) New York: McGraw-Hill, 1934.

JONES, A. J. *Principles of guidance.* (5th ed.) New York: McGraw-Hill, 1963.

KEMP, C. G. *Foundations of group counseling.* New York: McGraw-Hill, 1970.
LIFTON, W. M. *Working with groups.* New York: Wiley, 1961.
LIFTON, W. M. *Working with groups.* (2nd ed.) New York: Wiley, 1966.
MacLENNAN, B. W., & FELSENFELD, N. *Group counseling and psychotherapy with adolescents.* New York: Columbia University Press, 1968.
MAHLER, C. A. *Group counseling in the schools.* Boston: Houghton-Mifflin, 1969.
MAHLER, C. A., & CALDWELL, E. *Group counseling in secondary schools.* Chicago: Science Research Associates, 1961.
McKOWN, H. C. *Home room guidance.* New York: McGraw-Hill, 1934.
MORENO, J. L. Common ground for all group psychotherapists. What is a group psychotherapist? *Group Psychotherapy.* 1962, *15,* 263–264.
MORENO, J. L. (Ed.) *The international handbook of group psychotherapy.* New York: Philosophical Library, 1966.
MORENO, Z. T. Evolution and dynamics of the group psychotherapy movement. In J. L. Moreno (Ed.), *The international handbook of group psychotherapy.* New York: Philosophical Library, 1966. Pp. 27–125.
MURO, J. J., & FREEMAN, S. L. *Readings in group counseling.* Scranton, Pa.: International Textbook Co., 1968.
OHLSEN, M. M. Adapting principles of group dynamics for group counseling. *School Counselor.* 1966, *33,* 159–161.
OHLSEN, M. M. *Group counseling.* New York: Holt, Rinehart and Winston, 1970.
STRANG, R. *The role of the teacher in personnel work.* New York: Bureau of Publications, Teachers College, Columbia University, 1935.
SULLIVAN, D. F. (Ed.) *Readings in group work.* New York: Association Press, 1952.

Suggested Readings

ALLEN, R. D. A group guidance curriculum in the senior high school. *Education.* 1931, *52,* 189–194.
BONNER, H. *Group dynamics.* New York: Ronald Press, 1959.
CORSINI, R. J. *Methods of group psychotherapy.* Chicago: William James Press, 1957.
DREIKURS, R., & CORSINI, R. J. Twenty years of group psychotherapy. *American Journal of Psychiatry,* 1954, *110,* 567–575.
DURKIN, H. *The group in depth.* New York: International Universities Press, 1964.
HADDEN, S. B. Historic background of group psychotherapy. *International Journal of Group Psychotherapy,* 1955, *5,* 162–168.
MORENO, J. L. (Ed.) *The international handbook of group psychotherapy.* New York: Philosophical Library, 1966.
MORENO, Z. T. Evolution and dynamics of the group psychotherapy movement. In J. L. Moreno (Ed.), *The international handbook of group psychotherapy.* New York: Philosophical Library, 1966. Pp. 27–125.

2 | Theoretical Rationale

an Overview

Introduction

This chapter is intended to provide the reader with an overview of the general theory and rationale applicable to all age levels dealt with in this text. *Specific development tasks and coping behaviors appropriate for a given age group, plus details for counselee selection, and group composition, preferred size, location, and media utilized are described in each chapter devoted to a given age group. Also detailed in each chapter which is devoted to a specific age group are special leadership approaches and management of group process.*

Originally I planned to write a text on *group counseling* which presented a complete, or at least relatively complete, treatment of the application of group counseling to all age groups likely to be encountered in educational settings. However, two significant events influenced me also to undertake the task of presenting a method for initiating group guidance and illustrating how it can be used conjointly with group counseling.

The first event was a personal encounter with Dr. William Glasser which convinced me that he is on the right track in teaching teachers and administrators in the elementary schools to emphasize *success* experiences for young children through, among

others, a system of group (class) meetings which are oriented toward helping children achieve an identity of worthwhileness rather than one of failure and worthlessness. Details of how Dr. Glasser accomplishes this are outlined in his *Schools Without Failure.* In essence, he states that educators (namely teachers) must maximize success experiences for the young child especially but also for all students of all ages. Success experiences are maximized through the use of regular class meetings (a kind of group guidance or human relations class) in which students are taught to help each other solve problems which might interfere with success experiences of any and all children in the class. The sessions are problem-solving oriented and, in that sense, are similar to group counseling. The point to be made for these sessions, however, is that they are geared toward increasing cooperative experiences and the development of mutual love and respect and toward minimizing intra-group hostilities as well as competition or "grade seeking." In fact, Glasser (1969b) makes a strong case for the abolishment of letter grades in our educational system.

I concur with Glasser (1969a) that we in the helping professions shall never be able to "patch up" all the individuals who are suffering from experiences of failure which lead them to delinquency or mental illness or both. Thus our educational programs, especially the pupil personnel programs, must become increasingly oriented toward *prevention* rather than remediation. As I have defined group guidance and group counseling in Chapter one, both are aimed at prevention of personal-emotional problems—group guidance in particular. That is why I believe there must be a *rebirth* of group guidance or a substitute group movement such as "human relations" classes in the junior and senior high schools and a massive new program implemented in the preschool and elementary schools and in colleges and universities. Counselors must take the lead and work through school administrators and curriculum specialists to find a place in the curriculum for group guidance or human relations training and/or courses of study. In this text, I attempt to outline the conjunctive application of group guidance and group counseling in educational settings. A detailed group guidance program for junior and senior high schools is presented in *Group Guidance: A Critical Incidents Approach* (Gazda & Folds. 1968).

The second significant event which influenced the direction which I have taken in this text was the result of personal encounters with Dr. Robert Carkhuff and his method of Systematic Human Relations Training. Carkhuff (1969a, b) has outlined an approach

to training lay and professional helpers that is especially adaptable for use in training teachers and other school personnel and even students themselves to be group helpers or facilitators. In other words, Carkhuff provides a rationale and a systematic method to train teachers and others to serve the cause of prevention by functioning so as to produce the conditions for success experiences which Glasser reminds us should be the essence of public education.

Counselors and pupil personnel workers, as human relations specialists in educational settings, must take the leadership in training teachers and those who must serve as their intermediaries, as group guidance specialists and group facilitators (functional professionals). In order for counselors to become trainers they first must become trained as group facilitators in programs such as described by Carkhuff in Chapter six of this text.

Nature of Man

Two significant human conditions, especially, have influenced my philosophy of "helping" through the use of group counseling. First, and perhaps foremost, is my belief (stemming primarily from my religious convictions) that man is endowed with *free will* and thus has the capacity to make choices which may be for "good or evil." I believe further that some individuals because of their conditions of birth have a very limited sphere within which they can exercise their free will, whereas others, because of more favorable conditions of birth, have a much larger sphere within which they can exercise their free will. For example, the fatherless ghetto child may be hard pressed to survive and the degree to which he may exercise his free will is centered around his survival needs, whereas the child born of wealthy parents may exercise his free will on higher order needs and thus have an extended range within which he can utilize his free will.

The counselor or helper *a la* Carkhuff (1970) (whether in the group setting or individually) can assist a person seeking help to expand his repertoire of responses, i.e., learn new means to understand and to problem-solve and thus extend his sphere of free-will choices. This view of helping pervades my eclectic position outlined in this text. Whatever means a person uses to modify his attitudes and/or behavior, however, can usually be explained by some principle of learning. No single principle of learning holds the answer to all problems or behavioral conditions requiring

modification; therefore the counselor who intends to help a wide range of individuals must have a wide range of experiences and a thorough knowledge of the several means for helping through counseling.

Group counseling, of course, represents only one means for helping but it is a potent means because man is basically a gregarious animal who prefers to interact in small, close groups. This fact represents the second human condition which has influenced me and because of this I have proposed group counseling as the preferred mode of treatment for many individuals. By no means, however, am I proposing that there is no place for individual counseling. One can make just as strong a case for individual counseling as he can for group counseling. The research literature tends to show that a combination of group and individual counseling is the most potent form of treatment.

Man seeks to adjust to certain of his own conditions and to certain conditions of his environment. He also seeks to expand or improve his physical and mental properties just as he modifies his environment. In order to help man both adjust to as well as modify or expand himself and his environment when appropriate, the counselor has to be both flexible enough and possess the skills to recognize when the counselee is seeking somwhat limited and specific behavioral changes versus those occasions when he is struggling with the meaning of life or of his existence. In some respects the "adjustment" emphasis could be a part of the remedial focus of group counseling and the existential emphasis could be synonymous with the preventive focus (*cf* Chapter one).

A Developmental Approach

Heretofore, no systematic attempt has been made to provide an approach to *group counseling* and *guidance* which was applicable to all age levels. Previous attempts have 'singled out' methods of group counseling with children, with adolescents, *or* with adults. Slavson (1945), however, long ago recognized the need for differential treatment for different age groups in *group therapy.* "Group therapy," he said, "is practiced on different levels, and in discussing its functions in therapy, it is necessary that these levels be kept in mind" (p. 201).

My experience also has demonstrated the need for a position which allows for and accommodates a different emphasis with different age groups in group counseling and guidance. The devel-

opmental approach to group counseling and guidance, therefore, utilizes the developmenal task concept (Havighurst, 1948, 1952, 1953) with subsequent coping behaviors, to serve as broad guidelines for the group counselor and group guidance leader. Havighurst defines developmental task as follows:

> A developmental task is a task which arises at or about a certain period in the life of the individual, successful achievement of which leads to his happiness and to success with later tasks, while failure leads to unhappiness in the individual, disapproval by society, and difficulty with later tasks (1952, p. 2).

Havighurst (1952) also cites two reasons the concept of developmental task is useful to educators. His reasons seem equally applicable to counselors and guidance and counseling: "First, it helps in discovering and stating the purpose of education [group counseling and guidance] in the schools.... The second use of the concept is in the timing of educational [group counseling and guidance] efforts" (p. 5). He describes timing to mean teachable moment (1952, p. 5). Readiness for group guidance is determined by the developmental level of the individual and his corresponding need system, whereas readiness for group counseling is determined by the dissonance between the developmental task and its subsequent coping behavior.

Zaccaria (1965) gives a more comprehensive interpretation of developmental tasks than does Havighurst. His interpretation includes Havighurst's (1952) "bio-socio-psychological" emphasis, the "vocational developmental" emphasis of Super, et al. (1957, 1963), and Erikson's (1950, 1959, 1963) "psychosocial crises." Since Zaccaria's description of the developmental tasks concept is more inclusive than Havighurst's, I have utilized all three approaches in developing the guidelines for use by the counselor in assessing an individual's progress along his developmental pathways. Difficulty with the mastery of a developmental stage signals to the parent, teacher, counselor, and significant others that assistance or corrective action is necessary. Group counseling through the approach I have outlined in this text will help provide this assistance.

The developmental tasks or stages also serve as guideposts for the kinds of guidance information that the student requires at a given time. (For the convenience of the reader, Chapters three, four, and five contain charts of the developmental tasks with their corresponding appropriate coping behaviors.) If the group guidance leader will acquaint himself with these "guideposts," he will be in a position to provide accurate and timely information to the

student so that it assists the student to master successfully a given developmental task and thus truly serves the cause of prevention—the chief function of group guidance.

Our society and much of western culture is organized on the basis of an expected progressive development in the biological, sociological, and psychological realms of its citizens and, as such, the concept of developmental task has general applicability. For example, our schools are organized on a preschool and kindergarten, early elementary school, middle school, and high school basis; state laws govern marriageable ages of its citizens; federal laws govern legal retirement age; and so forth (Muuss, 1962).

Although there are wide ranges in the biological, social, and psychological development of individuals, there are classifiable periods between and within age groups. Several individuals (Blocher, 1966; Brammer & Shostrom, 1960; Erikson, 1950; Havighurst, 1952; Super, et al., 1957, 1963) have developed various classification schemes for the developmental phases. For group counseling and guidance purposes, the phases can be divided into (1) early childhood or preschool and early school, ages 5–9; (2) preadolescent, ages 9–13; (3) adolescent, ages 13–20; and (4) adult. That there is sometimes considerable overlap between age groups, is well documented. There is also a special discrepancy between the sexes at the end of the latency period and beginning of pubescence—beginning between ages 8–13 for girls and 10–15 for boys. The group counselor, therefore, must be alert to individual differences and organize his groups to accommodate them. Since "Little is known as to what the values of a group to a child of 3 or 4 may be" (Slavson, 1945, p. 203), the emphasis of my approach begins with the kindergarten child of age five.

Systematic Human Relations Training, *a la* Carkhuff (1969a, b), provides a theoretically and empirically sound method for training those professionals, e.g., teachers, who are not technically included among the "helping" professionals. When combined with the rationale and methodology of Developmental Group Counseling, it makes possible the training of "functional professionals" (Carkuff, 1970). Now this combined application of Carkhuff's Systematic Human Relations Training with Developmental Group Counseling is of vital importance because it makes possible the extension of Developmental Group Counseling through *functional professionals* (i.e., persons who do not have the paper credentials—certificates, degrees, or licenses—but who are in the fact capable of serving as facilitators or helpers) to the culturally different, the educationally deficient and even the mentally retarded.

The typical group counselor today is a middle-class WASP. He will be unable in many instances to transcend the racial, cultural, ethnic, economic, etc., barriers between himself and many who desperately need counseling assistance. Thus he must extend his role of group counselor to group trainer also (see Chapter six). In this role he can be prepared to be guided by the basic tenets of Developmental Group Counseling and Systematic Human Relations Training. For example, he will very often be alien, if not alienated, to the Black Community as a whole. Nevertheless, there will be those within the Black Community who could serve as functional professionals to reach those beyond the reach of a middle-class WASP. Somewhat analogous to AA and Synanon, volunteers from within a given cultural, or problem area (e.g., the Black Community, alienated youth, etc.,) must be given training to function as facilitators or helpers.

The expressed effort to go through others who are capable of reaching and assisting the culturally different, etc., is an example of "reaching" them by moving through media (persons, in this case) which are most "natural" to them whether or not their problem or potential problem is the result of inadequate coping behavior for a given developmental task or an alienated feeling towards those of different color, age-group, or economic condition.

In addition to stressing the necessity of reaching others through "functional professionals," the Developmental model described herein focuses on the need to utilize activities and media which are most natural to a given group—especially age group, *but also* ethnic, socio-economic, etc., group. Therefore, the potential group leader must be flexible enough and skilled enough to substitute an active sport or game such as basketball for a chess game for ghetto youth if he expects to approach or "reach" them through *activities* that are natural/comfortable for them.

Dynamics of Groups

Leadership

Counselor's Ability to Help

Recently Truax (1969) reported that one-third of trained professionals functioning in roles purported to be "helping" such as psychiatrists, counselors, social workers, etc., did in fact help their clients or persons seeking help from them; one-third actually harmed their clients; and one-third had no measurable positive or negative

effect. And he concluded that the more helpers we train with our old methods the farther behind we are getting. Further evidence to corroborate Truax's conclusion is presented in Truax and Carkhuff (1967), Carkhuff and Berenson (1967), and Carkhuff (1969a, b).

Essentially, the conclusion has been reached that traditional methods of preparing professionals in the field of human relations have not been at all effective and that considerably more care should be shown in certifying professional helpers. Carkhuff(1969a) has outlined the most comprehensive method to date for the selection and training of both lay and professional helpers. His conclusion, based on a vast amount of research (Berenson & Carkhuff, 1967; Carkhuff, 1969a, 1969b; Carkhuff & Berenson, 1967; Truax & Carkhuff, 1967; Rogers, Gendlin, Kiesler & Truax, 1967) suggests that the effective counselor or helper must offer high levels of the facilitative or "core" conditions of *empathy, warmth,* and *respect* as well as the more action- and activity-oriented conditions of *concreteness, genuineness,* appropriate *self-disclosure, confrontation,* and *immediacy* (Carkhuff, 1969a, p. 21).

In an earlier reference, Truax and Carkhuff (1967, p. 1) described the effective counselor as integrated, nondefensive, and authentic or *genuine* in his therapeutic encounter. They also described him as one who provides a non-threatening, safe, trusting, or secure atmosphere by his acceptance, unconditional positive regard, love or *nonpossessive warmth* for the client. And finally, he is able to "be with," "grasp the meaning of," or *accurately and empathically* understand the client on a moment-by-moment basis.

Perhaps most important from the several reports of research cited above is the concurrence that the counselor must first demonstrate that he is a healthy human being who has proven that he possesses the qualities described by Truax and Carkhuff (1967) and Carkhuff (1969a) and that his counselees or "helpees" *a la* Carkhuff (1969a), do in fact improve their behavior as a result of the help he provides them. Details for determining one's level as a helper are described in Carkhuff (1969a). It behooves every prospective helper to determine his level of functioning and, if it is not a facilitative level, to raise it or discontinue his role as a "helper."

Goldstein, Heller, and Sechrest (1966, Ch. 8) reviewed the research pertaining to the orientation of group psychotherapists and its effect on clients. They concluded that there was a major need to research the group therapist's orientation from a perspective which also considered the interacting influence of stage of

therapy, patient and therapist personality and behavioral characteristics, therapist and patient goals, and other related variables.

Leader Orientation

The qualities of a group counselor who is likely to be helpful were
outlined above. At this point emphasis will be placed on relating
the effects of his interaction to what happens in a counseling
group. Once more we need to turn to the group dynamics research
for direction. Goldstein, et al. (1966), following a review of research
in both group psychotherapy and group dynamics, concluded that
the research

> ... pointedly provides basic evidence for the prediction of more
> favorable patient response to a leader-centered versus a group-
> centered therapist orientation in the early stages of group
> psychotherapy. ... However, in spite of its less favorable early
> effects, there is a considerable body of group dynamics research
> suggesting that the group-centered approach is very likely to
> result in patient behavior much more highly related to a favor-
> able therapeutic outcome than would be the case if an essenti-
> ally leader-centered approach persisted beyond the first 10 to
> 20 therapy sessions (p. 377).[1]

The findings reported by Goldstein et al., are based to a considerable extent on patient expectancies of group leadership. In
this regard they found:

> In sum, these diverse studies focusing on leadership expect-
> ancies in psychotherapy and other settings appear to converge
> in the general conclusion that the more discrepant the expect-
> ancies, the less the attraction to the group, the less the satis-
> faction of group members, and the more the strain or negative
> affect between leader and led or therapist or patient (p. 375).[2]

If one can conclude that patients seeking group psychotherapy or,
similarly, counselees seeking group counseling will approach the
experience expecting direction and assistance from the leader, a
rule of thumb to follow would be for the group counselor to be more
active in the early group sessions and to move gradually from a
leader-centered approach to a group-centered approach as counseling proceeds. This practice should reduce counselee initial

[1,2]From Goldstein, A. P., Heller, K., & Sechrest, L. B. *Psychotherapy and
the psychology of behavior change.* New York: John Wiley & Sons, Inc.
1966. Reproduced by permission.

hostility, increase receptiveness, and provide the best overall plan for building a therapeutic climate.

This rule-of-thumb procedure is congruent with the model described by Carkhuff (1969a), the model which seems to have the greatest support for application to group counseling. Carkhuff, in describing guidelines for the communications of empathy (a prerequisite for developing a facilitative base), stated that especially at the beginning of helping the helper would find that by increasing his verbal responsiveness, he would not only provide a model for an increasingly active helpee but he would also serve to increase the probability of accuracy in communication.

In the beginning of a counseling group, the counselor is actively trying to build the facilitative base of mutual trust and caring through the utilization of interchangeable responses which incorporate the core conditions of empathy, warmth, and respect. As the counselees develop this base, they will provide cues that indicate they wish to explore their problems beyond the initial depth to a greater depth. The group counselor assists the counselees to move toward a greater depth of exploration which, in turn, leads to greater understanding and eventual positive action through the application of the more action-oriented core conditions of genuineness, appropriate self-disclosure, concreteness, confrontation, and immediacy (Carkhuff, 1969a).

STRUCTURING. Structuring refers to the counselor's orientation of group members. Research results support the use of the following procedures:

1| Be positive in building expectancy states. Group members should be told that (a) they most likely will like and be liked by other members of the group (Schachter, Ellertson, McBride, & Gregory, 1960); and (b) the group was set up to consist of individuals who share similar opinions and values (Festinger, Schachter, & Back, 1950).

2| Stress the hard work that will be involved in the group counseling process. This should increase the effort expended by counselees (Cohen, 1959; Yaryan & Festinger, 1961; Zimbardo, 1960).

3| Stress the careful screening that went into selection of the group members. (This procedure should increase the attractiveness of the group to the counselees—see research reviewed by Goldstein, et al, 1966, pp. 344–348.)

4| Define the norm of the group as different from the usual social norm: that is, that it is appropriate and beneficial to discuss one's personal concerns in the counseling group. Reinforcement of this new norm should make the transition to self-disclosure and revelation of one's problems more acceptable to group members (Bonney & Foley, 1963).

GOAL SETTING. Several studies have shown that clarity of group goals and means of achieving them increase the group's attraction for members, generate greater group cohesiveness, and reduce intra-group hostility. Is group cohesiveness, however, desired in group counseling? Truax (1961) studied the effects of cohesiveness in therapy groups and made the following observation:

> These results indicate that cohesion, long a central concept in the analysis of small group behavior, is also of importance in the analysis of group psychotherapy: successful group psychotherapy groups are cohesive. . . . These findings . . . point to a variable unique to the group setting and one which is susceptible to external manipulation (p. 16).

A counselee's purpose for seeking help or goal setting should be verbalized in initial interviews before he enters a group; however, he is encouraged to repeat these in the first session of the group. Therefore, to increase the possibility of goal achievement through group counseling, the counselor should encourage the counselees to verbalize their goals as specifically and concretely as they can in the beginning and to increase their specificity as clarity occurs through the counseling experience.

Berne (1966) has referred to goal setting as the therapist-patient contract. He considers the contract to exist between the therapist and the institution which employs him and between the therapist and patient. Therefore, the patient should know the therapist's institutional obligations which may impinge on the patient's goals. For example, if the counselor has an obligation to report use of drugs by counselees, the counselee should know this and thus not place himself in jeopardy. Berne (1966) also cautions that the contract between therapist and patient may need to be amended from time to time as determinants underlying symptoms or responses are made more explicit. The same opportunity for goal modification should be applied to group counselees.

Occasions arise wherein subgroups develop within a counseling group and frequently they begin to compete with each other to the point of creating severe friction within the total group. This

situation usually calls for reconstituting the group or instituting a superordinate goal such as the counselor's introducing a legitimate threat to the total group which is sufficient to bring together the warring factions in a total group effort to counteract the outside threat. The threat might be impending loss of a meeting place, the revocation of institutional time for group counseling, or some other administrative threat to the group's existence.

NORM SETTING. The concept of norm setting has particular relevance to group counseling in that it is equivalent to what is expected and/or allowable in the group. The norm may be either explicit or implicit, but in either case the group members know what they are permitted to do with its subsequent rewards and what they are forbidden to do with its subsequent punishments.

Included in the setting of group norms, of course, is the group counselor. He is active both in assisting the group develop the norms and is himself being influenced by the group with respect to the role or roles he will be expected to follow within the group. The counselor's actions are especially significant in determining group norms in the first few sessions. His own modeling such as responding empathically and showing warmth and respect to all members, supporting shy members, etc., can go a long way toward setting the climate for the group. That is, when the group is most in need of leadership early in its Exploratory Stage, the counselor has perhaps the greatest opportunity to influence its direction. Bonney (1969) contends that the leader

> should assume an active though not highly directive part in the formation of the group's norms. Ideally the setting of norms should emanate from the group itself. . . . The eventual accept-ance of a group norm should . . . be left to the consensus of the group and not forced by the leader, particularly in the early stages of the group's development (p. 167).

Stages of Group Development

A number of group therapists and group counselors (Bach, 1954; Bonney, 1969; Gendlin & Beebe, 1968; Mahler, 1969) have identi-fied stages or phases through which counseling and therapy groups purportedly pass, ranging from three phases (Gendlin & Beebe, 1968) to seven (Bach, 1954). The stages through which counseling groups progress are most clearly visible in closed groups, i.e., groups which retain the same membership throughout the duration

of the group's existence. In open groups or groups which add new members as old members terminate and especially when the influx of new members is frequent, the stage development is affected and, as Gendlin & Beebe (1968) have noted, the old members reach a Tired Phase because of the constant necessity of the old members assisting the new members through the Breaking Through Phase— the phase during which the member experiences an explosive freeing and growth process. With open groups, then, it is incumbent upon the counselor to know the potential effect of too rapid a turnover in an ongoing group. It is necessary to protect the Sustaining Phase (Gendlin & Beebe, 1968) or work phase of the core members of a group and to prevent them from reaching the Tired Phase.

Hill (1961, 1963, 1965) has developed an Interaction Matrix which is based on a hypothesis that therapy groups proceed along two dimensions of *content* and *work* and through approximately 16-20 cells or levels of interaction. The Hill model has many of the same elements which were included in the model developed by Carkhuff (1969a). The Carkhuff model, described under Leadership in this chapter and further elaborated by Carkhuff himself in Chapter six, emphasizes the necessity of building a facilitative base through high level expressions of empathy, respect, and warmth in the early phases of developing sound relationships. Building a facilitative base is prerequisite to the implementation of the action-oriented dimensions at later stages in helping relationships. The action-oriented dimensions are geared to changing behavior. The facilitative-action oriented dimensions include genuineness, specificity or concreteness of expression, and appropriate self-disclosure by the leader, whereas the action-oriented dimensions include the leader behavior just cited plus *appropriate* confrontation and immediacy or 'telling it like it is' between leader and helpees in the here-and-now.

The amount, the kind, and the timing of counselor intervention in groups, therefore, is related to the stage or phase of a group's development. It cannot be independent of the stage, however, since the group is influenced by counselor behavior and vice versa. It has been my experience that counseling groups go through four rather definite stages: (1) Exploratory Stage; (2) Transition Stage; (3) Action Stage; and (4) Termination Stage. These four stages are named similarly by others. For example, Bonney (1969) refers to the Exploratory Stage as the Establishment Stage and Mahler (1969) calls it the Involvement Stage. Both Bonney and Mahler have a second or Transition Stage. The Action Stage can be equated to

Mahler's Working Stage. The fourth or Termination Stage is equivalent to Mahler's Ending Stage.

Exploratory Stage

During this stage the group members introduce themselves and describe the goals that each hopes to achieve. They also agree on some basic ground rules. Following the initial session the counselees usually engage in social and superficial discussions about themselves each parrying with the other to present himself in an acceptable fashion. This is the kind of activity in which members assign to each other what Hollander (1964) has called "idiosyncratic credits." Bonney (1969) has referred to this as the "process by which the group, consciously and unconsciously, assigns power and influence, in varying degrees to each member of the group" (p. 166). It is also a means of establishing various roles that each person will first assume in the group. Hidden agendas also begin to emerge and the group begins to establish norms which will eventually become the unofficial but controlling ground rules.

It is especially important that the group counselor be actively helpful during the Exploratory Stage. He shows his helpfulness by clarifying goals for the group and the group means for achieving them, by telling the group something about himself and, most importantly, by modeling the facilitative dimensions of empathy, respect, warmth, and genuineness. In the Carkhuff (1969 a) sense, he gives consistently minimally facilitative or better responses, i.e., he consistently gives responses to each counselee that are *interchangeable* with those of the counselee—interchangeable especially with respect to the affect expressed by the counselee and also to the content or message expressed. It is during this initial or Exploratory Stage that a facilitative base of mutual trust and caring is built. Without this, the group fails to reach the next stage in its development.

Transition Stage

The Transition Stage occurs at a point when one or more counselees begin to self-disclose at a level significantly deeper than the 'historical' type of disclosures heretofore given in the group. At this point the group members experience a feeling of threat since the typical social group does not usually function in this manner. The members may attempt to block the self-disclosures with overly supportive responses or by attempts to change the subject—more

precisely to revert to the superficial conversation of a historical nature found in the Exploratory Stage.

To move the group as a whole through the Transition Stage to the Action Stage, or work stage, requires high levels of discrimination or sensitivity and accuracy in *timing* of counselor responses. The counselor must be able to encourage volunteers to self-disclose at a level that gives them a feeling of involvement and simultaneously he must be able to hold the anxiety level of the more threatened group members to a level that will not force their defense systems to overreact. Following the Carkhuff model for moving from counselee exploration to understanding to action, the counselor must be able to give responses that are at least minimally action-oriented, i.e., he must begin to add the facilitative action-oriented dimensions of genuineness, concreteness and appropriate self-disclosure to those of empathy, warmth, and respect. The counselor, himself, should be willing to self-disclose, when appropriate, at a depth equal to that of his most advanced counselee. In that way he models for the counselees who are beginning to involve themselves in the action-oriented dimensions of problem resolution, i.e., goal-related work.

Action Stage

The Action Stage is synonymous with the work or productive stage of a counseling group. Also, it involves the implementation of the action-oriented dimensions, *a la* Carkhuff's model, of confrontation and immediacy plus the facilitative action dimensions of genuineness, concreteness, and appropriate self-disclosures.

The group counselor must orient the counselees toward a belief that their condition will not change until they take definite steps (action) to modify it. Insofar as the counselee's goal can be achieved by modifying his behavior in the group itself, he should be encouraged to do so and rewarded when he does. In this regard talking about how he is planning to change is no longer defensible; he must demonstrate it in the here-and-now of the group experience. The counselor utilizes appropriate confrontations and shares with the counselee his here-and-now feelings about the counselee's ingroup behavior. He also encourages other group members to do likewise.

In the final analysis counselee action is goal related and dependent upon behavioral modifications to be employed outside of the group settings. It is encouraged in the form of *homework* to be done and then reported back to the group at the next session. Attempts which fail to achieve the desired goal can be appraised

and modified, even role-played in the group, until counselee satisfaction is achieved.

If the group counselor has involved all group members in the action phase of group counseling, he will seldom need to confront group members himself. Rather the group members will confront each other and the group counselor will be more of a gatekeeper of group safety. He will be one of the most expert timing devices in the group—the one who can best predict when a given counselee is ready to be confronted with decision making and/or action. In this view he not only confronts but solicits, through his openness, confrontation by the counselees.

Termination Stage

The Termination Stage begins with a tapering off of counselee self-disclosures, especially in new areas of concern. In a closed group with a preset termination date, the tapering off usually begins naturally two to three sessions before this date and frequently includes halfhearted attempts by the counselees to continue the sessions beyond the preset deadline. Not unusual during the last three or four sessions is the initiation of a "going around" procedure wherein each member solicits frank feedback from every other member. Also common during the Termination Stage is a general and spontaneous need of counselees to tell how much the group members and the group experience have meant to them. They are reluctant to see the group experience terminate and they usually make plans for a group reunion at some specific date in the future.

The group counselor's responsibility at termination is to reinforce the growth made by group members and to make sure that all group counselees have had the opportunity to work out their differences with the counselor and other group members before leave taking. If any member of the group, for whatever reason, continues to require counseling, the counselor must assume this responsibility or assist him in a mutually satisfactory referral.

Counselee Selection and Group Composition— General Guidelines

Frank (1952), Slavson (1953) and Hulse (1954) have pointed to our lack of knowledge in arriving at optimum composition for therapy groups. A similar observation can be made for group counseling. Research has not clearly demonstrated ideal combinations of

members for maximum growth through group counseling. Never-theless, certain guidelines have been utilized and are presented here for consideration, possible application, and research. My ex-perience leads me to concur with Lowrey and Slavson (1943) *that the most essential element in a therapy group is the skill and insight in grouping, and the second most important factor is the personality of the therapist.*

Based on a rather thorough review of the literature, Truax and Carkhuff (1967) concluded that conclusive research on the ques-tion of what type of client, patient or counselee would benefit most from counseling or psychotherapy has not been done; however, those counselees who are likely to improve or deteriorate can sometimes be predicted. Even then this may be more a factor of the leader's ability to provide a therapeutic relationship than a true picture of what the counselee is like. Nevertheless, they did find research data to support some *tentative conclusions* related to counselee selection for individual and/or group counseling. Their findings (Truax & Carkhuff, 1967, Ch. 5) are summarized as follows:

1| Matching of counselee and counselor types is critical where the counselor is quite restricted in his ability to show understanding, warmth, or genuineness to all but a narrow range of individuals.

2| Counselee readiness is a moderately good predictor of the degree of positive change. In this regard, coun-selees who have high expectations and high regard for the counselor tend to show the greatest immediate change while those who differ on the aims and meth-ods of counselor help tend to terminate treatment quickly.

3| The research evidence is unclear regarding the char-acteristics of counselees likely to benefit most from counseling or therapy. In general, the counselees with the greatest felt disturbance and the least overt disturbance show the greatest improvement at post-treatment.

4| The greater the initial psychological disturbance but the lesser the initial behavioral disturbance, the greater the predicted improvement *during* treatment.

5| Counselor liking or disliking for the counselee will af-fect outcome. Higher therapeutic conditions are of-fered to counselees who are liked by the counselor.

6| Social class variables (e.g., occupational and educational level, and intelligence) regarding type and duration of counseling offered, reflect general prejudices of the profession but do not necessarily reflect counselee response to counseling.

7| Counselee hope or initial expectations of help through counseling is a major factor contributing to the likelihood of its actually occurring.

8| Degree of counselee change is independently influenced *both* by the level of therapeutic conditions offered by the counselor and the initial degree and type of personal disturbance of the counselee.

9| Accurate empathic understanding seems to be more critical for outcome with nonverbal counselees while nonpossessive warmth and genuineness tend to be equally effective in producing preferred outcome with both verbal and nonverbal counselees.

10| The therapeutic conditions of accurate empathy, nonpossessive warmth, and genuineness are of equal importance in producing personality change in the most disturbed and least disturbed counselees.

11| Level of self-exploration by the counselee is a crude predictor of counselee outcome, i.e., the greater the degree of counselee self-exploration, the more likely the outcome will be positive. (The Truax Depth of Self Explorations Scale in Truax and Carkhuff, 1967, Chapter 5, can be used to obtain a measure of counselee level of self-exploration.)

The guidelines which have been cited above for rule-of-thumb selection of counselees come from both the individual and group counseling research literature and include characteristics of the counselee and counselor. However, the group setting is unique and creates greater problems for predicting possible counselee reaction(s). McGrath and Altman (1966), in their extensive review of small group research raised the "... old question of whether or not the individuals summate to form a group or whether the characteristics of individual members combine in some nonadditive but otherwise unknown way..." (p. 56). They concluded: "Actually very few data are available about the role of personality characteristics of members on various group phenomena. Rather, such properties should be studied with respect to the composition of the group" (p. 57). They further concluded "... there is very

little research on group composition, and what there is gives an unclear picture" (p. 60).

Regarding interpersonal attraction in small groups in general but not necessarily therapy or counseling groups, McGrath and Altman (1966) concluded:

> *In summary, the over-all picture suggests that interpersonal attractions, interpersonal communication, and perceptions of task success may vary interdependently, so that a manipulation of any one of them will lead to correlated changes in the other two. Successful induction of greater interpersonal attraction produces greater communication and increased perceptions of group task success. Similarly, successful manipulation of perceptions of group success produces greater interpersonal attraction and communication. Finally, it is possible that increasing the amount of communication among group members will lead to some favorable perceptions of other members and of the group's performance effectiveness, although the latter point is not established in the present body of research information. In these terms, we can suggest that attraction, perceived task success, and communication constitute an* interdependent system *of variables. We can further suggest that certain other variables—e.g., cooperative conditions, job autonomy and high member status—are associated with or are determinants of this system (p. 61).*[3]

With respect to the group counseling research, Anderson (1969) made this observation in his recent three-year review of the literature:

> *Group counseling research reflects little interest in client selection or client preparation as a major independent variable. The available data suggest that people who are affectively oriented, flexible, highly motivated to change, and sufficiently well-adjusted to interact rationally with others function well in counseling groups (p. 212).*

Following a comprehensive review of group dynamics and group psychotherapy research, Goldstein, et al. (1966) developed the following hypothesis concerning group composition: "On a variety of interactive, communicative and compatibility criteria, prediction of subsequent within-group behavior will be more accurate

---

[3]From McGrath, J. E., & Altman, I. *Small group research: A synthesis and critique of the field.* New York: Holt, Rinehart, & Winston, 1966. Reproduced by permission.

when based on direct behavioral measurement than on interview or psychometric measurement" (p. 329). In order to apply the above principle, they proposed three criteria as guidelines: (1) consistency or typical performance, (2) relation to task success, and (3) objective observation (1966, p. 333). To determine consistency of counselee behavior in a group, two means were suggested: (a) trial groups (see also Bell & French, 1955; Blake, Mouton, & Fruchter, 1954; Borgatta & Bales, 1955; and Gazda, 1968), and (b) simulated groups.

Trial or preliminary grouping is possible where there is a relatively large pool of potential counselees, such as in schools or other institutional settings. Potential counselees are placed in a large temporary group, observed for three or four sessions, and then placed in a permanent group based on their needs and contributions and the needs of the permanent group to which they are added (in the case of open-ended groups) or a new group (closed) when a new group is being organized.

The simulated method for screening consists of a prospective member's listening, via audio tape, to a simulated group experience and responding as if he were a member. This method allows the prospective group counselee to be observed regarding his reaction to type of group leadership and group members. Blake and Brehm (1954) and Bass (1960) describe this method in more detail.

To relate task or group success (therapeutic outcome) to group composition, Goldstein, et al. (1966) suggested the study and application of findings of characteristic rate of group member interaction, leadership behavior, the effects of group cohesiveness on outcome, and related therapy group dimensions.

Group cohesiveness was found by Truax (1961) to be one of three group conditions significantly related to intrapersonal exploration by counselees in groups. Most of the research in support of group cohesiveness as a powerful agent in affecting behavior is in the field of group dynamics or from non-therapy oriented groups (see Goldstein, et al., Chapter 9). Bach, a group therapist with a group dynamics orientation had this to say about group cohesiveness in therapy groups:

> *This principle of cohesiveness is most relevant to the therapy group, for much of the therapeutic process is mediated by all members. The most unique feature of group therapy is the co-therapeutic influence of peers, not of the doctor alone. Traditionally, the doctor is thought of as having the most influence, but in group therapy this is actually not necessarily so, because the relatively low degree of cohesiveness between doctor and*

patient as compared with the often very deeply involved peer relationships between the patients gives the co-patient a greater power of effective influence (1954, p. 348).[4]

After surveying individual therapy research, group therapy research, and group dynamics research Goldstein, et al. (1966) generated the following *hypotheses*[5] relative to the means of achieving cohesiveness in therapy groups:

1. Therapy group cohesiveness may be increased by inter-group competition (p. 407).

2. Therapy group cohesiveness may be increased by the temporary inclusion, within the therapy group of a "deviant plant" (p. 411).

3. Therapy group cohesiveness may be increased by dissolving or re-orienting diverging subgroups. The creation of a series of groupwide tasks characterized by superordinate goals with inherent task appeal and demanding interdependent linking across all group members for task completion will result in such subgroup dissolution or re-orientation (p. 417).

4. Therapy group cohesiveness may be increased by differential reinforcement by the therapist of patient group-oriented verbalizations versus individual-oriented verbalizations (p. 421).

Although the Goldstein et al. review of the literature which led to the generation of the above hypotheses did not include *group counseling* literature per se, there is little or no reason to doubt that the findings apply equally to group counseling. In order to achieve objective observations of group behavior for predicting outcome a number of interaction process scales were suggested by Goldstein et al. (1966), such as those by Bales, Carter, Heyns, Steinzer, Benne and Sheats, and Fouriezos, et al. A significant omission in their list is the Hill Interaction Matrix, HIM-A and HIM-B (Hill, 1961, 1963, 1965, 1967). Hill (1967) has stated that "With the HIM-B or HIM-A the pattern of preferences for a group leader or group member can be determined and, by extension, the composition of the group can also be determined and the compatibility of the members with each other and the leader can be measured" (p. 12). There is considerable evidence now building in the related literature to suggest that the Hill instruments, including HIM-G, can also be used to predict outcome of a counseling group

[4]From Bach, G. R. *Intensive group psychotherapy.* Copyright, 1954. The Ronald Press Company, New York. Reproduced by permission.
[5]From Goldstein, A. P., Heller, K., & Sechrest, L. B. *Psychotherapy and the psychology of behavior change.* New York: John Wiley & Sons, Inc. Reproduced by permission.

as a whole—though perhaps not for each individual participant.

Still another category for predicting an individual's behavior in a group consists of personal interviews and other measures of psychological appraisal. Research data (Goldstein et al., 1966) do not support this means as effective in predicting within-group behavior of members. However, Schutz's (1966) F I R O-B or three-dimensional theory of interpersonal behavior, with his several questionnaires, holds considerable promise as do the Indexes of Discrimination and Communication recently developed by Carkhuff (1969a, b). The use of biographical data such as used by Dr. Owens of the University of Georgia's Department of Psychology for predicting group interaction has not even been attempted and leaves an entire area open to research. Other techniques which already have been employed with limited success are Bach's (1954) use of MAPS Figure Grouping, the Life Space Drawings and a number of situational and psychodramatic tests described by Goldstein, et al. (1966, p. 326).

Both Ginott (1961) and Slavson (1964) feel that a person's capacity for "social hunger" is a primary prerequisite for placement in a therapy group. Ginott, in particular, applies this criterion in the selection of children for therapy groups. According to Slavson (1964), "Social hunger has the same relation to group psychotherapy as transference does to individual psychotherapy." I agree with Slavson's definition of social hunger in that ". . . the basic requirement for group psychotherapy [counseling] is social hunger; that is, the desire to be with people and belong with others" (p. 492).

Social hunger provides the group counselor with a good rule-of-thumb procedure for selecting group counselees; however, it is insufficient in itself, since it is difficult to appraise. Insofar as they are related to counselee readiness or hope, the previous guidelines, based on research cited by Truax and Carkhuff (1967), lend credence and specificity to their application in counselee selection.

Screening Interview

A diagnostic interview is held with each prospective group counselee to give the counselor an opportunity to describe the ground rules for and responsibilities of the group and to enable the counselor to ascertain the counselee's readiness and acceptability for a group counseling experience. The diagnosis is often useful for effective empathic understanding on the counselor's part and it

is essential for him also to know the degree of seriousness of the counselee's problem (Truax & Carkhuff, 1967), since prospective counselees experiencing a serious crisis in their lives should be seen individually. They tend to dominate a group with their immediate needs and prevent others from getting help and this often turns the group against them because they monopolized the time.

Not all counselors can help all counselees; therefore the group counselor must know himself and his limitations in this regard. The diagnostic interview permits the counselor to determine whether or not his prospective group counselee has a problem similar to one that the counselor has been unsuccessful in solving in his own life. The counselee should be referred to someone else if he has a problem which the counselor has proven inadequate in solving. Carkhuff (1969a) makes this point very succinctly:

> *If the helper cannot establish himself as a person who is himself living at more effective levels than the distressed person, if the helper cannot establish that given the same circumstances he could bring about a more effective resolution, there is no meaningful basis for helping (p. 45).*

The screening interview provides the counselor the opportunity to go over the ground rules of the proposed group with the candidate. The rules are carefully explained in this interview, are reviewed again at the beginning of the group during the first session and at other times throughout the counseling session as often as is necessary for their communication and clarification. The screening interview also serves as a hurdle to group membership which makes it more appealing upon admission—providing the initiation is not too severe (Goldstein, et al., 1966).

To heighten the candidate's appeal for the counseling group, he is told (after the counselor has decided to accept him) that he will very likely find the other group members to be congenial and helpful. A review of research by Goldstein, et al. (1966), suggests that this type of positive pre-membership structuring leads to increased acceptance of members for each other and resultant group cohesiveness.

Ground Rules

Following the counselor's hopeful and positive introduction in the screening interview, he reviews for the candidate the following ground rules that the candidate will be expected to follow as a member of the group.

1| That he will set a goal or goals for himself before he enters the group or, at the very latest, as early as he can isolate and define his direction of change. And that he will revise these goals as clarification and/or experience dictates.

2| That he will discuss as honestly and concretely as he can the nature of his troubles, including the successful and unsuccessful coping behaviors he has employed.

3| That, when he is not discussing his own difficulties, he will listen *intently* to the other group members and try to help them say what they are trying to say and to communicate his understanding, caring, and empathy for them.

4| That he is to maintain the confidentiality of all that is discussed in the group. (There are no exceptions to this rule other than those things that pertain to him only.)

5| That he will be on time and attend regularly until termination of the group (if a closed group) and until he has met his goals (if the group is open-ended).

6| That he will give to the counselor the privilege of removing him from the group if the counselor deems it necessary for the counselee's health and for the overall benefit of the group.

7| That he will concur that all decisions affecting the group as a whole will be made by consensus only.

8| That he should inform the group counselor in private, before the group is constituted, of individuals who would, for various reasons, constitute a serious impediment to his group participation. (I feel that the "cards should be stacked in the counselee's favor" as much as possible; therefore those individuals who could inhibit the counselee should be excluded from his particular group if at all possible.)

9| That he may request individual counseling interviews, but that what is discussed in these interviews should be shared with the group at the appropriate time and at the discretion of the counselor and himself.

Values and Uniqueness of Group Counseling

There are certain unique features and values of group counseling and psychotherapy in general which should be recognized. These

values and unique features are cited below with full awareness that they are not limited to Developmental Group Counseling and that all have not been experimentally validated. Lacking experimental validation, the value and unique features of group counseling (therapy) are supported by reference to agreement among experts.

Respondents to a national survey (Gazda, Duncan & Meadows, 1967) cited the following advantages—values and uniqueness:

1| Approximates a real life situation, or small community of peers, through which each member can test reality, practice identification, obtain feedback and support, share ideas, feelings, and concerns, leading to personal growth and improved interpersonal relations;

2| Provides for more economical and better use of counselor's time;

3| Facilitates an effective use of peer group pressure;

4| Makes certain individuals (e.g., the defensive, shy, dependent, and school behavior problem) more amenable to individual counseling;

5| Enables counselees to serve as cocounselors;

6| Provides a method for counselor training; and

7| Implements subsequent individual counseling.

Still other statements regarding the values and uniqueness of group counseling and/or group psychotherapy are reported in the literature and summarized as follows:

1| The client discovers that he is not alone or unique with his problems; that others have similar problems, too (Beck, 1958; Bennett, 1963; Broedel, Ohlsen, Proff & Southard, 1960; Cohn, Combs, Gibian, & Sniffen, 1963; Eiserer, 1956; Gawrys & Brown, 1965; Spielberger, Weitz, & Denny, 1964; Super, 1960).

2| The counselee is encouraged to attack his problems, etc., through the effect of the group acceptance and rewards—support (Andrews, 1964; Beck, 1958; Broedel et al., 1960; Bugental, 1962; Eiserer, 1956; Knowles, 1964; Ohlsen, 1964; Prados, 1953; Strang, 1958; Super, 1960).

3| The group represents a microcosm of social reality (real life) for the members and enables them to test

their behavior (interpersonal relations) against social reality (Andrews, 1964; Beck, 1958; Bennett, 1963; Berger, 1962; Bugental, 1962; Cohn et al., 1963; Eiserer, 1956; Gawrys & Brown, 1965; Ginott, 1961; Goldman, 1955; Hinckley & Herman, 1951; Knowles, 1964; Strang, 1958).

4| The group provides the counselees a relatively safe place to try out behaviors and experiment with possible changes (Beck, 1958; Bennett, 1963; Berger, 1962; Cohn et al., 1963; Gawrys & Brown, 1965; Goldman, 1955; Whitaker, 1964).

5| The counselee learns to give as well as receive help in the role of cocounselor (Bennett, 1963; Eiserer, 1956; Gawrys & Brown, 1965; Knowles, 1964; Ohlsen, 1964; Spotnitz, 1961).

6| The group counselees have the opportunity to learn from each other by observing how others attack and solve problems (Beck, 1958; Eiserer, 1956; Samuels, 1964; Spotnitz, 1961; Strang, 1958).

7| The group counseling experience may lead to the counselees' seeking further counseling on an individual basis (Cohn et al., 1963; Gazda & Ohlsen, 1961; Harris, 1965).

8| The counseling group may represent to some counselees a family group and thus provide the media through which the counselee can work through family problems (Knowles, 1964; Scheidlinger, 1948; Slavson, 1943).

9| Broedel et al., (1960), Kraft (1961), and Ohlsen (1964) emphasize the unique value that group counseling holds for the adolescent who has strong needs to identify with and be accepted by his peer group.

10| Group counseling or therapy sometimes provides a greater economy in the use of the counselor's or therapist's time (Beck, 1958; Bennett, 1960; Lodato, Sokoloff, & Schwartz, 1964).

Limitations and Disadvantages

The limitations and disadvantages of Developmental Group Counseling are not believed to be any different from those of any other form of group counseling or psychotherapy. For example, when

authors were asked to list the limitations and disadvantages of group counseling as a part of a survey questionnaire, their responses in order of frequency included the following:

> ... *inappropriate treatment for certain problem types, e.g., sociopathic or psychopathic children, and the severely disturbed; difficult to control confidentiality, depth of involvement, collusion of unhealthy effects, and anxiety level; requires a more skillful counselor, including a greater sensitivity and expertness in group dynamics; is difficult to select appropriate combinations of group members; permits certain participants, e.g., the shy and withdrawn, to refrain from participation; does not provide for adequate individual attention for some counselees; can be difficult, especially in the school setting, to arrange a convenient time for a group meeting; does not represent an economical use of counselor's time; may lead to acceptance of the group milieu which may become artificial; and it is difficult to train adequate practitioners (Gazda, et al. [1967], p. 307).*

Several other group counselors and group psychotherapists (who were not respondents to the survey questionnaire) point out possible limitations and disadvantages:

1| The group pressures may cause certain members to lose their individuality in their attempt to conform to group codes (Strang, 1958; Whitaker, Stock, & Lieberman 1964).
2| Some members may use the group to escape or as a refuge (Eiserer, 1956; Goldman, 1955).
3| The threat of group ostracism to some members may be overwhelming (Beck, 1958; Strang, 1958).
4| Improper grouping can lead to certain group members being harmed (Ginott, 1961; Samuels, 1964; Strang, 1958).

Still other limitations of group counseling and therapy are cited. Beck (1958) calls attention to the unsuitability of group therapy for those lacking communication skills; the lessened control of the group therapist, the unpredictability of group process, intragroup jealousies, and lack of opportunity for depth treatment at critical moments. Prados (1953) cites as a weakness the tendency of members to act out unconscious infantile impulses, and Spotnitz (1961) cites the tendency of some participants, because of group comfort and a decrease in the urgency to tackle their problems, to drop out of therapy prematurely.

Therapists who practice psychoanalytic psychotherapy on an individual basis frequently contend that the use of a group interferes with or makes impossible the development of a transference relationship and hence is not effective therapy. Some psychoanalytically-oriented group therapists feel that the transference relationship between counselees and therapist is sometimes interfered with by the presence of other counselees.

In summary, it seems possible that the same elements that make for a potent therapeutic climate and force are those that also add greater risks to the treatment; e.g., the presence of several counselees in a group decreases the counselor's control and thus subjects the counselees to greater risks of the group's ostracism, pressure, rivalry, breaking of confidence and the like, with the possible resultant harmful effects. Still other limitations or weaknesses of group counseling lie in the difficulty to bring together regularly a number of counselees at the same time and the reduced ability of the counselor to focus on nonverbal behavior.

Summary

A rationale for using group *guidance* and/or "human relations" classes in the prevention of personal disturbances, based on the assumption that rehabilitation is considerably less effective than prevention, was outlined. A developmental model encompassing the bio-socio-psychological, the vocational-developmental, and the psycho-social tasks and coping behaviors was described as a guidepost for keying the group worker to areas where help could be provided in a preventive way and, if problems were already apparent, serving as a focal point where remedial procedures could be introduced. This model is developmental in at least two ways; first in the developmental tasks sense just cited, and secondly in that it describes a complete group counseling and guidance approach based on different treatments for different age groups.

Effective group counseling and guidance requires a knowledge of good leadership principles, learning principles, and group dynamics principles. The research literature in each of these areas is reviewed and the findings are summarized to give the practicing group worker the most current and valid methods and techniques for application to group treatment. The essential qualities of a good group leader based on the core conditions of a helping relationship are described, and the importance of and techniques for leader structuring for effective learning are outlined.

The rationale for goal setting, norm setting, and developmental stages in group counseling has been presented in this chapter. The practicing group counselor should therefore be able to understand these group dynamics principles so that he can systematically incorporate them into his treatment model.

General guidelines for counselee selection and group composition are given with supporting research. In addition, specific instructions for screening group counselees and ground rules for group functioning are listed. The chapter closes with a section outlining values and uniqueness of group counseling contrasted by a section on limitations and disadvantages.

References

ANDERSON, A. R. Group counseling. In G. V. Glass and C. E. Thorensen (Eds.) *Review of Educational Research: Guidance and Counseling.* 1969, *39* (2), 209–226.

ANDREWS, E. E. Identity maintenance operations and group therapy process. *International Journal of Group Psychotherapy.* 1964, *14,* 491–499.

BACH, G. R. *Intensive group psychotherapy.* New York: Ronald Press, 1954.

BASS, B. M. *Leadership, psychology and organizational behavior.* New York: Harper, 1960.

BECK, D. F. The dynamics of group psychotherapy as seen by a sociologist, Part I: The basic process. *Sociometry,* 1958, *21,* 98–128.

BELL, G. B., & FRENCH, R. L. Consistency of individual leadership position in small groups of varying membership. In A. P. Hare, E. F. Borgatta, and R. F. Bales (Eds.), *Small groups.* New York: Alfred A. Knopf, 1955. Pp. 275–280.

BENNETT, M. E. Guidance and counseling in groups. (2nd ed.) New York: McGraw-Hill, 1963.

BERENSON, B. G., & CARKHUFF, R. R. (Eds.) *Sources of gain in counseling and psychotherapy: Readings and commentary.* New York: Holt, Rinehart & Winston, 1967.

BERGER, M. M. An overview of group psychotherapy: Its past, present and future development. *International Journal of Group Psychotherapy,* 1962, *12,* 287–294.

BERNE, E. *Principles of group treatment.* New York: Oxford University Press, 1966.

BLAKE, R. R., & BREHM, J. W. The use of tape recording to simulate a group atmosphere. *Journal of Abnormal and Social Psychology,* 1954, *49,* 311–313.

BLAKE, R. R., MOUTON, J. S., & FRUCHTER, B. The consistency of interpersonal behavior judgments made on the basis of short-term interactions in three man groups. *Journal of Abnormal and Social Psychology,* 1954, *49,* 573–578.

BLOCHER, D. H. *Developmental counseling.* New York: Ronald Press, 1966.

BONNEY, W. C. Group counseling and developmental processes. In G. M. Gazda (Ed.), *Theories and methods of group counseling in the schools.* Springfield, Ill.: Charles C. Thomas, 1969. Pp. 157–180.

BONNEY, W. C., & FOLEY, W. J. The transition stage in group counseling in terms of congruity theory. *Journal of Counseling Psychology,* 1963, *10,* 136–138.

BORGATTA, E. F., & BALES, R. F. Interaction of individuals in reconstituted groups. In A. P. Hare, E. F. Borgatta, and R. F. Bales (Eds.), *Small groups.* New York: Alfred A. Knopf, 1955. Pp. 379–396.

BRAMMER, L. M., & SHOSTROM, E. L. *Therapeutic psychology.* Englewood Cliffs, N. J.: Prentice-Hall, 1960.

BROEDEL, J., OHLSEN, M., PROFF, F., & SOUTHARD, C. The effects of group

counseling on gifted underachieving adolescents. *Journal of Counseling Psychology.* 1960, *7,* 163–170.

BUGENTAL, J. F. T. Five paradigms for group psychotherapy. *Psychological Reports,* 1962, *10,* 607–610.

CARKHUFF, R. R., & BERENSON, B. G. *Beyond counseling and therapy.* New York: Holt, Rinehart & Winston, 1967.

CARKHUFF, R. R. *Helping and human relations.* Vol. 1. *Selection and training.* New York: Holt, Rinehart, & Winston, 1969. (a)

CARKHUFF, R. R. *Helping and human relations.* Vol. 2. *Practice and research.* New York: Holt, Rinehart & Winston, 1969. (b)

CARKHUFF, R. R. Systematic Human Relations Training. In G. M. Gazda and T. L. Porter (Eds.), *Proceedings of a symposium on training groups.* Athens, Ga.: College of Education, University of Georgia, 1970. Pp. 77–110.

COHEN, A. R. Communication discrepancy and attitude change: A dissonance theory approach. *Journal of Personality,* 1959, 27, 386–396.

COHN, B., COMBS, C. F., GIBIAN, E. J., & SNIFFEN, A. M. Group counseling, an orientation. *Personnel and Guidance Journal,* 1963, *17,* 355–358.

EISERER, P. E. Group psychotherapy. *National Association of Women Deans and Counselors Journal,* 1956, *19,* 113–122.

ERIKSON, E. H. *Childhood and society.* New York: Norton, 1950.

ERIKSON, E. H. Growth and crises of the healthy personality. *Psychological Issues,* 1959, *1,* 50–100.

ERIKSON, E. H. *Childhood and society.* (2nd ed.) New York: Norton, 1963.

FESTINGER, L., SCHACHTER, S., & BACK, K. *Social pressures in informal groups.* New York: Harper, 1950.

FRANK, J. D. Group methods in psychotherapy. *Journal of Social Issues,* 1952, *8,* 35–44.

GAWRYS, J. J., & BROWN, O. B. Group counseling: More than a catalyst. *School Counselor,* 1965, *12,* 206–213.

GAZDA, G. M. A functional approach to group counseling. In G. M. Gazda (Ed.), *Basic approaches to group psychotherapy and group counseling.* Springfield, Ill.: Charles C. Thomas, 1968. Pp. 263–303.

GAZDA, G. M., & OHLSEN, M. M. The effects of short-term group counseling on prospective counselors. *Personnel and Guidance Journal,* 1961, *39,* 634–638.

GAZDA, G. M., DUNCAN, J. A., & MEADOWS, M. E. Group counseling and group procedures—Report of a survey. *Counselor Education & Supervision.* 1967, *6,* 305–310.

GAZDA, G. M., & FOLDS, J. H. *Group guidance: A critical incidents approach.* Chicago: Parkinson Div., Follett Educational Corporation, 1968.

GENDLIN, E. T., & BEEBE, J. Experiential groups: Instructions for groups. In G. M. Gazda (Ed.), *Innovations to group psychotherapy.* Springfield, Ill.: Charles C. Thomas, 1968. Pp. 190–206.

GINOTT, H. G. *Group psychotherapy with children: The theory and practice of play therapy.* New York: McGraw-Hill, 1961.

GLASSER, W. Reality therapy and group counseling. In G. M. Gazda (Ed.), *Proceedings of a symposium on group procedures for the disadvantaged.* Athens, Ga.: College of Education, University of Georgia, 1969. Pp. 1–73. (a)

GLASSER, W. *Schools without failure.* New York: Harper & Row, 1969. (b)

GOLDMAN, G. D. Group psychotherapy and the lonely person in our changing times. *Group Psychotherapy,* 1955, *8,* 247–253.

GOLDSTEIN, P., HELLER, K., & SECHREST, L. B. *Psychotherapy and the psychology of behavior change.* New York: Wiley, 1966.

HARRIS, W. K. A beginning counselor's experience with group counseling. *School Counselor,* 1965, *13,* 47–50.

HAVIGHURST, R. J. *Developmental tasks and education.* Chicago: University of Chicago Press, 1948.

HAVIGHURST, R. J. *Developmental tasks and education.* (2nd ed.) New York: Longmans, Green, 1952.

HAVIGHURST, R. J. *Human development and education.* New York: David McKay, 1953.

HILL, W. F. *Hill interaction matrix: Scoring manual.* Pocatello, Idaho: Author, 1961.

HILL, W. F. *Hill interaction matrix (HIM) scoring manual.* Salt Lake City, Utah: Dye, Smith & Co., 1963.

HILL, W. F. Hill interaction matrix (HIM). (Rev. ed.) Los Angeles: University of Southern California Youth Studies Center, 1965.

HILL, W. F. Group therapy for social impact: Innovation in leadership training. *American Behavioral Scientist.* 1967, *11*, (1), 1–43.

HINCKLEY, R. G., & HERMAN, L. *Group treatment in psychotherapy.* Minneapolis: University of Minnesota Press, 1951.

HOLLANDER, E. P. *Leaders, groups and influence.* New York: Oxford University Press, 1964.

HULSE, W. C. Dynamics and techniques of group psychotherapy in private practice. *International Journal of Group Psychotherapy,* 1954, *4,* 65–74.

KNOWLES, J. W. *Group counseling.* Englewood Cliffs, N.J.: Prentice-Hall, 1964.

KRAFT, I. A. Some special considerations in adolescent group psychotherapy. *International Journal of Group Psychotherapy,* 1961, *11,* 192–203.

LODATO, F. J., SOKOLOFF, M. A., & SCHWARTZ, L. J. Group counseling as a method of modifying attitudes in slow learners. *School Counselor,* 1964, *12,* 27–29.

LOWREY, L. G., & SLAVSON, S. R. Group therapy special section meeting. *American Journal of Orthopsychiatry,* 1943, *13,* 648–690.

MAHLER, C. A. *Group counseling in the schools.* Boston: Houghton Mifflin, 1969.

McGRATH, J. E. & ALTMAN, I. *Small group research: A synthesis and critique of the field.* New York: Holt, Rinehart, & Winston, 1966.

MUUSS, R. E. *Theories of adolescence.* New York: Random House, 1962.

OHLSEN, M. M. *Guidance services in the modern school.* New York: Harcourt, Brace & World, 1964.

PRADOS, M. Some technical aspects of group psychotherapy. *International Journal of Group Psychotherapy,* 1953, *3,* 131–142.

ROGERS, C. R., GENDLIN, E. T., KIESLER, D. J., & TRUAX, C. B. (Eds.) *The therapeutic relationship and its impact: A study of psychotherapy with schizophrenics.* Madison, Wisc.: University of Wisconsin Press, 1967.

SAMUELS, A. S. Use of group balance as a therapeutic technique. *Archives of General Psychiatry,* 1964, *11,* 411–420.

SCHACHTER S., ELLERTSON, N., McBRIDE, D., & GREGORY, D. An experimental study of cohesiveness and productivity. In D. Cartwright and A. Zander (Eds.), *Group dynamics.* Evanston, Ill.: Row, Peterson, 1960. Pp. 152–162.

SCHEIDLINGER, S. Group therapy—Its place in psychotherapy. *Journal of Social Casework,* 1948, *29,* 299–304.

SCHUTZ, W. C. *FIRO: A three-dimensional theory of interpersonal behavior.* New York: Holt, Rinehart, & Winston, 1960. (Republished: *The interpersonal underworld.* Palo Alto, Calif.: Science & Behavior Books, 1966.)

SLAVSON, S. R. *An introduction to group therapy,* New York: The Commonwealth Fund, 1943.

SLAVSON, S. R. Differential methods of group therapy in relation to age levels. *Nervous Child,* 1945, *4,* 196–210.

SLAVSON, S. R. Common sources of error and confusion in group psychotherapy. *International Journal of Group Psychotherapy,* 1953, *3,* 3–28.

SLAVSON, S. R. *A textbook in analytic group psychotherapy.* New York: International Universities Press, 1964.

SPIELBERGER, C. D., WEITZ, H., & DENNY, J. P. Improving the academic performance of anxious college freshmen. *Psychological Monographs,* 1964, *78,* No. 13 (Whole No. 590).

SPOTNITZ, H. *The couch and the circle.* New York: Alfred A. Knopf, 1961.

STRANG, R. *Group work in education.* New York: Harper, 1958.

SUPER, D. E. Group techniques in the guidance program. In G. F. Farwell & H. J. Peters (Eds.), *Guidance readings for counselors.* Chicago: Rand McNally, 1960. Pp. 345–357.

SUPER, D. E., CRITES, J., HUMMEL R., MOSER, H., OVERSTREET, C. B., & WARNATH, C. *Vocational development: A framework for research.* New York: Bureau of Publications, Teachers College, Columbia University, 1957, Monograph No. 1.

SUPER, D. E., STARISHEVESKY, R., MATLIN, N., & JORDAAN, J. P. *Career development: Self-concept theory.* New York: College Entrance Examination Board, 1963, Research Monograph No. 4.

TRUAX, C. B. The process of group psychotherapy. *Psychological Monograph,* 1961, *75* (Whole No. 511).

TRUAX, C. B. A new approach to counselor education. Paper presented at the Canadian Guidance and Counseling Association Convention, Edmonton, Alberta, Canada, June, 1969.

TRUAX, C. B., & CARKHUFF, R. R. *Toward effective counseling and psychotherapy: Training and practice.* Chicago: Aldine, 1967.

WHITAKER, D. S., STOCK, D., & LIEBERMAN, M. A. *Psychotherapy through the group process.* New York: Atherton Press, 1964.

YARYAN, R., & FESTINGER, L. Preparatory action and belief in the probable occurrence of future events. *Journal of Abnormal and Social Psychology,* 1961, *63*, 603–606.

ZACCARIA, J. S. Developmental tasks: Implications for the goals of guidance. *Personnel and Guidance Journal,* 1965, *24*, 372–375.

ZIMBARDO, P. G. Involvement and communication discrepancy as determinants of opinion change. *Journal of Abnormal and Social Psychology,* 1960, *60*, 86–94.

Suggested Readings

BLOCHER, D. H. *Developmental counseling.* New York: Ronald Press, 1966.

CARKHUFF, R. R. *Helping and human relations.* Vol. 1. *Selection and training.* New York: Holt, Rinehart, & Winston, 1969. (a)

CARKHUFF, R. R. *Helping and human relations.* Vol. 2. *Practice and research.* New York: Holt, Rinehart, & Winston, 1969. (b)

CARKHUFF, R. R. *The development of human resources: Education, psychology, and social action.* New York: Holt, Rinehart, & Winston, 1971.

CARKHUFF, R. R., & BERENSON, B. G. *Beyond counseling and therapy.* New York: Holt, Rinehart, & Winston, 1967.

ERIKSON, E. H. *Childhood and society.* (2nd ed.) New York: Norton, 1963.

GAZDA, G. M., & FOLDS, J. H. *Group guidance: A critical incidents approach.* Chicago: Parkinson Div., Follett Educational Corporation, 1968.

GLASSER, W. Reality therapy and group counseling. In G. M. Gazda (Ed.), *Group procedures for the disadvantaged.* Athens, Ga.: College of Education, University of Georgia, 1969. Pp. 1–73.

GLASSER, W. *Schools without failure.* New York: Harper & Row, 1969.

GOLDSTEIN, A. P., HELLER, K., & SECHREST, L. B. *Psychotherapy and the psychology of behavior change.* New York: Wiley, 1966.

HAVIGHURST, R. J. *Developmental tasks and education.* (2nd ed.) New York: Longmans, Green, 1952.

HAVIGHURST, R. J. *Human development and education.* New York: David McKay, 1953.

HOLT, J. *How children fail.* New York: Pitman Publishing Corp., 1964.

LEONARD, G. B. *Education and ecstasy.* Delacorte Press, 1968.

McGRATH, E., & ALTMAN, I. *Small group research: A synthesis and critique of the field.* New York: Holt, Rinehart, & Winston, 1966.

MIDDLEMAN, R. R. *The non-verbal method in working with groups.* New York: Association Press, 1968.

SUPER, D. E., CRITES, J., HUMMEL, R., MOSER, H., OVERSTREET, C. B., & WAR-
NATH, C. *Vocational development: A framework for research.* New York: Bureau
of Publications, Teachers College, Columbia University, 1957. Monograph No. 1.
SUPER, D. E., STARISHEVESKY, R., MATLIN, N., & JORDAAN, J. P. *Career de-
velopment: Self-concept theory.* New York: College Entrance Examination
Board, 1963. Research Monograph No. 4.
TRUAX, C. B., & CARKHUFF, R. R. *Toward effective counseling and therapy.* Chi-
cago: Aldine, 1967.
ZACCARIA, J. S. Developmental tasks: Implications for the goals of guidance.
Personnel and Guidance Journal, 1965, *24,* 372–375.
ZACCARIA, J. S. Some aspects of developmental guidance within an existential
context. *Personnel and Guidance Journal,* 1969, *47,* 440–445.

3 | Group Procedures for the Preschool and Early School Child[1]

Introduction

For purposes of group treatment, preschool and early school includes the ages from approximately five through nine. "Little is known as to what the values of a group to a child of 3 or 4 may be," according to Slavson (1945, p. 203); therefore until more information becomes available on how to treat the child of three or four in groups, one may risk extrapolating downward from age five and use basically the same rationale and group procedures for the period described in this chapter—at least for the more mature three- and four-year-olds.

The developmental tasks and coping behavior to be used as benchmarks for determining a child's progress or lack thereof are given in Tables 3.1–3.3 only for the period from ages five through nine. One should consult the same references used in this chapter if he extrapolates and uses similar group procedures with children in the infancy period.

The purpose of reproducing the developmental tasks and their coping behaviors for the age group covered in this chapter is to give the reader guideposts for evaluating a child's developmental progress and thus be in a position to spot potential trouble and introduce *group counseling* as a means of rectifying the

[1]Parts of this chapter are reproduced by permission from Gazda, G. M. & Folds, J. H. Group procedures in the elementary school. In G. M. Gazda (Ed.), *Theories and methods of group counseling in the schools.* 1969. Courtesy of Charles C. Thomas Publisher, Springfield, Ill.

trouble. And, perhaps even more important, the developmental tasks and coping behaviors provide the *group guidance* worker an outline of the kinds of guidance information a child needs and the time when he would be most ready and receptive to receive and utilize it. Appendix A provides the reader with additional help in isolating developmental tasks appropriate for levels below age 5 through age 15. Acceptable behavioral characteristics are listed as well as those showing minimal and extreme psychopathology for the child and parent(s).

The developmental tasks and their appropriate coping behaviors outlined in Table 3.1 represent Lilienthal and Tryon's (1950) and Tryon and Lilienthal's (1950) interpretations of Havighurst (1948, 1952, 1953). Erikson (1950, 1963), and Super, Crites, Hummel, Moser, Overstreet, and Warnath's (1957) developmental tasks are summarized in Tables 3.2 and 3.3 respectively. The ten developmental tasks and coping behaviors in Table 3.1 include early and late childhood. Lilienthal and Tryon (1950) contend that teachers in the first- second- and third-grade levels will be dealing with children in the stages of early and late childhood, and since this covers the age group treated in this chapter both stages are listed in Table 3.1.

TABLE 3.1

Bio-socio-Psychological Developmental Tasks[a]
Early, Middle and Late Childhood: Ages 5–9

Developmental Tasks	Coping Behaviors	
	Early Childhood[b]	*Late Childhood*[b]
1. Achieving an appropriate dependence-independence pattern	1. Adjusting to less private attention: becoming independent physically while remaining strongly	1. Freeing one's self from primary identification with adults *Example:* Viewing himself as something

[a](To avoid oversimplification and misunderstanding of the material shown in this table, the reader is directed to the ASCD 1950 Yearbook: *Fostering Mental Health in Our Schools* in which background material and a more complete rationale is given.)

From Tryon, C., & Lilienthal, J. W. Developmental Tasks: I. The concept and its importance. Association for Supervision and Curriculum Development, *Fostering mental health in our schools.* 1950 Yearbook Washington, D.C.: Association for Supervision and Curriculum Development, 1950. Pp. 77–89. Copyright © 1950 by the Association for Supervision and Curriculum Development. Reproduced with permission.

From Lilienthal, J. W., & Tryon, C. Developmental tasks: II. Discussion of specific tasks and implications. Association for Supervision and Curriculum Development. *Fostering mental health in our schools.* 1950 Yearbook. Washington, D.C.: Association for Supervision and Curriculum Development, 1950. Pp. 90–128. Copyright © 1950 by the Association for Supervision and Curriculum Development. Reproduced with permission.

[b]Early childhood overlaps the years 2–3–4 and late childhood overlaps preadolescent or early adolescence years 8–9–10.

TABLE 3.1 *(Continued)*

Developmental Tasks	Coping Behaviors	
	Early Childhood[b]	Late Childhood[b]
	dependent emotionally *Examples:* Being able to share his parents with new teacher, with other students, etc., and simultaneously learning rules of safety to give him greater mobility and physical independence	different from an adult and beginning to value opinions of other children, also beginning to demand the right to make choices
2. Achieving an appropriate giving-receiving pattern of affection	1. Developing the ability to give affection *Examples:* Takes pleasure in showing affection to parents, relatives, teachers, etc., as well as accepting affection from them	1. Learning to give as much love as one receives: forming friendship with peers *Examples:* Is able to give affection to peers as well as to adults other than parents, teachers and relatives, also able to give affection to animals
	2. Learning to share affection *Examples:* Learns to share affection of teacher with classmates	
3. Relating to changing social groups	1. Beginning to develop the ability to interact with age-mates *Examples:* Begins to take part in "parallel play" with another child or a small group of children	1. Clarifying the adult world as over and against the child's world *Examples:* Begins to realize importance of peer group and may begin to show defiance against adults
	2. Adjusting in the family to expectations it has for the child as a member of the social unit *Examples:* Learns good manners such	2. Establishing peer groupness and learning to belong *Examples:* Participates in cliques and gangs with age-mates

TABLE 3.1 *(continued)*

Developmental Tasks	Coping Behaviors	
	Early Childhood[b]	Late Childhood[b]
	as in eating and is more aware of his expectations in caring for family property	
4. Developing a conscience	1. Developing the ability to take directions and to be obedient in the presence of authority *Examples:* Becomes responsive to rewards and punishment of his parents and identifies strongly with his parents—especially with own-sex parent	1. Learning more rules and developing true morality *Examples:* Declining identification with adults and increasing identification with peer group leads to great interest in subsequent mastery of organized games and of their rules of participation—learning to apply abstract principles of fairness-unfairness, right-wrong
	2. Developing the ability to be obedient in the absence of authority where conscience substitutes for authority *Examples:* Through strong identification with parents and teachers their values become child's (Causes confusion for lower class child who tries to reconcile parent's values with teacher's values)	
5. Learning one's psycho-socio-biological sex role	1. Learning to identify with male adult and female roles *Examples:* Especially through play, girls show identification with mother and females in general and boys show identification with father and males in general.	1. Beginning to identify with one's social contemporaries of the same sex *Examples:* Boys and girls begin to separate into same-sex gangs. Boys begin to learn how to show affection to boys in masculine ways and girls to girls in feminine ways

TABLE 3.1 *(continued)*

Developmental Tasks	Coping Behaviors	
	Early Childhood[b]	*Late Childhood*[b]
6. Accepting and adjusting to a changing body	1. Adjusting to expectations from one's improving muscular abilities *Examples:* Is sensitive to his role of maturation and requires careful handling by adults to reduce competitiveness and resultant feelings of inferiority or superiority 2. Developing sex modesty *Examples:* Lapses in sexual modesty will require understanding on part of adults to prevent unhealthy attitudes towards one's body	"This is a period of relatively little bodily change. Sex interests are at their lowest ebb, and there is no real developmental task in this area at this time" (Lilienthal & Tryon, 1950, p. 111).
7. Managing a changing body and learning new motor patterns	1. Developing large muscle control *Examples:* Practices using his large muscles in numerous games and through enormous expenditure of energy— daredevil stage 2. Learning to coordinate large muscles and small muscles *Examples:* Begins to coordinate large and small muscles in such activities as tying shoelaces, dressing and undressing, picture painting, etc.	1. Refining and elaborating skill in the use of small muscles *Examples:* Uses finer muscles of hands and fingers in learning to write and uses finer eye mucles in learning to read
8. Learning to understand and control the physical world	1. Meeting adult expectations for restrictive exploration and manipulation of an expanding environment *Examples:* Restrictions on exploration	1. Learning more realistic ways of studying and controlling the physical world *Examples:* Frees himself from a reliance on fantasy and questioning and

TABLE 3.1 *(continued)*

Developmental Tasks	Coping Behaviors	
	Early Childhood[b]	*Late Childhood*[b]
	of places and things leads child to fantasy and to a considerable use of questions as he explores his environment, but he begins to make discriminations between space, weight, and time.	begins to make direct examinations of his physical world: he makes; he manipulates; he sees how it works as he perfects his abilities to perceive weight, space, and time
9. Developing an appropriate symbol system and conceptual abilities	1. Improving one's use of the symbol system *Examples:* Develops his vocabulary to approximately 3000 words by the end of this period, also his sentence length and structure increase in length and complexity from two to three words to five or six including compound and complex sentences; his talk is still egocentric, however	1. Learning to use language actually to exchange ideas and to influence one's hearers *Examples:* Moves away from egocentricity in establishing bonds with agemates; begins to show interest in problems of others; and is learning to manipulate written symbols and to improve sentence structure
	2. Enormous elaboration of the concept pattern *Examples:* Establishes rules of conduct and explores reality through ceaseless questioning; still has no definite concepts of space, time and cause and effect, and reality is vague, yet through his play especially, he begins to organize emotional, social, and mental realities. Egocentricity is still paramount and interferes with ability to listen and think (internalized conversation).	2. Beginning to understand real causal relations *Examples:* Focus of attention is still on action and movement, though cause-and-effect relationships are becoming better understood; consciousness is now associated with living things.
		3. Making finer conceptual distinctions and

TABLE 3.1 *(continued)*

Developmental Tasks	Coping Behaviors	
	Early Childhood[b]	Late Childhood[b]
		thinking reflectively *Examples:* Learns to differentiate between the absolute and the relative, grasps degrees of differences, is learning to apply concepts of right and wrong, and begins to separate the personal from impersonal
10. Relating one's self to the cosmos	1. Developing a genuine, though uncritical notion about one's place in the cosmos *Example:* Though his curiosity about his relationship to the universe is growing, he accepts at face value his parents' explanations of causal relationships.	1. Developing a scientific approach *Examples:* Begins to comprehend true causal relationships and develops a more realistic concept of the world. He begins to value objective investigations and no longer depends solely on adults for answers to his "why" questions.

TABLE 3.2

Psychosocial Developmental Tasks[a]
Early and Late Childhood: Ages 5–9

Developmental Tasks	Coping Behaviors
	Early Childhood
Autonomy vs. Shame & Doubt	Self-control is the basic strength and the basic virtue is willpower. Cooperation is also a coping behavior for this stage. *Guidelines:* From a sense of self-control without loss of self-esteem comes a lasting sense of good will and pride. A loss of self-control and foreign over-control produces a tendency for doubt and shame. Adults, therefore, should be "firmly reassuring," protect the child against his untrained sense of discrimination, and assist him to 'stand on his own feet' by protecting him against meaningless and arbitrary experiences of shame and self-doubt.

[a]Based on Erikson, Erik H. *Childhood and Society.* New York: W. W. Norton & Company, Inc., 1950, and Erikson, E. H. *Childhood and Society,* Second Edition, Revised. New York: W. W. Norton & Company, Inc., 1963.

TABLE 3.2 *(continued)*

Developmental Tasks	Coping Behaviors
	Early Childhood
	Late Childhood
Initiative vs. Guilt	Direction is the basic strength and purpose is the basic virtue for this period. The coping behaviors include goal-directedness, mastery, moral responsibility, and work identification. However, guilt is likely to result from goals contemplated and acts initiated because of one's enjoyment over new locomotor and mental powers. *Guidelines:* The child is especially amenable for learning and growth through sharing at this stage of development. Adult models, especially of the child's own sex, are important to him. Adults can assist the child in his direction, purpose, and mastery by guiding him into tasks that he is capable of successfully completing. Moral responsibility can be developed by providing the opportunity for mutual regulation where the child will not be inclined to overmanipulate himself, but where he can gain insight into the institutions, functions, and roles which will permit his responsible participation. Work identification behaviors permit initiative without too much infantile conflict or oedipal guilt and a more realistic identification based on a spirit of equality of doing things together.

TABLE 3.3

Vocational Developmental Tasks[a]
Pre-school, Early Childhood, and Late Childhood

Vocational Developmental Tasks	Vocational Life Stages (Coping Behaviors)
1. Increasing ability for self-help 2. Identification with like-sexed parent 3. Increasing ability for self-direction 4. Ability to undertake cooperative enterprises 5. Choice of activities suited to one's abilities	The self concept develops through identification with key figures in the family and in the school. Needs are dominant and roleplaying in fantasy is important.

[a]Reprinted with the permission of the publisher from *Vocational development: A framework for research* by D. Super, J. Crites, R. Hummel, H. Moser, P. Overstreet, and C. Warnath, New York: Teachers College Press, Copyright, 1957.

Group Guidance

Group guidance for the child in his first three or four years in school is not a common practice. Even where programs are avail-

able they are generally not called group guidance. This is also true for many programs that are being developed. This fact may be deliberate to avoid associating a new program with an established program of group guidance in the secondary schools which, for a variety of reasons, proved to be rather ineffective in the past. It may even be unwise to refer to a program in the early school years as group guidance. Education in human behavior, human relations education, mental health education, education in self-understanding, education in interpersonal relations, human development education, are a few of the names being used to describe what I have earlier (see Chapter one) defined as group guidance. I use group guidance to describe the large *group* activities in the realm of human relations education which must be instituted in our elementary schools, but I feel that any of those names given above would be equally appropriate. What the process is called is not of primary importance, but that it is done is of prime importance.

If educators are to use the classrooms of the early school years and, for that matter throughout all formal education through at least grade twelve, to teach self-understanding, self-worth, and ways of relating to others in a healthy manner, it will require a formal program that is a regular part of the curriculum. Otherwise, most teachers will not take the occasions in other classroom activities to promote self-understanding and understanding of others, or, if they do, it will be more incidental than planned. Studying about self and others should be a very exciting venture which will yield great dividends if it is done in a manner appropriate to the needs and age level of the child.

The developmental tasks with appropriate coping behaviors for the age group treated in this chapter serve as *guideposts* for the teacher or group guidance leader in choosing existing programs and/or developing a program based on the developmental needs of the children in a given school and grade. (Existing programs available to the group guidance leader are cited at the end of this chapter.) In-service programs to educate group guidance leaders (namely teachers at the age level dealt with in this chapter) will be required in addition to training that is described in Carkhuff's chapter of this text.

Children in the age group 5–9 are play- and action-oriented in addition to being spontaneous, open, and impressionable. Therefore, these natural inclinations should be utilized in any group guidance or human relations program developed for them as well as for any group guidance activities designed to enhance their emotional, social, and creative development which fit naturally into

their mode of behaving and offer an effective procedure for preventing maladjustment.

Since group guidance is intended to be oriented toward prevention of personal, social, emotional, and vocational problems, the emphasis is on cognitive understandings or the providing of accurate information about the behavior of self and others at a time when it is relevant—hence the necessity of using the developmental tasks as guideposts. Intensive involvement in a child's problems at a *deep affective* level is to be discouraged in guidance groups. Serious problems involving parents and relatives and other teachers are also to be avoided since confidentiality cannot be guaranteed in large classroom-size groups and also because there would be insufficient time and/or professional competency available to work through or resolve these kinds of problems in a classroom setting. Therefore a group guidance leader should not seek indiscriminately to open up a child in the classroom, but he should be alert to those children who have problems that are already interfering with their development and make a referral for individual or group counseling.

Group guidance classes should provide the kind of content and media for interpersonal interactions that would elicit behavior from the children which is appropriate as well as inappropriate. Those children exhibiting inappropriate thinking and/or behavior can be referred for more intensive assistance.

Selected Illustrative Studies of Group Guidance Activities.

The program described by Ojemann (1959) in *Developing a Program for Education in Human Behavior,* and the Bessell and Palomares (1967) program: *Methods in Human Development,* represent two programs that are comprehensive for the age group treated in this chapter. The other programs cited at the end of this chapter may be used to supplement one or the other of the above programs. In addition, a selected group of studies utilizing various group guidance techniques and media are described below which also may be used in any group guidance program for the age group 5–9.

Davis (1958) reported positive results in his experiment to modify children's reaction to school tasks through a puppet play teaching technique. The puppets were used to dramatize different behavior toward a study task. The subjects were kindergarten-level children, and the experiment was performed by the teachers. He concluded that the puppet lessons "contributed to verbal identification of specific behavior reactions that are negatively related

to accomplishment of school tasks" and that the technique is "a valuable asset in a group environment." Davis suggested applying the technique to a wide range of behavior problems in the school, such as taking turns, sharing, listening skills, and so forth.

Bender and Woltmann (1936) in a discussion of the use of puppet shows and puppet classes as a psychotherapeutic method for working with behavior problems in children called it a "most valuable" activity. The children with whom they worked seemed to respond more freely in groups than alone. The children were encouraged by the presence of other children with mutual experiences. Bender and Woltmann also felt that the activities centering around puppet classes (i.e., making puppets, writing plays, drawing puppet characters, and witnessing or producing puppet plays) had a therapeutic effect. Puppet shows apparently allow the child to express his own world.

Motion pictures were used by Denney (1959) in an attempt to reduce frustration in eighth-grade pupils. He found the activity successful with the eighth graders and recommended using this technique with pupils in other grade levels.

"Story-book counseling" is a group guidance procedure which has been used effectively in at least one school (Anderson & Schmidt, 1967). This approach was used with first-, second-, and third-grade pupils. They met one-half hour every third week in relatively small groups. At these meetings, the counselor read stories describing children in different behavior situations. These stories were useful in encouraging discussions, and the pupils seemed to be able to identify with the characters in the stories. For the most part, the materials used in these classes were based on the work of Ojemann (1959) and staff in their mental health series "A Teaching Program in Human Relations and Mental Health." In their description of the "story-book counseling" technique, Ojemann, Hughes, and Chowning, (1962) refer to *Children and Books* by Arbuthnot (1947, 1957, 1964) as another source for locating appropriate story materials.

The "Unfinished Story" is a similar guidance technique which encourages discussion and provides situations suitable for role-playing. Unfinished stories have been used by Folds and me (Gazda, 1969) with groups of pupils who were placed in remedial reading classes. For the most part, these pupils did not like school and did not participate in the cocurricular activities. These pupils seemed to be able to identify with the people in the unfinished stories and liked to discuss, write, or roleplay the possible solutions to the conflictual situation presented in the stories. In 1963,

the *NEA Journal* began publishing "Unfinished Stories" that are appropriate for use with elementary-level pupils. These stories seem to be appropriate especially for guidance in personal and social relationships.

Cole (1966) has presented a very personal approach to the use of various art media in the classroom. She described how to get the child to express himself in water colors, clay, story writing, dancing, and various other media. Cole's goal seemed to be to free the child to be himself. She has done this through establishing rapport by self-involvement and self-disclosure. She describes incidents from her own life and then uses these to stimulate the children to reveal their true feelings in whatever art media they are utilizing. This method of using art for classroom involvement gives valuable clues to the group guidance specialist or classroom teacher for using art as a therapeutic medium.

Sociodrama utilized in the resolution of group problems also appears to offer much to the group guidance leader in the elementary school. Corsini (1966) has defined sociodrama as "role-playing which focuses on the problem of the group" (p. 201). And, "if . . . a problem is acted out in a group and has meaning to all the members, the procedure is known as sociodrama" (p. 87). By contrast, Corsini has defined psychodrama as "role-playing by a person of his own past, present, or future situation" (p. 200). "Psychodrama occurs when an individual acts out his own problem" (p. 87). Corsini emphasized that roleplaying is a part of both psychodrama and sociodrama. His contention is that roleplaying is the inclusive term for spontaneity action techniques.

From the above definitions, one can conclude that the psychodrama is a more personal form of therapy than the sociodrama, i.e., the object of the treatment is the person himself rather than a symbol of persons or roles as represented through the sociodrama. Also, roleplaying is used in both sociodrama and psychodrama and is an action technique without regard to emphasis—personal or social, individual or group.

Based on the results of a pilot study of the use of sociodrama by classroom teachers, Shaftel and Shaftel (1949) succinctly described why the sociodrama is recommended for classroom teacher's use in the elementary school:

> *(1) sociodrama is a helpful elementary school teaching device that can be adequately used by inexperienced and relatively un-skilled teachers, and very effectively used by master teachers, if appropriate dramatic "warm-up" materials are provided for initial sessions; (2) enables the teacher to explore attitudes of*

her pupils in areas which do not usually enter classroom experiences (home and neighborhood life, for example) as a basis for further learning; (3) it fosters a permissive atmosphere in which pupils feel free to express their own feelings and attitudes for more socially acceptable generalizations; (4) it gives pupils an opportunity to express solutions in terms of their own drives and impulses which are often on a different level from their verbalizations (p. 252).[2]

In addition to the utility of the sociodrama as suggested above, Moreno's theoretical rationale emphasizes the value of *spontaneity* and the resultant catharsis assisting a person to encounter new situations with flexibility, confidence, and accuracy.

Corsini (1966) has listed simultaneity (creation of total involvement), spontaneity (learning while in a situation devoid of threat), and veridicality (approximation of reality situation) as unique values of roleplaying.

Based on the concept of developmental tasks, the classroom teacher or sociodrama leader can select those tasks of a social nature which a child must learn and assign the task or theme to the group for dramatization, and through a system of reinforcing acceptable behavior, condition the group to the mores of the culture or subculture. Barclay (1967), in a recent study, reported the successful application of reinforcement techniques through sociodrama and other means with low status fifth graders.

Application of a Developmental Approach to Group Guidance for Children Five to Nine Years Old

The following example illustrates how the concept of developmental task can be utilized in group guidance during the period of early childhood. The task is "Developing an Appropriate Symbol System and Conceptual Abilities" (Lilienthal & Tryon, 1950). During this period the coping behavior that the child needs to establish includes rules of conduct and the exploration of reality [causal relationships]. Lacking experience, the young child has no definite concepts of space, time, cause and effect, and his understanding of reality is also vague. He is trying to establish relationships between different things that he has seen and heard (Lilienthal & Tryon, 1950).

[2]From Shaftel, G., & Shaftel, F. R. Report on the use of a "practice action level" in the Stanford University project for American Ideals. In R. B. Haas (Ed.), *Psychodrama and sociodrama in American education*, Beacon House, Inc., Publisher, Beacon, New York, 1949. Reproduced by permission.

The group-guidance program developed by Ojemann (1959): *Developing a Program for Education in Human Relations,* is apropos for teaching causal relationships with emphasis on human behavior. In fact, this program is excellent through the period of early and middle childhood. It begins with kindergarten and carries through grade six. The program utilizes unfinished problem stories, role playing and sociodrama, student workbooks, and pertinent activities that are designed for use in language arts, social studies, science, the home environment, the playground, and so forth. There is also ample material to provide good imitative (modeling) behavior for the young child. (For additional stories to serve modeling purposes, see Peters, Shelley, & McCormick, 1966). The emphasis of the Ojemann program is on imparting of information and concepts which will enable the young child better to understand himself, others, and himself and others in relationship to their environment. It is preventive in nature.

One example of a causal relationship developed for the second grade deals with the story of a boy who did not finish his workbook because he had been ill with the flu. The class became involved when it was discovered that he marked his book arbitrarily just to finish in order for him to be eligible to attend the annual class party. (This story actually developed from the showing of two still life pictures around which the class created the incident —see Ojemann, Hughes, & Chowning, 1962). This means of involving the class enabled them to deal with problems that were current and meaningful to them. The teacher then was able to help the class develop an understanding of this kind of problem behavior (causal relationship) and a wholesome resolution of the problem. Similar stories and pictures for the spontaneous evocation of conflict situations are included in this approach to group guidance which utilizes student answers in workbooks, student demonstrations of problem resolution through role playing, etc. The emphasis is on the timely *involvement* of students in the problem for increasing understanding. Many of the methods utilized are *action-oriented* which appeals to this age group because of their natural receptiveness to play and activities. This activity and this program involved an entire second grade class and the emphasis was on cognitive or intellective understandings and prevention of maladaptive behavior—hence group guidance according to my definition.

PRINCIPLES OF LEARNING UTILIZED IN A GROUP GUIDANCE EXAMPLE. In the group guidance example above, a number of

learning principles are involved. First, the teacher must select pictures which are suggestive of a current class problem. Thus *readiness* for involvement is assured. Secondly, the teacher allows for and encourages student involvement. Participation in problem solving maintains the students' interest and motivation. (This could include presentation of a sociodrama which is a kind of 'play acting' for young children and for which they have a natural proclivity.) If a sociodrama is presented, several learning principles can be utilized. For example, a kind of *desensitization* is a part of the warm-up of a sociodrama. The sociodrama itself contains opportunities for rewarding *(conditioning)* positive attempts at problem resolution and not responding to poor attempts. It also allows for the application of *shaping* behavior by repeated replays of the sociodrama with subsequent verbal and nonverbal rewards for desired behavior. It also provides excellent opportunities for *modeling* in combination with conditioning methods, e.g., Jack (1934) and Page's (1936) combined use of modeling and social reinforcement procedures to increase the assertiveness of relatively inhibited children. Modeling alone could be instituted through stories—vicarious modeling (Bandura, 1965) or symbolic modeling (Chittenden, 1942). In addition, the existence of the classroom group maximizes the possibilities for stimulus and response generalizations so that the learnings in the classroom can be generalized beyond to similar settings.

Group Counseling

Play Techniques

The primary mode of group counseling for the age group 5–9 involves play and action. Slavson (1945, 1948) has advocated play group therapy for young children under twelve years of age and I concur with him. However, I prefer to refer to it as *group play techniques* or *play group counseling* when it is applied to basically normal children who are still able to function in a school setting. Although the basic rationale for emphasizing play and action techniques for this age group is the same whether it be play therapy or play techniques, or play group counseling, the degree of disturbance of the child, training of the therapist (counselor), and setting are different. I discourage school personnel from working with seriously disturbed children and from doing "therapy" in the school setting unless they are sufficiently trained at the doctoral

level in school counseling, school psychology, clinical psychology, or psychiatry. Nevertheless, when one considers the various processes of therapy that are currently practiced, save for psychopharmacological, electroshock, and surgical therapies, there is probably very little reason to insist that a therapist be required to receive training in medicine, or for that matter, at the doctoral level in other disciplines though doctoral level training should provide the therapist or counselor with greater sophistication of techniques, and hopefully with higher level ethical practices. In other words, there is no reason why most group play therapy techniques cannot be modified for use by counselors in the school setting, providing the group members are not seriously disturbed and that the counselor is trained in group counseling and play techniques, and has the appropriate playroom facilities and play media available.

Lebo (1955) has credited Rosseau as the first to recommend that children be educated through play, although Klein (1955) has taken credit for the development in 1919 of psychoanalytic play techniques. The reader should refer to the Suggested Readings at the end of this chapter for a representative sampling of the play therapy literature.

Harms (1948) has referred to play as the "language of childhood" (p. 237), and Frank (1955) has stated that "in play we ... observe various themes or schemes in which this [child's] immediate concerns are focused and more or less symbolically played out" (p. 585). Frank also has referred to play as "learning to learn: ... cope with life tasks," etc., (p. 583). It is generally agreed that all psychotherapy constitutes some form of learning. Axline (1955) succinctly conveys my feeling on this issue in the following assertion regarding learning and psychotherapy: "It [psychotherapy] seems to be a cumulative, compound, integrative, effective experience that can be used to illustrate many learning theories. At the same time, it raises many questions as to the adequacy of any existing theory to explain conclusively the learning experience that occurs during psychotherapy" (p. 622). In regard to therapeutic play, Conn (1951) has stated, "Every therapeutic play method is a form of learning process during which the child learns to accept and to utilize constructively that degree of personal responsibility and self-discipline necessary for effective self-expression and social living" (p. 753).

Lowrey (1955) has argued that "We should be more accurate if we spoke of 'activity' (or activities) instead of 'play' with reference to therapy. For it is the activity with its release of fantasy,

imagery, fears, hostility, and other feeling and thoughts which give us quick insights into the problems besetting our child patients" (p. 574).

Until now we have been speaking of play therapy without regard to its use in groups. What are the unique features or values that play in a group setting offers? Slavson (1945) has claimed that the function of the group in the treatment of young children lies in three areas: (1) play and activity; (2) association with other children of the same age; [and] (3) the role of the worker" (p. 208). The play and activity, according to Ginott (1961), should facilitate contact with the child, catharsis, insight, reality testing, and sublimation.

Slavson (1945) also has stated that in all instances the value of a group to children

> ... *lies in the fact it supplies a field in which the child may relate himself to others, thus helping him to break through isolation, withdrawal, and aggressive rejection of people ... to go out ... into the human environment, thus leading from egocentricity and narcissism to object relationships ... to test himself against others and discover the boundaries of his ego ... [and] offers the possibility of developing patterns of relationship with human beings of the same intellectual, emotional, and social development, in which the feeling of sameness and therefore of comfort and security is greatest ... (p. 209).*[3]

The role of the group leader or "worker," according to Slavson (1945), varies with the age of the children; he is more active with the young child who is dependent upon him for support, and of necessity, for young children, much of the authority must come from the therapist. His role changes both with the ages of the children and with their changing personalities. "While he functions at first as a source of security and support, his role changes to one of guidance and authority" (p. 209).

Some specific values attached to play therapy are suggested by Solomon (1955). It is his belief that through

> *the use of play, the child is able to express his own regressive tendencies, thereby lessening the need to act out such forms of behavior in his real life situation ... and the release of aggression or hostility with its appropriate emotion, that of anger, and the*

[3]From Slavson, S. R.: Differential methods of group therapy in relation to age levels. *Nervous Child*, 1945, *4*, 196–210. Reproduced by permission.

lessening of fears through the amelioration of the catastrophic results from the expression of the primitive impulses are well-established principles of gains which accrue from the judicious use of play therapy (p. 594).[4]

He has summarized the therapeutic value of play therapy as follows: "(1) release of hostility toward parents, siblings, etc.; (2) alleviation of guilt feelings; (3) opportunity to express freely all love fantasies; (4) incorporation of therapeutic suggestions in direction of growth; and (5) desensitization by means of repetition" (Solomon, 1940, p. 763).[5]

Amster (1943) has succinctly conveyed part of my purpose for advocating the use of play and action techniques when she stated that

Essentially play is an activity a child comprehends and in which he is comfortable, an integral part of his world, his method of communication, his medium of exchange, and his means of testing, partly incorporating and mastering external realities.

. . . Provision of play materials means the provision of a natural means of communication, through which the child's problems may be expressed more readily and the treatment more likely to succeed.

In treatment of children, play is always a medium of exchange and it is comparable to words, the adult's medium of exchange. It is not a therapy in itself any more than words can be. All therapies require a therapeutic relationship and a medium of exchange. The purpose of the play activity determines its role and importance in treatment. Therefore, play as a medium differs from play as a technique even as words differ from any purposive use of them. Play is a technique when it is used In treatment for definite diagnostic and therapeutic purposes *(p. 62).*[6]

Amster (1943, 62–67)[7] has listed and defined six uses of play as follows:

1. Play can be used for diagnostic understanding of the child . . . . *We can observe the child's capacity to relate to himself and others, his distractibility, his rigidity, his areas of preoccupation, his areas of inhibition, the direction of his aggression, his perception of people, his wishes, and his perception of himself. In the play his behavior, his ideas, feelings and expressions help our understanding of his problem and how he sees it (p. 63).*

2. Play can be used to establish a working relationship. *This use of play is helpful with the young child who lacks the adult's facility for verbal self-expression and with the older child who shows resistance or inability to articulate (p. 64).*

3. Play can be used to break through a child's way of playing in his daily life and his defenses against anxiety. *This use is helpful as an additional way of treating distortions in a child's way of playing (p. 65).*

4. Play can be used to help a child verbalize certain conscious material and associated feelings. *This use is helpful when a child blocks in discussing certain material and an impasse in treatment is created (p. 65).*

5. Play can be used to help a child act out unconscious material and to relieve the accompanying tension. *This cathartic use of play deals with symbolic material which has dangerous significance to the child. The therapist must be aware of how much release in play the particular child can tolerate without panic and must be aware of the kind of participation and interpretation in which to engage (p. 67).*

6. Play can be used to develop a child's play interests which he can carry over into his daily life and which will strengthen him for his future life. *This use of play has particular importance because of the correlation between the play and work capacities of an individual (p. 67).*

On the other side of the ledger, Bender (1955) wrote,

If the play technique used is important to the adult and gives him a tool with which he can understand the child and relate to him with confidence and warmth, the play setup will undoubtedly contribute to the relationship. Beyond this I doubt if there is any specific therapeutic value to the play procedures (p. 785).

Theoretical Rationale of Play and Action Methods for Group Counseling with the Child from Five to Nine

MODELING. A small group represents a slice of society. The composition of the group determines how closely the group will represent the society of a given group member. Group *counseling* provides a controlled opportunity for social learning or behavioral

change which is maximized because of the presence (modeling) of other individuals. Whether or not the group setting is the preferred mode for assisting a given individual improve his behavior and feelings of self-worth is contingent upon many factors which will be discussed later on in this chapter. The topic of import at this point is how to maximize opportunities for behavioral change for the young child from the ages of five to nine.

Play and action-oriented techniques such as sociodrama and psychodrama have been described earlier in this chapter as natural media or modes through which the young child communicates and expresses himself; therefore following the emphasis on developmental group procedures, the group counselor is encouraged to take advantage of these media in his treatment. In addition to maximizing his relationship-engendering procedures through the use of play and action methods, the group counselor must also use relevant learning principles if his counseling armamentarium is to be complete. In the following paragraphs a model will be developed which will assist the practicing group counselor in his understanding and treatment of young children in groups.

The young child has not developed his verbal facility to a high level and thus verbally loaded (interview-type) group treatment is of limited value. The young child in particular is dependent upon the imitation (modeling) of others for much of his learning both because of his relatively low verbal facility and also because of his relatively undeveloped behavioral response repertoire. However, as the child develops his verbal and behavioral repertoires, combinations of modeling and operant conditioning models may be used in modifying his behavior.

Modeling, sometimes referred to as no-trial learning or observational learning (Bandura, 1965), can be a very efficient method for changing behavior of the young child. A model can exhibit a preferred way of behaving, relating, problem solving, etc. This real-life model can be a peer or the adult group counselor or both. It is apparent that the peer and adult models must be capable of providing exemplary behavior and with respect to peers must be chosen with care to insure mutual helpfulness. The group counselor, too, must be able to model appropriately. (This subject is dealt with in Chapter two. Peer selection will be discussed under Selection in this chapter.)

In addition to modeling opportunities made available through group peers and the counselor, symbolic models can be presented in the playroom in the form of dolls, puppets, and verbally through counselor-read stories, counselor-led puppet plays and psycho-

drama. Structured play settings would give the counselor the greatest control over modeling since he would be able to recreate the setting, characters, etc., that have been responsible for precipitating and maintaining the child's problem behavior. (Structured play and modeling may be the equivalent of simulation or gaming techniques applied to older groups.) Since the structured problem situation may be anxiety producing for the young child, (perhaps comparable to the action dimensions of the Carkhuff model described in Chapter two), it should be introduced only after the group counselor has developed a strong base of mutual trust and understanding established in the free play situation utilized in the early stages of treatment. The free play situation can also provide the group counselor an opportunity to validate a diagnosis of the child's problem based on interview and case history data.

Research studies such as those of Chittenden (1942), Bandura, Ross and Ross (1963), Beach (1967), and Hansen, Niland and Zani (1969) demonstrated that symbolic or vicarious modeling can produce change similar to real-life models. In vicarious modeling the counselor or someone in a story, movie, or puppet play rewards certain characters for prosocial behaviors and punishes the characters in pantomime and/or verbally for asocial and antisocial behavior. Through the use of vicarious modeling the group counselor can structure the kind and amount of modeling opportunities that seem necessary to modify the child's behavior.

Psychodrama or roleplaying can also be used to involve all the members in the counseling or play group in minimally structured areas of problem behavior. In the psychodrama the group counselor is the director, one of the children is the protagonist or the person with an avowed problem and the other children become the auxiliary egos. A vicarious psychodrama can be created from puppet characters with the counselor assuming all roles and structuring the problem and its resolution as he chooses. (The relationship of psychodrama to learning principles will be described in more detail later in this section.)

Modeling as described herein is first of all a method for producing *new* learning. Bandura (1965) explains this occurrence by postulating the existence of *component responses* in the person's behavioral repertoire of prior learnings that are reproduced in unique combinations by new stimuli. Secondly, he postulates that:

> *Exposure to models may also strengthen or weaken inhibitory responses in the observer .... Reinforcers administered to a model undoubtedly serve a discriminative function signifying*

the probable reinforcement contingencies associated with the modeled classes of responses. In addition, rewarding consequences may result in vicarious extinction of inhibitory responses. Conversely, observed aversive outcomes tend to establish conditioned emotional responses . . . that help to support avoidant and inhibitory repertoires (p. 321).[8]

A third effect of modeling, according to Bandura (1965), is that

the behavior of models may elicit previously learned responses that match precisely or bear some resemblance to those exhibited by the model. This response facilitation effect *can be distinguished from disinhibition when the behavior in question is not likely to have incurred punishment and, therefore, any increase in responsivity is not attributable to the reduction of inhibitory responses (p. 321).*[9]

It is not my intention to portray modeling (real-life and/or vicarious) as the only method or learning principle applicable to the young child treated in a play group setting. Modeling and various conditioning procedures should be viewed as complimentary methods for modifying or shaping behavior. Illustrations of the combined use of modeling and social-reinforcement procedures to increase the assertiveness of relatively inhibited children are provided in early studies by Jack (1934) and Page (1936). Also, the acquisition of psychomotor skills which are governed largely by proprioceptive stimuli that are not observable nor easily described verbally requires more than modeling. Varying amounts of overt practice in addition to modeling are usually necessary in the acquisition of psychomotor skills (Bandura, 1965).

Since "self-administered primary and conditioned rewards may frequently outweigh the influence of external stimuli in governing social behavior" (Bandura, 1965, pp. 331–332), a child's self concept or feelings of worth may very well be a significant determinant of the ease and/or degree to which he can learn from a good model. Thus the necessity of "relationship therapy" or, as Carkhuff (1969 a,b) would describe it: building a strong facilitative base through the use of empathy, respect, warmth, concreteness, genuineness, and appropriate self-disclosure cannot be ignored in treatment. Otherwise the more action-oriented principles such

---

[8, 9]From Bandura, A. Behavior modification through modeling procedures. In L. Krasner and L. P. Ullmann (Eds.), *Research in behavior modification.* New York: Holt, Rinehart & Winston, Inc., 1965. Reprinted by permission of Holt, Rinehart & Winston, Inc.

as modeling and conditioning will prove to be of limited applicability. Arnold Lazarus (1968), a well respected behavioral therapist, has stated that "there is nothing in modern learning theory to justify withholding the combined advantages of interpretation and desensitization, or any other method or technique which seems to have beneficial effects" (p. 155).

Relationships Between Roleplaying (Sociodrama and Psychodrama) and Learning Principles Applicable to Group Counseling

Moreno (1949, 1963) has referred to the similarities between sociodrama and psychodrama and learning theory approaches to psychotherapy. Sturm (1965) also has described the similarities between psychodrama and behavior therapy. He asserts that "the basic principles underlying psychodrama can be seen to be like those of behavior therapy and indeed of all psychotherapy . . ." (p. 57).

Mowrer (1960) has introduced the concept of two-factor learning, but it appears feasible that what might account for the success of many different therapeutic approaches is multifactor learning. Sociodrama and psychodrama or *action-oriented procedures* are assumed to be very similar for purposes of comparing them with behavior therapy; however, in psychodrama there is a greater degree of emphasis on the personal problems of the individuals as contrasted with the social nature of the problems for the group in sociodrama. Action-oriented procedures of sociodrama and psychodrama are compared with behavioral therapies on the following pages. Column 1 (Table 3.4) contains the five basic elements of sociodrama and psychodrama and Column 2 shows their relationship to behavior therapy via various learning principles. These principles can be used to explain the basic elements of the sociodrama and psychodrama and vice versa.

The foregoing comparison between action methods (sociodrama and psychodrama or roleplaying) of therapeutic group approaches and learning concepts or principles of behavioristically-oriented approaches to counseling and therapy, is admittedly a forced one at the moment. However, there appears to be enough similarity and common elements present to warrant closer scrutiny through a systematic application of learning principles in conjunction with action-oriented group approaches to counseling. Barclay's (1967) use of sociodrama with certain reinforcement

TABLE 3.4

Comparison of Sociodrama, Psychodrama and Behavioral Therapies

Sociodrama And Psychodrama	Behavioral Therapies
1. Warm-up: Here the attempt is made to decrease the clients' fears and to encourage openness and spontaneity through physical touching, smiling, and pleasant talk including introductions and sometimes a description or clarification of client expectations prior to actual assumption of roles and the introduction of the clients' problems.	1. Systematic desensitization: The clients are encouraged to relax through physiological means and the general demeanor of the therapist in *preparation* for the introduction of mild anxiety into the relationship.
2. Catharsis through spontaneity: Here Moreno (1944) differentiates between catharsis in the sociodrama and psychodrama. Essentially, however, he intends the catharsis to evoke a positive feeling leading to *integration.* "A catharsis of integration is constituted by an increased action insight and greater ability for self-restraint and flexibility as the situation demands" (Moreno & Kipper, 1968, p. 59).	2. Reciprocal inhibition: Certain behavioral therapists encourage clients to make responses incompatible with anxiety including, among others, relaxation, assertiveness, eating, and the like.
3. Action through the socio- and psychodrama (role-playing): Roleplaying or dramatization is the essence of socio- and psychodrama, or as Corsini (1966) puts it, "The patient operates holistically, not partially" (pp. 12–13). The experiencing by the actor (protagonist) and the analysis by the director and group members constitute a system of rewards and punishment of the nature of operant conditioning, shaping, reciprocal inhibition, systematic desensitization, assertive training, emotive imagery, and still other versions of behavioristically-oriented therapies. Haas (1949) has described the use of roleplaying (psychodrama) to desensitize fifth graders to the fear of going from house to house soliciting papers for a paper drive. Drabkova (1966) has used psychodrama as a form of play therapy referred to as directed therapy through playing, and Blake (1955) has recommended its use for in-	3. It is feasible that most if not all versions of the behavioral therapists utilize one or more types of roleplaying since their emphasis is on the change of *overt* behavior, e.g., symptom modification and/or motoric modification through operant conditioning, etc. Bandura and Walters (1963) have suggested support for the assumption that there is a close relationship and/or utility between sociodrama (at least) and principles of conditioning when they stated, "Should one wish to produce discriminative social learning, the best procedure would undoubtedly be to set up actual or symbolic social situations and repeatedly reward desired responses to these stimuli, while punishing undesirable responses or letting these go unrewarded" (p. 248). Bandura (1965) and Lazarus (1968) also described the use of role-playing in assertive training, and Sturm (1965) has stated ". . . it

TABLE 3.4 *(continued)*

Sociodrama And Psychodrama	Behavorial Therapies
creasing a child's sensitivity and enhancing learning of social skills. Jennings (1950) has stated, "Any situations which hold a destructive emotional impact for most members of a given minority group require classroom exploration [sociodrama] to desensitize the individuals toward that experience, as much as to foster their cultivation of skills with which to face it" (p. 276).	appears that anxiety can be reciprocally inhibited within the psychodramatic technique of *roleplaying* . . ." (p. 59).
4. Group involvement: The group helps create a microcosm of the larger society and this creates a milieu for reality testing and also it provides a tremendous therapeutic lift through its peer support (reinforcement) of each counselee.	4. According to Lazarus (1968), "Generally speaking, in desensitization groups, therapy takes place primarily *in* but not *by* the group. . . . However, this is not true for assertive training groups. Here, the role of the therapist usually evolves from that of instructor to a participant observer" (p. 161). In assertive training groups, peer group support (reinforcement) is a very therapeutic element in change just as it is in sociodrama and psychodrama. Aside from the use of the group for reinforcement purposes, learning principles would support the probability of the group maximizing response and stimulus generalization.
5. Role-repetition or modifications of roleplaying, *e.g.,* doubling, mirror, and role-reversal techniques, provide the protagonist with the opportunity for re-experiencing a situation or event.	5. Role-repetition creates conditions which would appear especially appropriate for the application of shaping, also appropriate for discriminate training, assertive training, emotive imagery, and possibly even the broader concepts of operant conditioning, systematic desensitization, and reciprocal inhibition. In other words the possibility of replaying a role several times gives the group leader and group members the opportunity to reinforce and shape appropriate behavior and ignore or punish inappropriate behavior in various patterns and/or sequences as illustrated by the learning principles cited above.

techniques to improve the behavior of low-status children in the elementary school and Gittleman's (1965) use of roleplaying or *behavioral rehearsal* in a therapy group to reduce the acting-out behavior of a young boy are good examples.

In other words, action techniques such as sociodrama, psychodrama, and play techniques show promise of being explained by means of the laws of learning and certain learning-related principles of behavioral counseling and therapy. As play and action approaches to group treatment are supported through learning principles these methods of group counseling for young children will gain greater credence and scientific validity. The rapprochement offered herein is intended as a move in that direction.

Application of a Developmental Approach to Group Counseling for Children Five to Nine Years of Age

One of the developmental tasks for children from five to nine is "Achieving an appropriate dependence-independence pattern" (Tryon & Lilienthal, 1950). Using this task with its appropriate coping behaviors as an early warning system for detecting potential trouble for given children, a teacher has referred to us three children who are having difficulty performing appropriate coping behavior to accomplish successfully this task. The children are two boys and a girl. The girl is an eight-year-old shy, overly dependent child. One boy is aggressive and *too* independent for his own safety. He is seven years old. The other boy is nine years old and, prior to the recent birth of a male sibling, appeared to be making good progress in his dependence-independence functioning. With the arrival of a new baby brother, this nine-year-old boy become very dependent on his teacher (a female) and his parents and stayed very close to his teacher and his mother. The group counselor is a young female in her mid-twenties.

A group has been carefully selected to provide potential models for each child and also to contain some built-in-controls —namely an older boy whose age and size alone can assist the counselor in controlling the one younger but aggressive boy. The counselor also has obtained extensive case data on each child and has decided in interviews with the teacher and parents that the common problem for each child is a need to develop appropriate behavior to cope with the task of achieving a proper balance between dependence and independence.

The counselor uses a free-play setting for the first three or four sessions. She meets the group for 45 minutes and holds the sessions in a playroom. During this time the children can play with a variety of toys and materials. The counselor shows an in-

terest in each child and makes every effort to establish rapport or build the base of mutual trust and liking for one another. After the base has been established, the counselor begins to structure the last half of each play session. At first she does this through story reading and telling and through the use of puppets. She introduces vicarious models in this way and verbally rewards appropriate dependence-independence behavior. Moving from puppets to dolls, she structures situations and asks the children to use the dolls to work out solutions. She rewards appropriate solutions verbally and asks for re-plays of inappropriate solutions until they approach appropriate coping behavior for dealing with the dependence-independence task.

As the children show progress with vicarious modeling, she also sets up sociodramas and psychodramas revolving around school and family situations for the group to use in modifying their behavior. Finally, the counselor moves into the realm of the here-and-now relationships between herself and each child and those between each child. She models for the child by encouraging their appropriate independence from her and by rewarding appropriate dependence also.

The play and action-selected media are used to promote relationship development and problem resolution and are not, therefore, in themselves the primary focus of the treatment. The counselor is always conscious of the timing of her moves and of the purpose of her techniques. She moves from the least threatening situations in the beginning to the more threatening but more relevant procedures as the children show signs of growth. The above procedure or model provides ample opportunity for vicarious and real-life modeling and numerous opportunities for implementing other learning principles of desensitization, shaping, operant conditioning, discriminate and assertive training, and reciprocal inhibition. The deliberate use of these principles represent the science of play group counseling, whereas the when and how of implementing them represent the art of this form of treatment.

Selection and Group Composition

This topic was dealt with in a general way in Chapter two. My purpose at this point is to focus on selection criteria and group composition most relevant to the five to nine age group. As with other age groups there is virtually no sound research on preferred ways

of selecting and composing a counseling group for the child from five to nine. During this period of development, except for the more mature children in the nine-year-old bracket, the child relies heavily on the adult or older siblings as his model(s). For this reason, the group counselor has more direct control over what happens in a counseling group with five to nine year olds than with other age groups. Nevertheless, careful selection and grouping for maximum positive mutual influence is still of prime importance.

The following suggestions are given as guidelines for selecting children for play group counseling:

1| The best predictor of what a child will do in a play group is what he in fact does in a similar group such as a trial group similar to the treatment or play group. The best combinations or those who show the greatest mutually therapeutic interactions should be selected, as soon as they can be identified, for the permanent group.

2| When open-ended groups are conducted, the counselor must try to replace a child who has completed treatment with one who can fill the role being vacated. This choice should be based on previous group behavior of the prospective group member, but actual behavior may require removing the child from the group if his behavior is detrimental to himself and the group.

The concept of role balancing is suggested as a rule of thumb to follow. This means that one should avoid overloading a group with a particular behavioral type, such as aggressive, hyperactive children, but rather include a hyperactive or aggressive child in a group including a calm, self-reliant child as well as a withdrawn child and perhaps one other child of a behavioral type that will provide a model for one of the other three. In support of this procedure, Ginott (1968) has stated,

> *An effeminate boy needs to identify with more masculine playmates. The dependent child needs the example of more self-reliant groupmates . . . . Agressive youngsters need groupmates who are strong but not belligerent. Fearful children need to be placed in a group of more mature youngsters (p. 177).*

3| Slavson (1943) and Ginott (1968) both consider the basic prerequisite for admission to a therapy group the presence or capacity for *social hunger* within the child. This concept would help the play group counselor in screening out only the most anti-social children. Usually these kinds of children are obvious potential 'wreckers of groups' and would not be considered for group treatment unless it could be rigidly controlled in a mental hospital or child guidance clinic. Nevertheless, children who show little self-restraint, shallow feelings towards others, and little conscience, should be considered lacking in social hunger and poor risks for play group counseling.

4| Age and sex constitute two additional categories that the group counselor must consider when composing a group for treatment by play and action techniques. Ginott (1968) has recommended that preschool children can be placed appropriately in mixed sex groups, whereas school-age children should be separated by sexes. This procedure may prove more appropriate for a clinic population served by Ginott; however, I have found little need to separate the sexes until they approach latency or roughly the age of nine or ten. At this point the girls are beginning to mature more rapidly than the boys and their sexual aggressiveness interferes with treatment when placed with less physically mature boys.

For the most part, children of the same age constitute the most therapeutic grouping. Exceptions are made deliberately to place more aggressive children in older age groups and some immature children in groups with children younger than themselves but not immature. A general practice to follow would be to compose groups in which there is no more than a year's range in the chronological age.

5| Differences in ethnic backgrounds, race, and intelligence do not pose serious problems for young children. However, grouping those with *gross* differences in intelligence, such as inclusion of retarded youngsters with those of average to better than average in intellectual ability, should be avoided.

6| Children who have been labeled "unsuitable for group therapy," according to Ginott (1961, p. 27), are chil-

dren who, as infants, were deprived of close contacts with their mother, children with murderous attitudes towards their siblings, sociopathic children, children who have shown accelerated sexual drives, children who have been exposed and/or involved in perverse sexual experiences, those who habitually steal, the extremely aggressive child, and the child who suffers from severe or acute trauma leading to the development of gross stress reactions such as inappropriate terror to a family pet (following being bitten by a dog), refusal to enter an automobile (following a recent auto mishap), etc.

Group Size

The size of a group of young children composed for the purpose of play group counseling should be considered in the light of counselor control. Young children have not developed to any large degree the social graces of listening while others are talking, taking turns, being considerate of others who may be suffering emotional stress, etc. Since fewer built-in controls exist within each child at this age, the counselor must be prepared to exercise control so that the group does actually function as a growth group. In addition to his lack of social controls, the young child also lacks adequate controls for his own and others' safety. The counselor, therefore, must be alert to the safety needs of each child. The fearful child, especially, requires this kind of safety assurance.

To focus intently on what each child attempts to communicate requires eternal vigilance on the part of the counselor. Since the young child depends on his play and non-verbal means for much of his communication, the counselor must control the number of such stimuli if he is to be in touch with each child in the group and with the group as a whole. When the counselor moves to structured play and socio- and psychodramatic techniques, it is vital that he maintain the kind of control over these media that will serve the purpose of counselee growth.

The larger the number in a play group the fewer the opportunities for the development of close, intimate relationships among the children and between a child and the counselor. Therefore, the larger the number, the slower the development of group cohesiveness, and group cohesiveness appears to be critical in the development of a growth group (Goldstein, et al., 1966). Among young

children, cohesiveness is especially difficult to achieve since each child is so self-centered. In fact it often appears that in play group counseling the counseling is individual counseling within the group setting rather than *group* counseling, *per se*.

Another factor which could increase or delimit counselor control is the nature of the counselees in the group. Although this problem should be controlled through role balancing, one or two rather aggressive and/or hyperactive youngsters in a group would necessitate more counselor vigilance and control than a group of less aggressive or hyperactive children. When all the above considerations are given to group size, a good practice to follow is not to exceed five regardless of experience and competence, and to include no more than two or three children if one is just beginning to practice play group counseling.

Frequency, Length, and Duration of Group Sessions

Play group counseling (techniques) is, as described in Chapter one, both prevention- and remediation-oriented. It is prevention-oriented to the degree that a child is having some difficulty acquiring adequate coping behaviors to master successfully a given developmental task. It is remedial to the degree that a child has failed to develop appropriate coping behaviors for a given developmental task and therefore is beginning to experience difficulty in intra- and interpersonal relationships. The counselor, in setting up a play group, should determine the degree to which his group is composed of children who require preventive or remedial treatment. The former usually does not require as intensive treatment or as much counselor intervention as the latter.

When combined with a supportive group guidance program, preventive play group counseling could be effective on a forty-minute to one hour a week basis over a period from three to twelve months. Play group counseling which is primarily remedial requires greater intensity of treatment and intensity of treatment, all other variables being equal, varies directly with length and frequency of group sessions. Therefore, two group sessions of forty to sixty minutes, equally spaced throughout the week, are recommended.

The duration of treatment is difficult to predict; however, periodic evaluations should be made with parents, teachers, and significant others to appraise the child's progress. Usually, too

much is expected by teachers, parents, and even counselors. Counselors often terminate treatment at the first sign of progress thus creating an excellent possibility of a relapse on the part of the child. No minimum time can be set for remedial treatment in play groups, but the counselor should consider six to nine months a reasonable treatment period. Since children are referred for help at different times in the course of a school year, the school counselor who operates on a nine-month schedule must vary the frequency of weekly meetings for a group depending on the time remaining in the school year. Nevertheless, he should try to allow at least three months for any play group.

Media

Having previously developed the rationale for using play and action techniques for group work with young children, the emphasis here will be on identifying specific materials for inclusion in the playroom. The purposes for the use of play and action facilitating media are:

1| to facilitate relationship building or to establish the facilitative base between the children and the counselor,
2| to increase the potential for communication between the child and counselor and among the children themselves by capitalizing on the natural medium of child play,
3| to assist the child in recognizing and/or understanding the difference between appropriate and inappropriate coping behavior—opportunity for reality testing,
4| to protect the child's degree of self-disclosure through encouraging a certain degree of vicarious expressiveness and experiencing,
5| to provide occasions for symbolic or vicarious modeling,
6| to facilitate the occurrence of responses that can be rewarded by the counselor, *i.e.*, to maximize the opportunity to use the principles of operant conditioning and shaping, and
7| to maximize the controlled use of "release therapy" when appropriate.

Much has been written regarding the use of play and action producing media for use with the young child, but virtually no carefully controlled investigations have been done which have demonstrated the superiority of one toy over another or one action technique over another. Nor can one expect to find this kind of exacting information, since different toys are likely to be preferred for different problem types. Beiser (1955) studied the free choice of a selected group of toys of 100 children, 79 boys and 21 girls, ranging from 2 to 12 years of age. The range of cases was quite broad, but were of the type referred to the Chicago Institute for Juvenile Research. Each toy was tabulated according to the number of children who played with it (Popularity), a ratio of popularity and total dynamic interpretations stemming from play with a toy (Communication Value), frequency with which the toy stimulated fantasy on the child's part (Fantasy Stimulation), the breadth or number of dynamic interpretations that a therapist could make from a child's play with an individual toy (Dynamic Spread), and a Combined Total ranking of the toys. The highest ranking toys are shown in Table 3.5 and the lowest ranking in Table 3.6. Beiser warned that her finding should be interpreted with caution until further study could relate the influence of degree of disturbance, age, sex, and intelligence, to play patterns.

Certain toys and materials are provided for "release therapy." These usually include plastic inflatable figures for punching, pop guns for releasing hostility, finger paint for smearing and messing, pounding tools and boards for releasing aggression, etc. These media should be used with caution since the aggressive child may be stimulated to greater aggression, hostility, and destructiveness if the use of the toy or medium *reinforces* these qualities within him rather than serving as cathartic release.

Pupil personnel workers of the Baltimore County (Maryland) School System (Board of Education, 1963) have categorized play media under three areas: (1) *toys for release of aggression* (bop bags, guns, soldiers, rubber puppets, finger paints, clay, and play dough); (2) *real life toys* (doll house, family dolls, animals, medical kit, play money, cars, trucks, black board and telephones); (3) *toys for enhancement of self concept* (play logs, erector set, puzzles, and maps). Ginott (1961, 1968) has advocated the use of specific toys for the development of the objectives of a therapeutic relationship, i.e., catharsis, insight, reality testing, and sublimation. To convey the permissiveness of the counselor in his attempt to establish a good *therapeutic relationship*, the counselor makes heretofore forbidden toys available to the child such

TABLE 3.5

Highest Ranking Toys[a]

Popularity	Communication Value	Fantasy Stimulation	Dynamic Spread	Combined Total
64% doll family	1.41 Nok-Out Bench	55% doll family	11 doll family	doll family
62% soldiers	1.14 doll family	54% paper and crayon	10 animals	soldiers
60% gun	1.13 gun	48% clay	9 planes	gun
55% Nok-Out Bench	1.0 soldiers	46% blocks	8 clay	clay
51% trucks	0.88 paper and crayons	43% planes	8 trucks	paper and crayons
50% goose	0.83 clay	39% soldiers	8 gun	animals
46% telephone	0.79 large baby doll	35% animals	8 Nok-Out Bench	planes
46% animals	0.65 animals	29% trucks	8 goose	Nok-Out Bench
46% planes		29% furniture		trucks

[a]From Beiser, H. R. Therapeutic play techniques: Play equipment for diagnosis and therapy. *American Journal of Orthopsychiatry*, 1955, *25*, 761–770. Copyright the American Orthopsychiatric Association, Inc. Reproduced by permission.

TABLE 3.6

Lowest Ranking Toys[a]

Popularity	Communication Value	Fantasy Stimulation	Dynamic Spread	Combined Total
3% pencil	0.0 pencil	0 pencil	0 pencil	pencil
8% scissors	0.2 crayons (only)	0 ball	1 paste	paste
9% paste	0.26 furniture	9% Nok-Out Bench	3 scissors	scissors
13% blocks	0.26 telephone	11% paste	4 blocks	ball
13% ball			4 ball	

[a]From Beiser, H. R. Therapeutic play techniques: Play equipment for diagnosis and therapy. *American Journal of Orthopsychiatry,* 1955, *25,* 761–770. Copyright the American Orthopsychiatric Association, Inc. Reproduced by permission.

as noise-making toys, including drums, pegboards, xylophones, air rifles and cap guns. Other forbidden toys such as a typewriter, flashlight, tool kit, according to Ginott, serve the purpose of establishing a good relationship. A doll family also serves this end.

Materials included in the playroom for release or *catharsis* must be carefully chosen to fit the child's basic problem. Care should be taken not to include materials which lead to diffuse hyperactivity. Ginott cautions that catharsis in children almost always leads to mobility and acting out and that acting out in and of itself has no curative effects aside from pleasure and release. For the hyperactive child Ginott recommends materials which will focus his energies such as pegboards, building blocks, rifles for shooting, nails for driving, wood for sawing, construction boxes and the like. For the fearful and fragile child, Ginott recommends materials that can be handled without the aid of tools such as water, paint, sand, play dough, dolls, chalk, and crayons. These materials also have the added advantage of permitting the child to conceal certain of his feelings and to erase or remake or refine certain of his productions.

Toys alone do not provide the child *insight;* therefore Ginott suggests that the counselor structure play situations which will enable the child to gain insight into the dynamics of his behavior. This can be done, for example, by providing only one gun which will likely bring out a conflict. The counselor also might structure a task that requires cooperation of all the children if it is to be accomplished. This might include, for example, preparing puppets for a puppet show. Ginott (1968) cautions the counselor to avoid treating the child suffering from a character disorder with insight methods.

For *reality testing* toys should be chosen so that the playroom is furnished with those of graded difficulty. Complex puzzles and toys should be excluded from the playroom, especially for the child whose self-image and ego strength is low.

> *In order for play therapy to be an experience in social learning, children should be provided with situations and materials that demand exploration of others as well as themselves. Most children at times in their therapy, should be exposed to peers, resistive materials, and planned scarcity of tools, so that they can test themselves in relation to social actualities (Ginott, 1961, p. 60).*

Finally, Ginott recommends sand, water, paint and clay as essential media for *sublimation* of children's urethral and anal

drives. A variety of outlets to promote sublimation are suggested by Ginott. He cites the need for sublimating anger through the punching of dolls or plastic bounce back toys as well as the possibility of destroying clay figures or composing critical poems and writing murder mysteries.

In addition to the usual toys which are included in a typical playroom, consideration should be given to the use of other action-oriented media including sociodrama and psychodrama, story telling and books for the child's use and for group listening when read by the counselor, the construction and use of puppets for symbolic or vicarious sociodrama and psychodrama, short films and filmstrips, music, and tape recordings. These media offer the counselor the opportunity to introduce models vicariously through puppet shows, stories, audio and video tapes, and films or filmstrips, which the children can use to imitate. These vicarious models are especially useful when the group is lacking in appropriate peer models. The sociodrama and psychodrama are action techniques that the counselor can structure for the playroom in which the models or participants (protagonist and auxiliary egos) are the group members themselves.

For the mature eight-year-old and the nine-year-old child, media and techniques appropriate for the preadolescent may be more appropriate than those suggested for the young child. The reader should refer to this section in Chapter four for a discussion of appropriate media.

Application of Play Media—An Example

Clinical experience also provides us with certain crude indices which can guide us in our selection of toys and action media for certain purposes and for certain kinds of children. Based on the rationale developed earlier in this chapter, the first few sessions of play group counseling should be rather unstructured to provide the child opportunities for free play and to enable the counselor to build his facilitative base and to diagnose further the child's problem areas. To build the best facilitative base the counselor tries to respond on a level that is interchangeable with that expressed verbally and/or symbolically by the child. The counselor communicates that he understands the child by expressing in words and actions a message that is interchangeable with that expressed by a given child. For example, if a young girl begins to punish verbally and/or symbolically, a baby brother in doll play, the counselor expresses verbally that he understands how the baby brother can

sometimes require so much of Mommy and Daddy's attention that there is little left for sister, etc. Symbolically, the counsellor can show that he understands by taking the baby brother out of sight of the mother and father doll and putting a little girl doll in their presence.

To follow up the example just cited, the counselor can, through roleplaying with the dolls and, eventually with the child, show how to use appropriate ways of gaining mother and father's attention without having to resort to the inappropriate and ultimately self-defeating behavior of punishing baby brother. Reinforcement of appropriate coping behaviors, in this case, can be provided through models who are rewarded by the counselor or story characters if the story is read rather than told. Direct reinforcement can be given when the child's doll play or relationships with other children in the group warrant it.

The Playroom

The playroom should be located in an area of the school or clinic where the noise will not distract other adults or children. It should be designed such that there is complete privacy from onlookers (except for authorized adult observers who are behind a one-way mirror), and it should be soundproof (Meeks, 1967). The playroom should be neither too small nor too large since cramped quarters force children into continuous close contact, which creates occasions for irritation as well as lack of privacy, whereas a room that is too large engenders running and rough-housing. With these considerations in mind, Ginott (1961) recommends a room of 300 to 400 square feet.

The room should be furnished with certain permanent or at least semi-permanent facilities. The room itself and all of its furnishings should be constructed with the physical safety of the children and the counselor in mind. The room should be well lighted and ventilated. Any glass in the windows and light fixtures should be protected by wire mesh. The walls should be easily cleaned and repaintable and the floor also should be easily cleaned but not treated with wax or other types of polish which would make it slippery. Indoor-outdoor carpeting may be suitable in some cases where safety factors are pre-eminent.

Each playroom should be equipped with at least one study table and a long wooden bench for use as a table or work area. A chalkboard should be fastened to a wall and a sturdy easel should

be fastened so that it will not fall or collapse. Chairs should be of wood or plastic and noncollapsable. A small area should be set aside for a floor sand box, including seating space on the edges. A sink with running water should be included in one area of the room. The faucets should be easily controlled by a young child. A large doll house is included as a part of the permanent facilities in a playroom, although it could be portable and stored in a cabinet. Bathroom facilities should be in an easily accessible adjoining room. A large, sturdy cabinet should be set against one wall or in a corner for the storage of supplies and toys, or an adjoining closet should be available for storage. Finally, electrical outlets should be placed above the reach of the children, but accessible to the counselor for the use of tape recorders, slide projectors, record players, etc.

Beiser (1955) has developed a "portable playroom" which consists simply of a box which includes special toys arranged for a given child. The child can then pick up his box and use the toys and materials in a playroom equipped with the permanent fixtures described in the preceding paragraph. This "portable playroom" permits greater individualization of counseling but incurs the added problem of promoting jealousies among the children.

Selected Illustrative Research Studies

Research studies using play- and action-oriented approaches with young children in groups are rare in the published literature. My inclusion here of selected studies in the area of play group counseling and those in which the emphasis was on sociodrama and psychodrama is twofold: to support the use of these approaches and to provide the reader with a sampling of the techniques, settings, age groups, etc., in which these approaches have been found helpful. First, I shall present a sampling of studies where the emphasis was on play in counseling or therapy groups. This section will be followed by selected studies in which the chief medium was sociodrama or psychodrama.

Play Group Counseling Studies

Eleven third-grade boys were randomly assigned to three play therapy groups by Clement (1967). The boys had been referred by their teachers because of shy, withdrawn behavior. One group of

four Ss met in a playroom and received tangible reinforcements (tokens) for socially approved behavior. Another experimental group of four Ss received verbal reinforcement from the play therapist for socially approved behavior. A third or control group met in a playroom in the absence of a play therapist. Fourteen play sessions were held for each group.

The Token Group exhibited an increase in social approach behavior and a decrease in discrete, problem behavior. The Verbal Group increased slightly in social approach behavior. The Control Group showed no change on the objective measures used for evaluation. All groups, however, failed to demonstrate changes in "productivity," "anxiety," and "general psychological adjustment."

Jensen (1958) utilized a combination of play therapy (music, art, drama, and dance) and interview group counseling with underachieving primary school children in grades 2, 3, and 4. The Ss were ten children with normal measured intelligence, but their classroom behavior was not conducive to learning. Their behavior ranged from silent withdrawal to hyperactive, disruptive participation.

The children were given a combination of academic remedial instruction for one hour each of four days a week and one hour of group counseling during the second hour for four days a week. The experimental program consisted of approximately 60 to 80 periods during the year. The membership in the counseling groups was varied from one session to another. Sometimes the group would be given a task which required group cooperation; on other occasions the counselor would initiate a discussion designed to produce analysis and discussion about social relationship problems that might apply to some of the group members, and at still other occasions, music, art, drama or dance therapy was used.

Eight of the ten pupils benefited from this treatment program. One child was dropped from the program because of irregular attendance and failure of the family to cooperate and a second child was referred for psychiatric treatment. Jensen concluded that pupils with problems involving social relationships can be "restored" to adequate classroom performance within a relatively short time if the *right* counseling is given at the *right* time. She also stressed, among other things, the importance of diagnosis and counseling by a competent person such as small-group counseling by a trained school counselor and the close communication and working relationship throughout the treatment between the child's teacher and the group counselor.

Koenig (1949) carefully screened ten children from grades three through six for inclusion in a play group counseling experiment in a public school setting. The children were referred because of various problems, e.g., nonconforming classroom behavior, truancy, chronic tardiness, infantile behavior, nervousness, aggressive behavior, emotional disturbances, stealing, inattention, etc.

Koenig modified a regular classroom for use as the playroom. Various media were employed including handiwork, music, puppetry, sociodrama, clay modeling, drawing and painting, making puppet characters and a puppet stage, and quiet periods for story-telling, writing letters, reading books and conversation. During holidays, parties were held in the playroom and the counselor gave appropriate gifts to each child. The counselor functioned from a permissive frame of reference in which she permitted the children to choose their own media and interpersonal contacts. The setting itself was considered conducive to emotional adjustment. Explanations and interpretations were given only under special circumstances. Unrestraint in activity was permitted only in the beginning of treatment.

The treatment period consisted of one hour per week for a period of six months. The group counselor kept anecdotal records of each child and after three sessions a note was sent to each teacher concerning the child in her class in which his pattern of behavior was described and suggestions for assisting him in the classroom were given.

Significant improvement in nine of the ten children was noted by the counselor, teachers, and classmates. Four months following termination of treatment, seven of the ten still showed significant improved behavior although two had begun to slip back into previous behavioral patterns. Consequently, the counselor recommended a longer treatment period of at least one school year.

A project utilizing play group techniques in the public school setting has been described by Schiffer (1957). It concerned the treatment of emotionally disturbed children who came from a slum area created by a rapidly shifting population in New York City. The children ranged in grades from one through six; however, they were grouped generally by grades and by sex, except in the lower grades. The groups were open ended and thus several groups met over three or four years.

Teachers who volunteered to work with the children served as the group leaders. These teachers were supervised by a person trained in group therapy and group dynamics. Supervision was

held weekly during which time all aspects of the project were dealt with including intake, group organization, supplies, analysis of verbatim reports, evaluations, etc.

A playroom was set up in the school building for exclusive use of the play groups. It included the usual furnishings such as tables, chairs, work benches, sandbox, sink, etc. For lower grade children, doll families, doll furniture, paints, easels, sand, clay, paper, toys, and games were available. Woodworking tools and games for older children were provided.

The play groups were unstructured with the teacher-leader assuming a permissive, accepting, neutral role. Overt aggression was permitted within limits acceptable to the children and setting. Each play group met for one hour once a week.

Schiffer acknowledged that the play groups as constituted for this project, were not appropriate for deeply rooted symptoms nor were they intended as a complete therapeutic program. "Nevertheless," he stated, "our experience indicates that therapeutic effects do emerge and many of the children function better in the classroom and in the neighborhood as a result of their participation in the specialized play group" (1957, p. 193).

Selected Illustrative Studies Using Socio- and Psychodramatic Techniques

As early as 1941, Alpert (1941) described a teacher's application of "spontaneous dramatizations" and group therapy discussion to kindergarten children suffering from an unwholesome use of scatological language. Alpert reported that the treatment led to a decrease in the use of scatological language and that the "educational group therapy," in addition to the removal of the symptom, helped free the children from guilt and anxiety through the teacher's interpretations and universalizing of the symptom which permitted the children to abreact it in their play and obtain relief and release.

Gillies (1948) has reported the successful application of "therapy dramatics" in drawing out and involving normal first-grade children of six and seven years of age. To stimulate dramatization, Gillies started the groups with simple nursery rhymes, such as "There was a Crooked Man," and "Sing a Song of Sixpence." This was followed with appropriate stories, such as, *Daddies: What They Do All Day* by Helen Walker Puner, and piano music or self-devised rhythm bands.

Brunelle (1949) has utilized a literary source book: *Reading*

Ladders for Human Relations published by the American Council on Education, to select objective *conflict* situations in human relations to be roleplayed in the elementary school classrooms. After reading a given conflict situation, selection of roleplayers was made by the classroom teacher, and the session was roleplayed, discussed, and replayed until the students and teacher were satisfied with the handling of the conflict situation. Brunelle concluded, "Research indicates that there is considerable carryover from the training situations to real life situations when roleplaying is used. It is this *carryover* that makes role playing such a significant educational technique" (p. 237).

Roleplaying or psychodrama, later called the spontaneity approach to creative teaching, was used successfully by Cole (1949). She used it to desensitize fifth graders to rebuff and discouragement.

Teachers in the elementary schools of Inglewood, California utilized sociodrama developed around vocational, travel, family conflict, classroom conflict topics to "explore key children in action," and discovered that former uncooperative children frequently gave good sociodramatic performances, and that insights pass between pupil and pupil and between pupil and teacher. The teachers discovered "how problems of human relations could be resolved openly through group enactment and evaluation as well as how social skills could be built, through spontaneity practice, by children who needed them" (Haas, 1949, p. 262).

Wells (1962), a school administrator, has described her successful application of roleplaying counseling (psychodrama) in the elementary school. She used a variety of the psychodrama situations which included on the spot, future enactment, and "here and now," with children from first to eighth grade. She also utilized role reversal, double ego, soliloquy, and conscience in the roleplaying. Usually the group psychodramas consisted of only two or three children, sometimes a teacher or parent, and the director (Cecilia Wells). The problems of these normal children included, "quarrels over possessions, rivalry for position in a game or line, tripping or hitting each other—especially on the playground, interference with each other's classroom activities, classroom behavior unacceptable for the learning situation, and academic inadequacies" (p. 244).

Boyd and Youssi (1958) used five open-ended problem stories dealing with home situations, school incidents, and the school community to learn more about the attitudes and values of class members, and to study the reactions of the class toward individual

members. They recommend that the elementary school teachers use these procedures as a diagnostic technique and to improve understanding of the values, attitudes, maturity, etc., of their students.

Summary

This chapter was written to stand on its own. However, to comprehend it fully it should be read in conjunction with Chapter two. In Chapter three, I have tried to provide the reader with all the information that is required to develop a rationale for group guidance and counseling with the young child from five through nine years of age. The theoretical approach outlined in this chapter is based on the hypothesis that both prevention and remediation of problems in young children can best be served if considerations are given to the developmental stages and coping behaviors appropriate to the given age group.

A further hypothesis has been promulgated in this chapter and throughout this text. It is that group guidance is the most economical and efficient means within the area of the *helping relationships* to serve the cause of problem prevention. Group counseling is viewed as a preventive-remedial approach in the helping relationships. It is not promoted as a form of treatment that is preferred over individual counseling. It is presented as a procedure with unique offerings appropriate for some and inappropriate for others, and it is sometimes most efficaciously used in conjunction with individual counseling.

The bio-socio-psychological developmental tasks of Havighurst as interpreted by Lilienthal and Tryon and Tryon and Lilienthal, the psychosocial developmental tasks of Erikson, and the vocational developmental tasks described by Super, et al., all in conjunction with their appropriate coping behaviors, are outlined in three separate tables. The reader of this text is requested to use these tables as guideposts or guidelines for determining the group guidance and counseling needs of children five through nine years of age.

Since the major thrust of this text is on group counseling, group guidance is treated less completely. Even so, I have presented a rationale for group guidance which utilizes the play and action orientation of young children. A sample group guidance session is given which attempts to portray the simultaneous use of developmental levels and learning principles appropriate for

the systematic application to group guidance with young children. Selected research studies are summarized to illustrate the successful use of play- and action-oriented approaches, e.g., sociodrama and psychodrama, to group guidance. Group guidance resources are cited both within the chapter and at the end of the chapter under suggested readings and programs.

A theory and a method of group counseling consistent with the developmental needs of young children are described in some detail. Play and action techniques are considered the media most consistent with the natural interests and inclinations of young children. The values and limitations of toys and play materials are documented from theoretical and research literature and from personal clinical experiences.

The special learning principles which appear to be most applicable to changing behavior in the young child are named and illustrated. Modeling, in particular, is presented as a principle of learning most applicable to young children.

Sociodrama and psychodrama or roleplaying and action-oriented procedures are compared with principles of learning illustrated in the behavioral therapies. The conclusion reached from this comparison is that they are not contradictory principles but rather are complimentary in their application to group counseling.

Selection and group composition, group size, media, and the playroom, are separate topics systematically dealt with in this chapter. Each section is developed to be consistent with the theoretical rationale outlined for group counseling in this text and especially for the age group treated in this chapter.

An example of the application of play media to the treatment of young children through group counseling is given to illustrate the developmental model, including how learning principles can be systematically employed in modifying behavior. Selected research studies are also summarized to illustrate successful application of related group approaches.

Suggested readings and programs are given at the end of the chapter to assist the reader in the location of materials for implementation of the group guidance and counseling program described herein. Also, additional theoretical references are cited for the reader who wishes to expand and/or further research the position expounded in this chapter.

References

ALPERT, A. Education as therapy. *Psychoanalytic Quarterly*, 1941, *10*, 468–474.

AMSTER, F. Differential uses of play in treatment of young children. *American Journal of Orthopsychiatry*, 1943, *13*, 62–68.

ANDERSON, J., & SCHMIDT, W. I. A time for feeling. *Elementary School Guidance and Counseling*, 1967, *1*, 47–56.

ARBUTHNOT, M. *Children and books.* Chicago: Scott, Foresman, 1947.

ARBUTHNOT, M. *Children and books.* (2nd ed.) Chicago: Scott, Foresman, 1957.

ARBUTHNOT, M. *Children and books.* (3rd ed.) Chicago: Scott, Foresman, 1964.

AXLINE, V. M. Play therapy procedures and results. *American Journal of Orthopsychiatry*, 1955, *25*, 618–626.

BANDURA, A. Behavioral modifications through modeling procedures. In L. Krasner & L. P. Ullmann (Eds.), *Research in behavior modification.* New York: Holt, Rinehart & Winston, 1965. Pp. 310–340.

BANDURA, A., ROSS, D., & ROSS, S. Imitation of film-mediated aggressive models. *Journal of Abnormal and Social Psychology*, 1963, *66*, 3–11.

BANDURA, A., & WALTERS, R. H. *Social learnings and personality development.* New York: Holt, 1963.

BARCLAY, J. R. Effecting behavior change in the elementary classroom: An exploratory study. *Journal of Counseling Psychology*, 1967, *14*, 240–247.

BEACH, A. I. The effect of group model-reinforcement counseling on achievement behavior of seventh and eighth grade students. Unpublished doctoral dissertation, Stanford University, 1967.

BEISER, H. R. Therapeutic play techniques: Play equipment for diagnosis and therapy. *American Journal of Orthopsychiatry*, 1955, *25*, 761–770.

BENDER, L. Therapeutic play techniques: Discussion. *American Journal of Orthopsychiatry*, 1955, *25*, 784–787.

BENDER, L. & WOLTMAN, A. G. The use of puppet shows as a psychotherapeutic method for behavior problems in children. *American Journal of Orthopsychiatry*, 1936, *6*, 341–354.

BESSELL, H., & PALOMARES, U. H. *Methods in human development.* San Diego, Calif.: Human Development Training Institute, 1967.

BLAKE, R. R. Experimental psychodrama with children. *Group Psychotherapy*, 1955, *8*, 347–350.

BOARD OF EDUCATION OF BALTIMORE COUNTY, MARYLAND, GUIDANCE DEPARTMENT. *Elementary school counseling*, 1963. (Mimeo)

BOYD, A., & YOUSSI, M. Peer group regulates role playing. *School Counselor*, 1958, *6*, 11–18.

BRUNELLE, P. Action projects from children's literature; An indirect approach to intercultural relations in the elementary school. In R. B. Haas (Ed.), *Psychodrama and sociodrama in American education.* Beacon, New York: Beacon House, 1949. Pp. 235–242.

CARKHUFF, R. R. *Helping and human relations.* Vol. 1. *Selection and training.* New York: Holt, Rinehart & Winston, 1969. (a)

CARKHUFF, R. R. *Helping and human relations.* Vol. 2. *Practice and research.* New York: Holt, Rinehart & Winston, 1969. (b)

CHITTENDEN, G. E. An experimental study in measuring and modifying assertive behavior in young children. *Monograph of Social Research and Child Development.* 1942, 7 (1, Whole No. 31).

CLEMENT, P. W. Group play therapy and tangible reinforcers used to modify the behavior of eight-year-old boys. *Behavior Research and Therapy*, 1967, *5*, 301–312.

COLE, N. R. Exploring psychodrama at fifth grade level. In R. B. Haas (Ed.), *Psychodrama and sociodrama in American education.* Beacon, New York: Beacon House, 1949. Pp. 243–245.

COLE, N. R. *Children's arts from deep down inside.* New York: John Day, 1966.

CONN, J. H. Play interview therapy of castration fears. *American Journal of Orthopsychiatry*, 1955, *25*, 747–754.

CORSINI, R. J. *Roleplaying in psychotherapy.* Chicago: Aldine, 1966.

DAVIS, C. D. *A group technique for the modification of certain behavior reactions (kindergarten level).* (Doctoral dissertation, State University of Iowa) Ann Arbor, Mich.: University Microfilms, 1958. No. 57–1608.

DENNEY, E. W. A study of the effectiveness of selected motion pictures for reducing frustration in children. *Dissertation Abstracts*, 1959, *19*, 3170–3171.

DRABKOVA, H. Experiences resulting from clinical use of psychodrama with children. *Group Psychotherapy*, 1966, *19*, 32–36.

ERIKSON, E. H. *Childhood and society.* New York: W. W. Norton, 1950.

ERIKSON, E. H. *Childhood and society.* (2nd ed.) New York: W. W. Norton, 1963.

FRANK, L. K. Play in personality development. *American Journal of Orthopsychiatry*, 1955, *25*, 576–590.

GAZDA, G. M., & FOLDS, J. H. Group procedures in the elementary school. In G. M. Gazda (Ed.), *Theories and methods of group counseling in the school.* Springfield, Ill.: Charles C. Thomas, 1969. Pp. 21–55.

GILLIES, E. P. Therapy dramatics for public schoolrooms. *Nervous Child.* 1948, *17*, 328–336.

GINOTT, H. G. *Group psychotherapy with children: The theory and practice of play therapy.* New York: McGraw-Hill, 1961.

GINOTT, H. G. Group therapy with children. In G. M. Gazda (Ed.), *Basic approaches to group psychotherapy and group counseling.* Springfield, Ill.: Charles C. Thomas, 1968. Pp. 176–194.

GITTLEMAN, M. Behavior rehearsal as a technique in child treatment. *Journal of Child Psychology and Psychiatry*, 1965, *6*, 251–255.

GOLDSTEIN, A. P., HELLER, K., & SECHREST, L. B. *Psychotherapy and the psychology of behavior change.* New York: Wiley, 1966.

HAAS, R. B. (Ed.) *Psychodrama and sociodrama in American education.* New York: Beacon House, 1949.

HANSEN, J. C., NILAND, T. M., & ZANI, L. P. Model reinforcement in group counseling with elementary school children. *Personnel and Guidance Journal*, 1969, *47*, 741–744.

HARMS, E. Play diagnosis: Preliminary considerations for a sound approach. *Nervous Child*, 1948. 7, 233–246.

HAVIGHURST, R. J. *Developmental tasks and education.* Chicago: University of Chicago Press, 1948.

HAVIGHURST, R. J. *Developmental tasks and education.* (2nd ed.) New York: Longmans, Green, 1952.

HAVIGHURST, R. J. *Human development and education.* New York: David McKay, 1953.

JACK, L. M. An experimental study of ascendant behavior in preschool children. *University of Iowa studies in child welfare,* 1934, *9*, 3–5.

JENNINGS, H. H. Sociodrama as an educative process. In *Fostering mental health in our schools: 1950 Yearbook, ASCD.* Washington, D.C.: Association of Supervision and Curriculum Development, 1950. Pp. 260–285.

JENSEN, G. E. Small-group counseling for under-achieving primary school children. In H. I. Driver (Ed.), *Counseling and learning through small group discussion.* Madison, Wisc.: Monona Publications, 1958. Pp. 286–290.

KLEIN, M. The psychoanalytic play technique. *American Journal of Orthopsychiatry*, 1955, *25*, 223–237.

KOENIG, F. G. A group therapy experiment in a city elementary school. *Understanding the child*, 1949, *18*, 40–44.

LAZARUS, A. Behavior therapy in groups. In G. M. Gazda (Ed.), *Basic approaches to group psychotherapy and group counseling.* Springfield, Ill.: Charles C. Thomas, 1968. Pp. 149–175.

LEBO, D. The development of play as a form of therapy. *American Journal of Psychiatry*, 1955, *12*, 418–442.

LILIENTHAL, J. W., & TRYON, C. Developmental tasks: II. Discussion of specific tasks and implications. In *Fostering mental health in our schools: 1950 Yearbook, ASCD,* Washington, D.C. Association of Supervision and Curriculum Development, 1950. Pp. 90–128.

LOWREY, L. G. Therapeutic play techniques: Introduction. *American Journal of Orthopsychiatry,* 1955, *25,* 574–575.

MEEKS, A. Dimensions of elementary school guidance. *Elementary School Guidance and Counseling.* 1967, *1,* 163–187.

MORENO, J. L. Sociodrama: A method for the analysis of social conflicts. *Psychological Monographs,* 1944, No. 1.

MORENO, J. L. The spontaneity theory of learning. In R. B. Haas (Ed.), *Psychodrama and sociodrama in American education.* Beacon, New York: Beacon House, 1949. Pp. 191–197.

MORENO, J. L. Behavior therapy. *American Journal of Psychiatry,* 1963, *120,* 194–196.

MORENO, J. L., & KIPPER, D. A. *Group psychodrama and community-centered counseling.* In G. M. Gazda (Ed.), *Basic approaches to group psychotherapy and group counseling.* Springfield, Ill.: Charles C. Thomas, 1968. Pp. 27–79.

MOWRER, O. H. *Learning theory and behavior.* New York: Wiley, 1960.

OJEMANN, R. H. *Developing a program for education in human behavior.* Iowa City, Iowa: State University of Iowa, 1959.

OJEMANN, R. H., HUGHES, J .E., & CHOWNING, K. *A teaching program in human behavior and mental health: Book II, handbook for second grade teachers.* Iowa City, Iowa: State University of Iowa, 1962.

PAGE, M. L. The modification of ascendant behavior in preschool children. *University of Iowa studies in child welfare.* 1936, *9,* 3–65.

PETERS, H. J., SHELLEY, M., & McCORMICK, R. *Random House program for elementary guidance.* New York: Random House, 1966.

SCHIFFER, M. A therapeutic play group in a public school. *Mental Hygiene,* 1957, *41,* 185–193.

SHAFTEL, G., & SHAFTEL, F. R. Report on the use of a "practice action level" in the Stanford University project for American ideals. In R. B. Haas (Ed.), *Psychodrama and sociodrama in American education.* New York: Beacon House, 1949. Pp. 245–253.

SLAVSON, S. R. *An introduction to group therapy.* New York: The Commonwealth Fund & International Universities Press, 1943.

SLAVSON, S. R. Differential methods of group therapy in relation to age levels. *Nervous Child,* 1945, *4,* 196–210.

SLAVSON, S. R. Group therapy in child care and child guidance. *Jewish Social Service Quarterly,* 1948, *25,* 203–213.

SOLOMON, J. C. Active play therapy: Further experiences. *American Journal of Orthopsychiatry,* 1940, *10,* 763–781.

SOLOMON, J. C. Play techniques and the integrative process. *American Journal of Orthopsychiatry,* 1955, *25,* 591–600.

STURM, I. E. The behavioristic aspects of psychodrama. *Group Psychotherapy,* 1965, *18,* 50–64.

SUPER, D. E., CRITES, J. O., HUMMEL, R. C., MOSER, H. P., OVERSTREET, P. L. & WARNATH, C. F. *Vocational development: A framework for research.* New York: Bureau of Publications, Teachers College, Columbia University, 1957.

TRYON, C., & LILIENTHAL, J. W. Developmental tasks: I. The concept and its importance. In *Fostering mental health in our schools: 1950 Yearbook of ASCD.* Washington, D.C.: Association for Supervision and Curriculum Development, 1950. Pp. 77–89.

WELLS, C. G. Psychodrama and creative counseling in the elementary school. *Group Psychotherapy,* 1962, *15,* 244–252.

Suggested Readings

AXLINE, V. *Play therapy.* (Rev. ed.) New York: Ballantine Books, Inc., 1969.

BANDURA, A. Behavioral modification through modeling procedures. In L. Krasner and L. P. Ullmann (Eds.), *Research in behavior modification.* New York: Holt, Rinehart & Winston, 1965. Pp. 310–340.

BARCLAY, J. R. Effecting behavior change in the elementary classroom: An exploratory study. *Journal of Counseling Psychology,* 1967, *14*, 240–247.

BENDER, L. Therapeutic play techniques: Discussion. *American Journal of Orthopsychiatry,* 1955, *25*, 784–787.

BENDER, L., & WOLTMANN, A. G. The use of puppet shows as a psychotherapeutic method for behavior problems in children. *American Journal of Orthopsychiatry,* 1936, *6*, 341–354.

BLAKE, R. R. Experimental psychodrama with children. *Group Psychotherapy,* 1955, *8*, 347–350.

BRUNELLE, P. Action projects from children's literature: An indirect approach to intercultural relations in the elementary school. In R. B. Haas (Ed.), *Psychodrama and Sociodrama in American Education.* Beacon, New York: Beacon House, 1949. Pp. 235–242.

COLE, N. *Children's arts from deep down inside.* New York: John Day, 1966.

CROSBY, M. (Ed.) *Reading ladders for human relations.* (4th ed.) Washington, D.C.: American Council on Education, 1963.

DINKMEYER, D. C. *Guidance and counseling in the elementary school: Readings in theory and practice.* New York: Holt, Rinehart, & Winston, 1968.

DRABKOVA, S. H. Experiences resulting from clinical use of psychodrama with children. *Group Psychotherapy,* 1966, *19*, 32–36.

FAUST, V. *The counselor-consultant in the elementary school.* Boston: Houghton-Mifflin, 1968.

FRANK, L. K. Play in personality development. *American Journal of Orthopsychiatry,* 1955, *25*, 576–590.

GAZDA, G. M., & FOLDS, J. H. Group procedures in the elementary school. In G. M. Gazda (Ed.), *Theories and methods of group counseling in the schools.* Springfield, Ill.: Charles C. Thomas, 1969. Pp. 21–55.

GILLIES, E. P. Therapy dramatics for public schoolroom. *Nervous Child,* 1948, *17*, 328–336.

GINOTT, H. G. *Group psychotherapy with children.* New York: McGraw-Hill, 1961.

GINOTT, H. G. Group therapy with children. In G. M. Gazda (Ed.), *Basic approaches to group psychotherapy and group counseling.* Springfield, Ill.: Charles C. Thomas, 1968. Pp. 176–194.

GLASSER, W. Reality therapy and group counseling. In G. M. Gazda (Ed.), *Group procedures for the disadvantaged.* Athens, Ga.: College of Education, University of Georgia, 1969. Pp. 1–73.

GLASSER, W. *Schools without failure.* New York: Harper & Row, 1969.

HAAS, R. B. (Ed.) *Psychodrama and sociodrama in American education.* New York: Beacon House, 1949.

HANSEN, J. C., & STEVIC, R. R. *Elementary school guidance.* Toronto, Ontario: Macmillan, 1969.

HARMS, E. Play diagnosis: Preliminary considerations for a sound approach. *Nervous Child,* 1948, *7*, 233–246.

HILL, G. E. Agreements in the practice of guidance in the elementary schools. *Elementary School Guidance and Counseling,* 1967, *1*, 188–195.

HOLT, J. *How children fail.* New York: Pitman Publishing Corp., 1964.

HOLT, J. *How children learn.* New York: Pitman Publishing Corp., 1967.

JENNINGS, H. H. Sociodrama as an educative process. In *Fostering mental health in our schools: 1950 Yearbook ASCD.* Washington, D.C.: Association for Supervision and Curriculum Development, 1950. Pp. 260–285.

KAWIN, E. *The wise choice of toys.* Chicago: University of Chicago Press, 1934.

KRISE, M. Creative dramatics and group psychotherapy. *Journal of Child Psychiatry*, 1952, *2*, 337–342.

KRUMBOLTZ, J. D., & THORESEN, C. E. *Behavioral counseling: Cases and techniques.* New York: Holt, Rinehart, & Winston, 1969.

LEBO, D. The development of play as a form of therapy. *American Journal of Psychiatry*, 1955, *12*, 418–442.

LILIENTHAL, J. W., & TRYON, C. Developmental tasks: II. Discussion of specific tasks and implications. In *Fostering mental health in our schools: 1950 Yearbook, ASCD,* Washington, D.C.: Association for Supervision and Curriculum Development, 1950. Pp. 90–128.

LIPPITT, R. Psychodrama in the kindergarten and nursery school. *Group Psychotherapy*, 1954, *7*, 262–289.

LOTT, A. J., LOTT, B. E., & MATTHEWS, G. M. Interpersonal attraction among children as a function of vicarious reward. *Journal of Educational Psychology,* 1969, *60*, 274–283.

MORENO, J. L. The spontaneity theory of learning. In R. B. Haas (Ed.), *Psychodrama and sociodrama in American Education.* Beacon, New York: Beacon House, 1949. Pp. 191–197.

MORENO, J. L., & KIPPER, D. A. Group psychodrama and community-centered counseling. In G. M. Gazda (Ed.), *Basic approaches to group psychotherapy and group counseling.* Springfield, Ill.: Charles C. Thomas, 1968. Pp. 27–79.

MOUSTAKAS, C. E. *Psychotherapy with children.* New York: Harper, 1959.

MUNSON, H. L. *Elementary school guidance: Concepts, dimensions, and practice.* Boston: Allyn & Bacon, 1970.

MURPHY, G. Play as a counselor's tool. *School Counselor*, 1960, *8*, 53–58.

NELSON, R. Physical facilities for elementary school counseling. *Personnel and Guidance Journal*, 1967, *45*, 552–556.

O'CONNOR, R. D. Modification of social withdrawal through symbolic modeling. *Journal of Applied Behavior Analysis*, 1969, *2*, 15–22.

PETERS, H. J., SHERTZER, B. & VanHOOSE, W. *Guidance in elementary schools.* Chicago: Rand McNally, 1965.

SOLOMON, J. C. Active play therapy: Further experiences. *American Journal of Orthopsychiatry*, 1940, *10*, 763–781.

SOLOMON, J. C. Play techniques and the integrative process. *American Journal of Orthopsychiatry*, 1955, *25*, 591–600.

STURM, I. E. The behavioristic aspect of psychodrama. *Group Psychotherapy*, 1965, *18*, 50–64.

TRYON, C., & LILIENTHAL, J. W. Developmental tasks: I. The concept and its importance: In *Fostering mental health in our schools: 1950 Yearbook, ASCD.* Washington, D.C.: Association for Supervision and Curriculum Development, 1950. Pp. 77–89.

WELLS, C. G. Psychodrama and creative counseling in the elementary school. *Group psychotherapy*, 1962, *15*, 244–252.

WOODY, R. H. *Behavioral problem children in the schools.* New York: Appleton-Century-Crofts, 1969.

Group Guidance Programs

A Teaching Program in Human Behavior and Mental Health

Manual: Ojemann, R. H. *Developing a program for education in human behavior.* Iowa City, Iowa: State University of Iowa, 1959.

Kindergarten and Grade 1: *Handbook for Kindergarten and First Grade Teachers.*
Grade 2: *Handbook for Second Grade Teachers.*
Grade 3: *Handbook for Third Grade Teachers.* (Rev. Ed.).

Focus on Self-Development

Publisher: Science Research Associates, Chicago, Illinois
Grades K-2: Stage One: Awareness

Preschool and Early Elementary School Human Development Program

Bessell, H., & Palomares, U. H. *Methods in human development.* San Diego, Calif.: Human Development Training Institute, 1967.

Program for Elementary Guidance

Peters, H. J., Shelly, M., & McCormick, R. *Random House program for elementary guidance.* New York: Random House, 1966.

Developing Understanding of Others (DUSO)—D. Dinkmeyer.

DUSO Kit D-1 Social-Self Ages 5–7.
DUSO Kit D-2 Social-Self Ages 6–8 (Available soon)
American Guidance Services, Inc.
Dept. PGJ-4 Publishers Bldg.
Circle Pines, Minn. 55014

Suppliers of Play Media

ABC School Supply, Inc., 437 Armour Circle, N. E., P. O. Box 13084, Atlanta, Georgia 30324

Creative Playthings, Div., of Columbia Broadcasting System, Inc., Princeton, New Jersey.

Fisher-Price Toys, Inc., East Aurora, Erie Co., New York, 14052

Milton Bradley, Co., Springfield, Mass. 01101

Playskool, Inc., Div. of Milton Bradley Co., Chicago, Ill. 60618

Tonka Corp., Mound, Minn.

4 | Group Procedures for the Preadolescent

Introduction

The preadolescent is the child in the latency years of approximately 9–13. During the latter years of this period in particular or with the beginning of pubescence, the developmental gap between boys and girls is most noticeable, with the normal girl developing secondary sexual characteristics in advance of the normal boy by one to two years. Thus girls in the latter years of the latency period may be better described as early adolescents. The same holds true for more rapidly developing boys. Any of the classifications used to differentiate different age groups and developmental levels must be considered only as a norm with exceptions especially prominent at either end of the age group. Nevertheless, if we are to understand better and assist a given age group, we still need to employ what we know about the *typical* child in a particular age group.

Because boys and girls do vary greatly within the developmental levels, the group leader is also encouraged to make use of the guidelines of developmental tasks and appropriate coping behaviors for the age group preceding and also for the age group immediately above the one in which he works. Hence, the group leader of preadolescents would need to appraise himself of the developmental levels of the child 5–9 years of age as well as the adolescent or the child above the age of 13.

The child in latency is often the neglected child because he

has entered into a period of quiescence. His natural group consists of peers of the *same* sex. He is in the so-called homosexual age of his development wherein boys prefer to be with boys and girls prefer to be with girls. Cub and Boy Scouts become important for boys and girls' clubs, Brownies, and Girl Scouts are important to the girls.

The school grades most representative of latency or pre-adolescence are grades 4, 5, and 6, or the middle school. Junior high school overlaps at least in the seventh grade but for the early maturing boys and especially for the girls, eighth grade finds them in the early adolescent phase of development. When working with thirteen-year-olds, therefore, the group leader must use developmental guidelines and group techniques for both the preadolescent and the early adolescent.

The guideposts of developmental tasks, with appropriate coping behaviors, outlined in the following three tables are intended to be comprehensive. They include the bio-socio-psychological tasks and coping behaviors of Havighurst (1948, 1952, 1953), as interpreted by Lilienthal and Tryon (1950) and Tryon and Lilienthal (1950); the psychosocial stages of Erikson (1950, 1963), and the vocational developmental stages of Super, et al., (1957). In addition to these tables, Appendix A contains descriptions of appropriate and inappropriate behavior for children from infancy through age 15.

Group Guidance

The preadolescent, referred to earlier as the neglected age group, is in a crucial phase of his development even if it does represent the quiet period before the storm which comes with the onset of puberty and adolescence. The school in particular must show a keener interest in the preadolescent because it is during the middle grades especially that the child begins to look toward school as a chore rather than a delight. It is here that the excitement stemming from new learnings and friendships (peers and teachers) can and must be given concerted attention; otherwise many children begin marking time in the classroom.

Some form of a systematic program devoted to helping the preadolescent understand himself and others is recommended as a deterrent to the crushing of the child's interest in school at this stage of his development. With a group guidance program instituted in every classroom every child and every teacher will have

TABLE 4.1

Bio-Socio-Psychological Developmental Tasks[a]
Preadolescence: Ages 9–13

Developmental Tasks	*Coping Behaviors*
	Early Adolescence
1. Achieving an appropriate dependence-independence pattern	1. Establishing one's independence from adults in all areas of behavior *Examples:* He wants to do a number of things completely on his own, e.g., going to bed when he pleases, going where he pleases. To support his independence he supplements his allowance through paper routes, mowing lawns, etc. He resents adult interference with his plans and avoids conflicts with parents by being away from home frequently. He is eager to become independent but feels inadequate and must have the security of the apron strings when he needs it.
2. Achieving an appropriate giving receiving pattern of affection	1. Accepting one's self as a worthwhile person, really worthy of love *Examples:* Because of his dramatic physical changes, the preadolescent must find his apparent new self—learn to love his new self. In the process he becomes very egocentric and preoccupied with himself. He uses his friendships (very unstable) to gain understanding of himself. He gets crushes on teachers, adults and other adolescents. As he grows more self-confident his affection and confidence in others grow.
3. Relating to changing social groups	1. Behaving in accordance with a shifting peer code *Examples:* In the pre-pubertal period the boys are about one or two years behind the physical development of girls. Exclusion of girls or to "hate" girls is the thing to do. Boys at this period must avoid being sissy and therefore must be ready to fight as well as to dress in an unkempt fashion. Girls must learn to make a turnabout in former patterns—being demure is no longer a means of

[a](To avoid oversimplification and misunderstanding of the material shown in this table, the reader is directed to the ASCD 1950 Yearbook: *Fostering Mental Health in Our Schools* in which background material and a more complete rationale is given.)

From Tryon, C., & Lilienthal, J. W. Developmental tasks: I. The concept and its importance. Association for Supervision and Curriculum Development, *Fostering Mental Health in Our Schools*. 1950 Yearbook. Washington, D.C.: Association for Supervision and Curriculum Development, 1950. Pp. 77–89. Copyright © 1950 by the Association for Supervision and Curriculum Development. Reproduced with permission.

From Lilienthal, J. W., & Tryon, C. Developmental tasks: II. Discussion of specific tasks and implications. Association for Supervision and Curriculum Development. *Fostering Mental Health in Our Schools.* 1950 Yearbook. Washington, D.C.: Association for Supervision and Curriculum Development, 1950. Pp. 90–128. Copyright © 1950 by the Association for Supervision and Curriculum Development. Reproduced with permission.

TABLE 4.1 *(Continued)*

Developmental Tasks	Coping Behaviors
	Early Adolescence

	achieving status, she must become sophisticated and glamorous or become a jollygood fellow with less mature boys.
	As postpuberty approaches, both boys and girls must achieve popularity with the opposite sex. Boys must be seen with girls, must learn to dance, avoid fights (except for lower class boys), etc.
4. Developing a conscience	(There is no marked development of conscience; however, the pre- and early adolescent must achieve control over his emotions—rapidly becoming more intense—through strong reassertion and extension of the principles and rules already mastered.)
5. Learning one's psycho-socio-biological sex role.	1. Strong identification with one's sex mates *Examples:* Identification with members of his own sex is the first order of business in adolescence; however, boys will make snide remarks to girls and girls manage to get into scuffling proximity to boys. 2. Learning one's role in heterosexual relationships *Examples:* As sexual organs begin to mature during pubescence, first physical contacts are touching each other on arms and shoulders in attempts to get to know one another. Since the girls are usually more physically mature, they are forced into an aggressive role with boys in their classes—a role contrary to our culture for girls, yet normal. Some girls withdraw into romantic fantasy rather than break the feminine role pattern. Early maturing boys get along well with maturing girls, but the late maturing boys have a difficult time.
6. Accepting and adjusting to a changing body	1. Reorganizing one's thoughts and feelings about one's self in the face of significant body changes and their concomitants *Examples:* Children vary enormously as to chronological age at which they reach puberty. Some girls reach puberty at 9½ years and some boys do not achieve it until they are 18.
	Slow maturing boys worry over their small physical size and lack of secondary sexual characteristics. Fast maturing girls worry about their large size and prominent secondary sexual characteristics. Pre- and early adolescents need to recognize the wide range of normalcy at this period of development so they do not feel they are abnormal or "queers." Most obvious changes at end of preadolescence for boys are growth of external genitals and body and facial hair, and a deepening of the voice and general increase in body size and weight. For girls, breasts grow and hips become wider, menstruation begins and there is a growth of body hair.

TABLE 4.1 *(Continued)*

Developmental Tasks	Coping Behaviors
	Early Adolescence
	2. Accepting the reality of one's appearance *Examples:* The pubescent child is very self-conscious, especially over his looks. The boys are concerned about muscle-building, hair, and complexion. The girls show their concern with their personal appearance by spending many hours dressing and primping.
7. Managing a changing body and learning new motor patterns	1. Controlling and using a "new" body *Examples:* Pubescence brings on rapid physical growth and an adolescent clumsiness. Games for boys such as baseball, basketball, and football provide them with the kind of strenuous exercise needed to gain control of their "new" bodies. Girls, likewise, turn to strenuous activities such as swimming and tennis. A boy or girl who backs away from these strenuous physical activities during this crucial period may never master the developmental stage and lose his chance for status with his peers as well as remain physically inferior throughout his life.
8. Learning to understand and control the physical world	(This area recedes in significance at this stage as the pre- and early adolescent must concentrate his energy on tasks in other areas. However, he continues the enlargement of his development begun at the previous stage by perfecting his skills in getting around the city, traveling away from home, etc.)
9. Developing an appropriate symbol system and conceptual abilities	1. Using language to express and to clarify more complex concepts *Examples:* Early adolescents are learning new words rapidly; they are becoming more adept at expressing their thoughts in writing; their sentences become longer, averaging 15–16 words near the end of this period. 2. Moving from the concrete to the abstract and applying general principles to the particular *Examples:* Causal relations are understood in a more mature way; ideas or relations whose content is symbolized in abstract terms are comprehended more fully; causation is considered in terms of abstractions; more mechanical and logical deductions are being made; and what constitutes "proof" is being better understood.
10. Relating one's self to the cosmos	(Research shows that there are probably no developmental tasks in this area at this stage of development. Boys and girls at this age are primarily concerned with themselves and with changing relations to peers and adult authority. They seem less concerned about their relations to the cosmos than to their relations to real people.)

TABLE 4.2

Psychosocial Developmental Tasks[a]
Preadolescence

Developmental Task	Coping Behaviors
	Latency
Industry vs Inferiority	Method or a *modus operandi* is the basic strength and competence is the basic virtue for this stage. *Guidelines:* With latency the normal child sublimates his need to get what he wants by direct attacks. He learns how to gain recognition by producing things; he begins to recognize that he must go outside his family for his future and thus he is amenable to developing skills and tasks in productive work as well as play. His ego boundaries now include his tools and skills and the pleasure derived from attention to their development. He begins to learn the technological aspects of his culture, including tools and utensils, and the first sense of the division of labor. He learns of the necessity to become educated—(literate) and to accept the role played by school in this. Violent drives during this stage are dormant. During this latency stage of development the child faces the danger of developing a feeling of inadequacy and inferiority regarding his potential mastery of the tools of the society and his anatomy or physical equipment to use these tools. To protect him from developing inferiority, his family must prepare him for school life and the school must fulfill the promises of his earlier expectations. This is socially a most decisive stage since he must learn that industry requires doing things with others (division of labor), and he must also learn of the differential opportunities awaiting him. However as his understanding of the *technological ethos* develops, he must not accept work as his only obligation and "what works" as his only criterion of worthwhileness.

[a]Based on Erikson, Erik H. *Childhood and Society.* New York: W. W. Norton & Company, Inc., 1950, and Erikson, E. H. *Childhood and Society, Second Edition, Revised.* New York: W. W. Norton & Company, Inc., 1963.

special time to concentrate on understanding each other. A group guidance program takes this important, perhaps most important, requirement for successful living out of the realm of a chance occurrence and places it squarely in the mainstream of the school curriculum where it should be.

The developmental tasks and coping behaviors outlined earlier in this chapter are intended to serve as guidelines against which any organized group guidance program can be evaluated. The program may be "packaged" as are those listed at the end of

TABLE 4.3

Vocational Developmental Tasks[a]
Preadolescence

Developmental Tasks[b]	*Vocational Life Stages (Coping Behaviors)*[b]
1. Ability to undertake cooperative enterprises	For ages 11–12, likes are the major determinant of aspirations and activities. For ages 13–14, abilities are given more weight, and requirements, including training, are considered.
2. Choice of activities suited to one's abilities	
3. Assumption of responsibility for one's acts	
4. Performance of chores around the house	
5. Further development of abilities and talents	

[a]There is no clear demarcation for vocational developmental tasks and appropriate coping behaviors for preadolescents; therefore this table shows an overlapping of the higher order tasks of the elementary school child and the lower order tasks of the high school child.

[b]Reprinted with the permission of the publisher from *Vocational development: A framework for research* by D. Super, J. Crites, R. Hummel, H. Moser, P. Overstreet, & C. Warnath, New York: Teachers College Press, Copyright, 1957.

this chapter, or it may be developed for the specific needs of a given school and supplemented by the prepared group guidance materials. The emphasis in this book is on group counseling; therefore a thorough treatment of group guidance is not intended. It is included only to develop briefly a theoretical rationale consistent with that of the rationale developed for group counseling and to call attention to the importance of including group guidance or human relations education in any complete guidance program.

Consistent with the developmental paradigm of this text, any group approach must be congruent with the needs of a given age group and the approach must also maximize the natural proclivities of that same age group. Even though the preadolescent is more verbal than the child from five to nine, but less verbal than the adolescent and adult, a group approach which depends *primarily* on verbal means for conveying information, which can serve the cause of prevention, is to be avoided. The preadolescent is play- and action-oriented just as is his younger counterpart, but his play now is dominated by a group or team emphasis. Team sports and

group games involving the same sex fit his developmental interests, and any theory or technique for working with groups at this age must capitalize on these facts. Accordingly, I have developed this position in the following section concerned with group counseling. Suffice it to say here, that group guidance procedures should include special attention to developing cognitive understandings through simulation (gaming) and games as well as other action-oriented approaches such as sociodrama and roleplaying.

Nesbitt (1968) differentiates among simulation, roleplaying and games as follows: "Simulations are operating models of physical or social situations . . . The word simulation can also refer to the use of symbolic models of social situations." . . . such as the model of a free market system to illustrate the operation of supply and demand (p. 3). Stated another way, according to Nesbitt, ". . . a simulation is a selective representation of reality, containing only those elements of reality that the designer deems relevant to his purpose" (1968, p. 4).

Roleplaying is confused with simulation, according to Nesbitt (1968), "largely because of the fact that virtually all simulations designed for use in the classroom involve roleplaying. . . . Roleplaying qualifies as a simulation only to the degree that the roles being acted out correspond to or represent the functioning of some real process or system" (p. 5).

Dr. Clark C. Abt, a leading designer of educational games, defines a game as a

> contest (play) among adversaries (players) operating under constraint (rules) for an objective (winning, victory or payoff). Stated less formally, a game might be defined as something enjoyable—however serious—involving competition for specified objectives and observing rules.
> A game can be physical, like baseball, or mental, like chess, or a game of luck, like dice . . . (Nesbitt, 1968, p. 5).

In the classroom, elements of simulation, games, and roleplaying are usually combined as students follow certain rules and assume certain roles in a simulated environment. For this reason, teachers generally follow the rule of using "simulation games" or use the words interchangeably (Nesbitt, 1968).

The emphasis on simulation or gaming for implementing a group guidance program for this age level in particular, may be so interesting as to rekindle the preadolescent's interest in school in general. A beginning has been made in the application of gaming to guidance in the form of the Life Career Game (Varenhorst,

1968). Similar adaptations to other guidance needs are quite feasible in addition to the vocational needs of students. And, although instruction through simulation constitutes what appears to be a breakthrough in educational processes for all age levels, it is probably most appropriate to the natural tendency towards games and gaming of the preadolescent.

In keeping with my emphasis on group guidance as prevention-oriented, I quote Varenhorst (1968): "The Game by its very purpose is preventive rather than crisis-oriented. Students are experiencing that by getting information, looking at consequences, and following certain paths, they can avoid problems, not just in the Game, but in their own lives" (p. 362). Although Varenhorst has adapted the Life Career Game for *group counseling* purposes in the high school, she has also used a modified version with success in the junior high school. Also, she has acknowledged that "With proper assistance, the game can be used for groups of 30, or more. This means that the game could be used in a classroom situation, avoiding all the detail work of gathering students from a variety of classes" (Varenhorst, n.d., p. 10).

Further evidence of the applicability of the Life Career Game to group guidance is given by Varenhorst (n.d.) as follows:

> It has been demonstrated that the game meets some of the needs that were lacking in the group guidance sessions. It provides for involvement, both rationally and emotionally. Students are learning where and how to seek information and to evaluate the information they are getting in terms of which decision to make. Students are receiving immediate outcomes of their decisions. They are able to see the consequences of those decisions and are learning how to adapt future decisions on the basis of the outcomes of past decisions (p. 10).

The use of simulation or gaming as it is detailed in the Life Career Game is only one example of what is possible for this technique in group guidance. The developmental tasks of the preadolescent delineate several areas of concern to the preadolescent that can be adapted for simulation. For example, "relating to changing social groups" can be a task around which a game can be developed to assist the preadolescent to understand and safely practice appropriate coping behaviors in this important realm of his development. Thus the tasks present the *topic* for a game and the coping behaviors outline the *critical areas* around which the framework of the game is constructed.

The development of strategies for games has taken place in a

little more than ten years, but there is nothing new about "gaming" itself. War games, for example, are as old as gladiators and knights. Authorities have traced war gaming back to the game of chess, which is thought to have originated in India (Carlson, 1969).

Since simulation and game designing for educational settings is a relatively new venture, there are few guidelines to follow in the design of a game. "Games for Learning" by Dr. Clark Abt (1966) gives some help in game design, and Nesbitt (1968, p. 11–12)[1] offers the following seven objectives for classroom simulation game construction:

1| Identification of objectives, e.g., dramatizing some part of reality or acquainting the participants with the difficulties of decision-making.

2| Construction of a simplified, manipulatable, and significant model of the process or system that will best serve the objective.

3| Actors or teams must be identified according to number and classroom needs that would most effectively demonstrate the model. For example the Parent-Child game requires two participants, whereas the Life Career Game can accommodate two or three teams.

4| There must be resources, e.g., money, votes, or information, that can be exchanged in competition with other players. Most of these resources are given a precise value so points or success-failure can be evaluated at the conclusion of the game.

5| The game participants must have clear objectives or goals to direct their trading of resources. An example of a goal would be improving one's lot in life.

6| Limits or rules must be set on what is permissible behavior; time limits must be set for various stages of play and procedures for exchanges must be described.

7| The stage for the game might be set so as to instruct the actors. In the Life Career Game, for example, the teams are given a profile of a hypothetical student whose life they are to plan for the next eight to ten years.

The decision-makers in the school classroom are usually students. Although computers are being simplified for student ap-

---

[1] From Nesbitt, W. A. *Simulation games for the social studies classroom.* Vol. 1 *New dimensions.* New York: Foreign Policy Assoc., 1968. Reproduced by permission.

plication to gaming, the decisions possible should be within their group since *learning outcomes* of the game are usually based upon the strategy developed. Chance factors should be no greater than would be the case in real life.

Selected Studies of Group Guidance Activities

Roleplaying, dramatizations, and pantomimes were the chief media used by Crystal (1969) in reaching preadolescent low-income Negro children in central Los Angeles. The children were sixth graders who saw school as a prison. Their behavior was unruly and their attitude toward the teacher was hostile. For the most part, they were also quite hostile toward each other. Fighting inside and outside the classroom was prevalent. Roleplaying was initiated by the classroom teacher because it "provides experience in seeing the relationship between cause and effect . . . . The informality, the humor, and the empathy-arousing drama catch young people's interest, involve them, and hold their attention" (Crystal, 1969, pp. 170–171).

Pantomime by the teacher was used first as a warm-up for roleplaying. Chesler and Fox's (1965) *Role-Playing Methods in the Classroom* provided suggestions for the pantomime during the fourth week of school. During the tenth week of school, "But Names Will Never Hurt Me," from Shaftel's (1967) *Role-Playing for Social Values* was introduced. The story provoked a good discussion of possible solutions or endings, each being acted out by volunteers. Following the procedure, the children began to make up their own plays which introduced problems pertinent to these preadolescents. However, these kinds of plays became so detailed that interest dissipated and more simple plots were required.

Crystal found that spontaneous skits inserted at a point when things began to 'drag' were quite successful. Since roleplaying leads to increased activity by the children, break periods or recess following roleplaying was inserted.

Although roleplaying and its variations did not in one semester change behavior, the children did appear to enjoy school more than before. Perhaps the time was too short to produce other behavioral changes; however, Crystal hypothesized that the roleplaying enabled the children to, in effect, build up their response repertoire to the point that they could later recall solutions in the dramas that would be applicable to their immediate problems. She referred to the experience as providing the children . . . a storehouse of human experiences in human relationships [they] would not otherwise have (1969, p. 179).

Barclay (1967) studied the effects of brief interventions on the behavior of low sociometrically chosen fifth graders. One treatment procedure included the training of the teacher in social reinforcement principles and the application of these principles by two school psychology interns. The treatment period was for five weeks only and included setting up situations, among others, wherein low-status children could participate as equals or as superior to high social desirability students. Sociodrama was used on several occasions to cast low-status children in hero roles. The sociodramas were received with enthusiasm and significant discussions followed which permitted praising of the low-status children for their performances. The teacher also used the low-status children as hall monitors, errand runners, etc., and reinforced appropriate behavior.

The children in this study showed significant gains in sociometric ratings, femininity, and degrees of happiness, among others. This is a prime example of using learning theory principles to change behavior in the classroom. Also, the use of sociodrama with fifth graders provided the occasion to reinforce preferred behavior. Other reinforcement procedures used in this study also produced desired changes, but the point to be emphasized is that the sociodrama provides innumerable opportunities for setting up behavioral contingencies for reinforcement which may lead to differences in operant behavior and possible changes in one's personality.

Boocock (Carlson, 1969) tested the social-psychological impact of the Life Career Game and the Game of Legislature on approximately 1,200 4-H Club delegates while they were attending a national conference. Half the conferees took part in the games and half were the control group. Boocock found that the participants developed greater feelings of efficacy which she hypothesized was related to giving young people the confidence needed to act upon the intellectual information that they had acquired during the game.

In accord with the informational emphasis of group guidance, Carlson's (1969) evaluation of the value of gaming and simulation as an educational aid, based on his comprehensive survey of games as tools for learning seems apropos:

> . . . When used in conjunction with other materials, they [games] can provide useful points of departure for discussion. At best, then, games can supplement other educational programs, making real and vivid material that often seems abstract in a textbook. If nothing else, they can convey to the player a feeling for

*the complexity and multiplicity of factors that must be consid-
ered in decision-making. And conceivably they may increase the
confidence of young people to deal with real world problems
that seem impossibly remote from their lives (p. 173).*

Group Counseling

Development of Activity Group Approaches

One of the first psychotherapists, if not the first, to recommend the
use of activity as a means of creating a therapeutic climate was
Moreno (1946). Moreno's activity-oriented approach led to the
development of sociodrama and psychodrama. Slavson (1954),
however, pioneered and expanded the application of media such
as arts and crafts, table games and outdoor activities such as
field trips and excursions in the treatment of adolescents and preadolescents. He referred to this treatment procedure as activity
group therapy and activity-interview group therapy. Gabriel (1939),
along with Slavson, was one of the first to use activity group work
in the treatment of behavioral disorders. She also used field trips,
clay, painting, and related activities in treating adolescents in
groups.

Slavson (1945) made the following comment relative to the
value of activity groups for the preadolescent:

> *What little children gain through play and acting out, young
> children in their latency period and early adolescence achieve
> through manual activity, creative expression, and free play and
> interaction with one another. Older adolescents and adults re-
> quire verbal expression and insight to gain the same results
> (p. 202).*

Galkin (1937) also contributed to the field of activity group
therapy. He used the natural medium of outdoor play and a camp
environment of the preadolescent and adolescent in activity group
therapy.

In recent years, Ginott (1961, 1968), has followed the lead of
Slavson and has added additional activity media to the treatment
of the preadolescents. In addition to the usual arts and crafts,
table games, etc., he has introduced penny arcade-type machines
such as rifle galleries and electric bowling tables and modern
communication devices such as the walkie-talkie and typewriter.

An activity group approach within the context of *counseling*

has been described by Blakeman and Day (1969). They have borrowed from the activity group therapy literature "the need for communication through a natural and spontaneous activity" and combined this with counseling within a group setting. Their process is defined as follows: "Activity group counseling refers to the group process which improves communication through natural, spontaneous activity whereby peers participate in the developmental, behavioral, and attitudinal concern of the individual members of the counseling group" (Blakeman & Day, 1969, p. 61). Thus activity group therapy has been used as the model for the development of activity-oriented procedures for counseling. Although Blakeman and Day have named their procedure activity group counseling, had they followed Slavson's (1964) lead they might have more appropriately named it activity-interview group counseling a la Slavson's activity-interview group psychotherapy, its forerunner. Actually, Blakeman and Day used activities such as darts, basketball, swimming, rifle shooting, and table games such as chess and various card games to generate interaction among the preadolescent boys with whom they worked. The activity was then followed by group discussion of the personally-relevant interactions. This method is similar to Slavson's activity-interview group psychotherapy approach.

No single "activity" approach to group counseling seems to include the several options possible. In view of this situation, I have proposed two activity-oriented approaches to group counseling for the preadolescent. Each is developed on the hypothesis that has been described earlier in this chapter, viz., that group games, both highly physical and sedentary, are the most natural media and means through which the preadolescent communicates freely and spontaneously.

Activity-Interview Group Counseling

Activity-interview group counseling is a composite of activity group therapy a la Slavson and interview group counseling. In essence an activity, such as darts, is used to involve the group and to lower the inhibitions and defenses of the group members. The activity itself may provide an opportunity for physical catharsis or a nonsystematized desensitization. It serves the same purpose as systematic desensitization practiced by behaviorally-oriented counselors and therapists. In addition to providing a means for tension reduction through physical catharsis, the activity also pro-

vides an opportunity for interpersonal interactions which are the concern of the counselor and members in the group "interview" period following the game or activity.

Activity-interview group counseling, like all other variations of group counseling described in this text, is a combination of prevention and remediation: thus it is intended for preadolescents, in particular, but also for adolescents and some adults, who are not suffering from debilitating emotional problems.

The activities may be many and varied. They should be chosen by the group counselor according to the needs of the group members. Care should be taken to vary the games or activities in order to provide some success experiences to all members of the group. The athletic-type preadolescent should have the opportunity to demonstrate his talents in team sports like basketball, touch football, and volley ball. In like fashion, the less athletic preadolescent should have an opportunity to experience success in table games such as electric bowling, ping pong, chess, checkers, and the like. Still other activities such as dancing and swimming (especially for females) and arts and crafts should be used for those who may have talents apart from the physical or intellective.

Simulation and gaming constitutes a new and promising medium for use in group guidance, especially, but also group counseling for the preadolescent in particular. Games such as the Life Career Game (Varenhorst, 1968) can be adapted for small counseling groups and would provide the less physically competitive preadolescent with a substitute means for showing ability or excellence, such as in problem solving. It would also appeal to the group counselor who has less interest and enthusiasm for the more physically active team sports.

Simulating problem-resolution can serve as a means of vicariously conditioning preadolescents by rewarding choices or decisions which lead the hypothetical person to success experiences and not rewarding or vicariously punishing the hypothetical person's inappropriate choices, decisions, etc. Thus, this medium could serve much like roleplaying, to protect the real counselee, but go beyond it in complexity of problems, external factors affecting decisions, etc. The use of action mazes (see Appendix B for a sample maze) using two or three members as a team could be arranged and when warranted competition between or among teams could be encouraged. To facilitate total group understanding of appropriate and inappropriate moves through the maze, total group discussions could follow the completion of the maze.

Since the activity itself in activity-interview group counseling

represents only part of the treatment, those activities which involve simultaneously several, if not all the group members, should be most utilized. The discussion or interview-group counseling session following the game or activity constitutes the second part of the treatment. During this period the counselor helps the group members focus on the nature of the interactions that occurred during the activity phase of the treatment. The behavior that occurred during the activity is related to the life style of a given group member in the sequence described in Chapter two. That is, the counselor builds a strong facilitative base with high levels of empathy, respect, and warmth and only after having established a feeling of mutual trust and caring does he move the group member into the planning and action phase of the treatment through appropriate self-disclosure, genuineness, concreteness, confrontation, and immediacy *a la* Carkhuff (1969, a. b).

The interview or discussion phase need not be held in a formal setting such as a conference room, although such a room should be available when movement from an activity setting is required. The conference room can also be set up as a dual-purpose room including equipment and materials for group activities as well as chairs for the interview phase.

The following protocol illustrates the dual-purpose setting used with a group of black preadolescent "problem students[5]," ranging in age from 11 to 14. The protocol includes portions taken from the sixth group session. The setting is a dual purpose room in which six black boys are milling around the room. Some are reading; others are drawing; one is throwing darts. J. (the subject of discussion) is very active.

Protocol[2]

J.   I'm not gonna' tell anything in the meeting today because everytime I do, R. tells Mr. A.

R.   I did not tell!

Co.   Let's hear about this.

J.   I am not going to say anything.

R.   He went and shot off his big mouth, and because I told Mr. A. now he is mad at me.

J.   Ah, Peanut, that isn't either what happened. That isn't the first time you've done this, Peanut. I've been playing with you

[2]From Blakeman, J. D., & Day, S. R. Activity group counseling. In G. M. Gazda (Ed.), *Theories and methods of group counseling in the schools.* 1969. Courtesy of Charles C. Thomas, Springfield, Ill.

all day and you've been doing it all along. Every time you touch him he gets mad. Just touch him a little bit and he gets mad; he's a baby.

Co. How about that Group? How would you handle this?

W. J. is to blame; he is always to blame. He's a great big bully.

J. I didn't touch him. I know what I'm gonna' do about it! I'm just not gonna' associate with anybody in this group anymore.

R. Don't worry; it will pass over.

J. No, it won't pass over, R. I'm the only one around this school that even likes you a little bit, and I don't see how I can like you now. You're gonna' be so lonely. I'm the best friend you got and you did me dirty and that's all I'm gonna' have to do with you.

Co. It sounds like J. is pretty mad this time.

M. I think they are both at fault. I think they are both babies.

Co. Let's talk about the basketball game we played yesterday.

J. I'm not gonna' talk. Every time I talk, somebody tells on me. I've been in the office more than anybody this year, more than any of you punks.

Co. J., it sounds like maybe you are blaming R. for some of your problems.

J. This is part of the office and every time I may do something wrong, R. goes to Mr. A. and tells him all about it.

Co. Do you consider this part of the office? Is this like the principal's office?

J. It was before you came. I don't mind if he tells you, but I don't want him telling Mr. A., and I don't want him telling the principal.

R. J., you think I am the cause of all your problems.

J. The way I feel about it, if I weren't around you everything would be all right. That's what I'm gonna' do; stay away from you.

Co. J., it sounds like R. is responsible for everything you have had to go wrong this year.

J. Most all of 'em, anyway.

Co. Most all of them?

J. Yes, all of them. Everything I've been in trouble with is 'cause of him.

Co. It sounds like J. and R. have had everything to say, so far. What do some of the rest of you think? I wonder if some of the other boys might not be able to help you out.

J.   Every time I see two or three boys beat up on him, fight him, Jump on him, I help him. Now, first time things go wrong, he runs in and tells Mr. A. I'm through with him.

Co.   We don't seem to be getting very far with this argument; why don't we try something. Why don't we try J. and R. just being quiet for a minute and let some of the other boys give some of their opinions of how they might handle a situation like this.

J.   No, I'm not through yet. I want to talk some more. I don't like Peanut, and I'm not having any more to do with him.

R.   I think Mr. Counselor has a good idea; let's try that.

T.   I think they both got problems. I think they both need to work on 'em.

M.   I think we ought to put them together and let them fight it out.

Co.   It seems to be a lot of buzzing, but no one wants to say anything directly to J. or R. about the situation. I get the idea that all of you would like to, but you're kinda' frightened of what they might say back.

J.   I think the way to settle this whole thing is if I don't associate with R. anymore. When he gets tired of not associating with me, he'll come around and say, "Let's make friends again;" then we'll be friends.

Co.   I'm still puzzled about your saying R. is responsible for all your problems.

J.   Yes, he is. And even though you want me to say something, I'm not gonna' say nothing different. He is responsible for all my problems. Let's do something different; I'm tired of this. I don't want to be talking all day long. I'm mad at this group.

Co.   It seems like J. doesn't feel like the group is satisfying him any more. How do the rest of you feel?

Group: It's great; it's what we want. Let's do it.

W.   Let's get J. out of the group if he doesn't like it.

H.   If he wants out, let's get him out.

L.   Yeah, let's get him out, if he doesn't want to be in the group; let's get him out.

Co.   I guess the boys are saying, J., that the door is open.

J.   Well, one thing about this group is that when we do play basketball or football, we got a sorry bunch of players. None of them really want to play ball. They're just a bunch of goofoffs. We got a sorry bunch of players.

M.   That's what you say. You shoot all the time anyway, how would you know? You never pass it to anyone.

M. Why don't you try to teach some of the boys how to play, rather than chewing at them all the time?

R. Well, I'd like to say something. I tell you this. When J. has the ball, even if you're wide open, he won't pass it to you. He won't pass it to any little boys. All he wants to do is shoot or pass it to one of the big boys. He keeps on dribbling like he don't even hear. All he does is shoot.

M. I think J. and I are the best basketball players in here and I think we play harder than any of the other boys. I think J. doesn't like the other boys. He never passes. I try at least to be good to them.

J. Yeah, W., L., & T., they're no good. They won't even play. They lose interest in the game, and if you don't keep on them all the time, they won't even play. No sense to pass to them, anyway. They just dribble and lose it. They're no good anyway.

L. The group wasn't formed just for basketball. There is other reasons, too. Someone else might be good in football. You just want to be the hog in everything you do, J.

Co. It seems like some of you boys felt like being good in basketball was the main purpose in the group, while others seem to think that there are other purposes in the group.

T. Yeah, keep us out of trouble.

J. I'd like to talk now. Now, you say I don't pass the ball, but who in here does pass the ball? Every time I pass to T. or W., they lose the ball. Every time. So why pass to them? Just lose it if I pass it to them.

W. What are you talking about boy? You don't even know what you are talking about.

J. Now you answer that, W. Why should I pass it to you? Now ... if you see somebody that ain't gonna' do no good with something that is given to them, why give it to them? Why do it? Why give it to them?

Co. It seems like J. sees a different purpose for the group. He wants to be a good basketball player and have a basketball team. Some of the rest of you don't feel that way.

M. Well, I think anybody that don't know how to play ought to learn, and I think that this is a good place to learn to do things. I think J. is wrong. I think we ought to be teaching boys to learn.

J. The time to learn is not while you're playing the game. The time to learn is on your own in your own yard. Besides that, you can't teach boys that don't want to learn. Some of these

boys would rather play dodge, so go let them play dodge, but when they come on a basketball floor, they ought to play basketball and they ought to try to be good. If they don't show a lot of interest, they shouldn't ought to be out there.

W. I'm no good at basketball, but I think that I'd have a lot of fun playing basketball if J. weren't there.

R. J. always shoots the ball so when we get back to this meeting, he can just talk all the time and brag about what he did during the game.

Co. Let's take a look now, boys, at what we are doing. It seems as though everybody is ganging up against J., and it seems like we're trying to tell him that he's not a very good sport when it comes to playing basketball. I think maybe we're being a little hard on him.

J. Don't worry about me. I don't feel bad.

M. I think this is good because I think J. needs help. I think he needs help badly not only in basketball but all over.

J. I don't think I need no help.

M. Yes, you do need some help. You need lots of help.

J. You can't help me.

Co. M., what do you see he needs help in?

M. He needs to learn how to keep his mouth shut, and he needs to learn how to act.

J. I don't need no help from none of you. I don't want any help from anybody.

Co. You don't want any help, from any of us?

R. That's his main problem. When somebody tries to help him, he won't let them. It is the same thing he was saying. If he won't help himself, how can we help?

J. Be quiet. Oh, shut up, Peanut. Peanut, will you shut up! I'm leaving this group. I'm through with this group. This group can't help me. I don't like any of you, and I'm not gonna' be in this group. I am through with you, and I don't want anything to do with you or anybody in this group.

Co. Sorry you feel that way, J. It sounds like we have been a little hard on you today. It seems like the boys had a lot on their minds.

H. Yes, it is true.

J. I'm quitting. I don't want anything more to do with you. I don't want to come to any more of the group meetings. Count me out.

Co. We'll leave it up to you, J. Whatever you decide is all right with us. I think though that we should leave it open if you would like to come back.

J. I won't come back, and I won't have anymore to do with it.

M. I hope you do come back, J. I like you. I just think there are some things you need to work on.

W. Yeah, we like you, J. I'm sorry that you are so mad.

R. I like you too, J., even if you are mad at me. And if you don't want to be in the group, I don't think you should have to be.

Meeting ends. J. says that he is quitting and is very angry. J. comes back to counselor during the week, however, and apologizes for getting angry. He comes back to the group and is a model group member.

The protocol illustrates a very action-oriented approach on the part of the counselor. He assumed that he had a good base built with J. and the group. The counselor and the group members showed empathy, warmth, respect, self-disclosure, genuineness, concreteness, immediacy and confrontation—with a rather heavy emphasis on confrontation. If J. had not previously experienced the counselor and group members as helpful individuals, the result of this session would not have been so positive.

Application of a Developmental Approach to Activity-Interview Group Counseling

The protocol cited above highlights a couple of developmental tasks of the preadolescent with which he is being assisted in mastering. The principle task is "achieving an appropriate giving-receiving pattern of affection" with the concomitant coping behavior of "accepting one's self as a worthwhile person, really worthy of love." During the latter stages of preadolescence dramatic physical changes often occur within the individual, and he must *find* his apparent new self—learn to love his new self. In the process he sometimes becomes very egocentric and preoccupied with himself. He uses his friendships to gain understanding of himself (Tryon & Lilienthal, 1950).

Also closely tied with the developmental task just cited, are the following tasks: "accepting and adjusting to a changing body" and "managing a changing body and learning new motor patterns." The protocol illustrates how these tasks with both appropriate and inappropriate coping behaviors can be isolated and how the peer group can be utilized to help each other through a healthy adult model in the person of the counselor.

The confrontations of the peer group, though appearing hurtful, were genuine and mixed with expressions of caring. J. was rewarded for his positive behavior and physical attributes, but he was punished (verbally) for his inappropriate attitudes and behavior. One must be reminded that without a strong base to begin with, confrontation would produce unhealthy responses rather than the healthy response by J.

Activity Group Counseling

Activity group counseling is akin to Slavson's activity group therapy which is illustrated very well in the film "Activity Group Therapy," directed by him and available from Columbia University Press. Once again "counseling" is used in this text in lieu of "therapy" because the degree of deterioration or disturbance among the clientele to be served is not so severe as is the case when therapy or "reconstruction of a personality" is involved.

Activity group counseling is different from activity-interview group counseling to the extent that the counselor is much less active on a verbal level. He is present as a catalyst and source of safety or control but the composition of the group and the selection of activities, materials, and other media are chosen more carefully than would be necessary for activity-interview group counseling. Activity group counseling requires a greater skill in social engineering because the group members and the media must be relied upon more heavily as agents of change.

The setting and media must accommodate in particular the needs of the overinhibited and the belligerent preadolescent (Ginott, 1968). The "engineering" requires a careful balance of group members including some overinhibited and some belligerent with some who fall between these two extremes. If the balance is incorrect, the hyperactive and belligerent preadolescents threaten the overinhibited and cause them to withdraw even further. If a group is composed totally of overinhibited preadolescents, there are no aggressive peer models for them to imitate and thus the counselor would be the only model for positive change. Since preadolescents are separated by sex for group treatment, we are herein describing all male and all female groups.

The overinhibited, shy, withdrawn, sexually inadequate preadolescent boy will require media such as fire for fire play, walkie-talkies, tape recorders, and various penny arcade-type machines —rifle gallery, electric bowling table, and the like (Ginott, 1961,

1968). These media are captivating and serve to involve indirectly the overinhibited preadolescent with others until he can move to direct personal confrontations. In addition, some of these media permit him to release latent hostility.

On the other hand the aggressive and belligerent preadolescent boy needs to learn how to sublimate and control his hostile feelings. Fire play, rifle galleries, boxing machines, and the like provide him with acceptable media to release his aggression without infringing on the rights of others. Shop materials including hard substances such as wood for sawing and hammering and similar substances are thought to serve as media for sublimation for the belligerent preadolescent (Slavson, 1955). Slavson also recommends for the less belligerent clay, water colors, appropriate molds for making ashtrays, large sheets of paper and equipment for cooking of simple refreshments. Ginott (1961, 1968) has found it necessary to add to the traditional facilities pioneered by Slavson. As mentioned previously he has found that the aggressive and acting-out preadolescent, in particular, requires media such as fire for fire play, rifle galleries, boxing machines, and the like. These kinds of media appeal to the masculine identification of the aggressive, hostile, and acting-out preadolescent. They tend to view water colors, clay, and fine arts materials as sissy and avoid them.

A new and promising substitute for the media just described is the concept of simulation and gaming. Although not commercially available for counseling purposes, the simulation and gaming model would appear to be especially appropriate for the preadolescent who has a natural interest in games and related activities. For example, one could devise a series of steps such as action mazes through which to take the overinhibited or shy preadolescent. Emphasis would be on a vicarious or simulated problem resolution which focuses on his need to become more assertive if he is to complete the action maze with the greatest ease and success. In a similar way, the belligerent and overly aggressive preadolescent might discover the value of controlling his aggression as he works out problems through action maze-types of simulations and games. To encourage socialization for both the overinhibited and the belligerent, group members could be paired to work on the action maze together and total group discussions could be based on the reasons certain choices or moves were made by paired members. The discussion phase, however, is emphasized more in activity-interview group counseling.

Selection and Group Composition

The preadolescent age group is the one age group that definitely calls for separation of the sexes in the group treatment plan. There also might be some reason to separate the sexes in the age group from 5 to 9; however, this would most likely be true for those reaching the latency period around age nine. The preadolescent age represents the time when boys prefer to be with boys and girls prefer to be with girls, i.e., their *natural* choices are for members of the same sex. This preference should be respected when placing preadolescents in counseling groups.

Activity groups, I contend, are the preferred modes of treatment for the preadolescent. The majority of counselees in the age group are boys and games and activities are their most comfortable ways of relating. This tends to be a *masculine* preference, however, and activities, though relevant, are not as necessary in the group counseling of preadolescent girls. Except for the more aggressive preadolescent girls, interview group counseling, the preferred mode of counseling for adolescents and adults, may be used effectively with preadolescent females.

As with other age groups, role balancing and the provision of models for mutual imitation are of prime importance in activity-oriented group counseling. Hansen, Niland and Zani (1969), in a study of model reinforcement group counseling with elementary school children of low sociometric ratings, had this comment on group composition:

> *When none of the students exhibit successful classroom behavior, it is difficult to learn acceptable behavior from each other. This may be true of other group counseling studies using different criteria in which all persons in the group share a common problem. Thus, group composition may be a major reason why so many group counseling studies report null results (p. 744).*

Although proper group composition is important in *activity-interview* group counseling, it is even more critical in the "engineering" of therapeutic elements for *activity* group counseling because of the greater emphasis of the peer group members on each other and the less active role of the group counselor. The best predictor of the performance or functioning of a preadolescent in a group is some observable behavior during a trial or preliminary group placement (Gazda, 1968).

The preadolescent can be placed in an oversized newly

formed group for a trial period of three or four sessions. The best participant combinations, based on direct observation of interaction, can be retained for the duration of the group. The others can be continued on an individual counseling basis until an opening in an open-ended group becomes available or until enough counselees are available for the formation of a new group.

Certain preadolescents do not make good candidates for group treatment. Ginott (1968) has labeled as unsuitable for group treatment (1) preadolescents with accelerated sexual drives such as those with premature and persistent preoccupation with sexual matters; (2) preadolescents who have actively engaged in homosexual activities; (3) psychopathic preadolescents; (4) destructive preadolescents whose aggressiveness is deep-rooted in hostility toward self (masochism) or others (homicidal); (5) preadolescents with long histories of stealing outside the home. (Preadolescents who steal only at home may be bidding for affection or a temporary act of revenge. These preadolescents may be placed in a group treatment setting.); (6) preadolescents who have been involved in a recent trauma or catastrophe; and (7) preadolescents suffering from *intense* sibling rivalry.

The chronological age difference of preadolescents in group treatment should not exceed two years (Ginott, 1968). The social age and the intellectual age of the group members must also be considered in the composition of a group. Since both types of activity-oriented group counseling approaches utilize the physically active games as well as sedentary games with neither predominating, the socially mature but physically small preadolescent is guaranteed some game or activity in which he has a chance to compete and excel.

The greater the emphasis on activities in the treatment plan, e.g., activity group counseling versus activity-interview group counseling, the less the importance of intellectual differences. Nevertheless, "normals" should not be placed in groups with mental retardates and vice versa.

Some chronologically younger preadolescents are often deliberately placed in a group with older preadolescents when the younger preadolescent is overly aggressive and requires the control of older groupmates. Likewise, some chronologically older but immature preadolescents are sometimes placed in groups with younger groupmates.

Generally, siblings and close relatives and friends should not be placed in the same group. When siblings are present in the same group, they sometimes feel compelled to look after each

other and thus reduce their independent participation. Also, there is the greater possibility of one telling on another especially when angered or hurt in a family quarrel. The presence of close friends and/or relatives poses the problem of trying to maintain the image which had been developed. This image-maintenance behavior interferes with the counselee's freedom to be real and spontaneous rather than role-dominated.

Setting and Media

Consistent with the developmental emphasis of this text, all settings should be, insofar as possible, "natural" to the counselee. Activity group approaches to counseling require large rooms and open outdoor areas where a variety of activities by several counselees may be engaged in simultaneously. Schiffer, for example, suggests that a room of approximately 600 square feet is of optimal size (Ginott, 1961). The room should be of sufficient size to accommodate work benches, and tables, table tennis, penny arcade-type machines, space for crafts and a meal table and perhaps a phonograph with records (especially for females). The typical school does not have rooms such as that just described. The typical school, however, does have an industrial arts shop and a home economics suite. These rooms with their media and materials can be adapted to the preadolescent.

In addition to the school shop and home economics suite, the gymnasium, swimming pool, and athletic fields and various game courts all provide areas that can be utilized by the activity group counselor. A small conference room capable of comfortably accommodating six or seven people should be available to the activity group counselor, especially when he is using the activity-interview approach. This room would serve as a place to which to retire for the interview phase following a physical activity. The dual-purpose room described earlier in this chapter could serve equally as well for a conference-activity room.

The activity group counselor should view the entire community as his treatment setting. Camping and field trips should be included whenever possible. The therapeutic use of fire building by the preadolescent has been cited earlier, but unlike the artificial setting of building a fire in a sink, the camp with its campfire would provide a more natural means of using fire as a treatment medium. Visits to community fairs or penny arcades may also be more

naturally utilized as treatment media than would be their use in a school setting. Nevertheless these types of games should be available in one setting or the other and preferably convenient for repeated use.

Gump and Sutton-Smith hypothesized that certain behaviors (respondent behaviors) were made more likely by given physical settings or, more specifically, that the amount and kind of social interaction is significantly affected by variation of activity-settings. Their subjects were 23 boys, aged 9½ to 11½ years, who had adjustment difficulties. They had been sent to the University of Michigan Fresh Air Camp. They found that *amount* and *kind* of interaction differed significantly between swimming and crafts. Swimming produced significantly greater interactions; however, when compared to counselor involvement, crafts produced significantly greater involvement than swimming.

The researchers concluded: "The general implication for recreational and therapeutic work with children is that choice of activities per se is very important; this choice will markedly affect the children's relations to one another and to the leader or therapist" (1955, p. 759). For example, in the swim setting the counselor was more often called upon to admire and recognize assertive actions, to settle or supervise conflict interactions, and less often be involved in helping interactions whereas in crafts the opposite tended to be true. According to Gump and Sutton-Smith,

> *The counselor learns from such data that a "prescription" of swimming will send a child to a "robust" social climate in which total interaction is high and in which assertion and attacking are highly likely. A crafts "prescription," on the other hand will place a child in a "mild" social climate in which total interaction is low, assertive and conflict interaction minimal, and dependency (helping—being helped) interaction high (1955, p. 759).*

Obviously, then, the choice of setting *as well as choice of media utilized* within the setting should be made carefully to accommodate the needs of the group members. As recommended under the Media section of this chapter, settings as well as media should be varied to meet the needs of *all* group members.

For the more sedentary games such as card games, chess, and simulated games like the Life Career Game and Family Game, small tables should be available to permit the group to divide into subgroups and to spread out the materials included in the game

kits. Of course, a sufficient number of chairs should be available for the number involved in the group. With more and more simulation games being produced and with their inclusion of filmstrips and sound films, a filmstrip projector and a movie projector with screens would be appropriate accessories.

Group Size

Many of the considerations discussed in the section for the child from 5–9 years of age apply to the preadolescent child from ages 9–13. Although the average child from 9–13 has become more socialized than the child from 5–9 years of age, he still does not have the same degree of self-control that the adolescent and adult have mastered. For this reason, the group counselor will need to limit the number of group participants in this age group so that he can control the therapeutic group processes.

Another consideration given to group size for activity groups is the nature of the activity itself and the possible controlling and/or safety conditions of the activity. Activities such as touch football, softball, and basketball permit physical movement over a wide range or area and detract from the control and resultant safety extended by a group leader, whereas table games such as cards and table tennis localize the group and make it possible for the activity group counselor to retain more overall control of the group members as well as control the safety factor. Activities such as touch football and softball are difficult to play with a small group and, unless another group can be obtained to serve as the opposition, some of the larger team sports would prove inappropriate for activity group counseling.

Providing models for each member in the group is another condition of group counseling which must be considered when determining size for activity groups.

If each preadolescent has a model in the group, we can readily see that each time we add a person we are in fact adding him plus his model unless certain individuals are serving as models for more than one group member. This, in fact, is quite feasible.

No systematic research has been completed regarding size of preadolescent activity groups; however, I have found five to seven to be an optimum number. Under certain circumstances, especially if a co-counselor is employed, as many as ten may be included in an activity counseling group.

Frequency, Length, and Duration of Group Sessions

The degree of disturbance of the group participants is probably the best indicator of the frequency and duration of treatment through activity group counseling. As with other types of group counseling, activity group counseling, in my opinion, is both prevention- and remediation-oriented. The degree to which remediation is necessary or the degree to which coping behaviors must be varied or initiated will determine how often and how long a group should meet.

I have found that activity-interview group counseling or activity group counseling require approximately six months to one year of meeting 1½ to 2 hours a session at least once a week. Twice a week sessions of approximately 1½ hours is recommended especially in the beginning of a group until cohesiveness or *esprit de corps* has developed. These time periods are only rough guidelines for closed activity groups. Of course, open-ended groups could go on indefinitely just as long as the member turnover was calculated and very gradual—approximately one new member added with the termination of a group member, every three months.

Selected Illustrative Studies of Activity-Type Group Counseling

Epstein (1960) reported the successful application of an activity group approach to the treatment of a group of institutionalized boys ranging in age from 11½ through 13. The members were screened to provide group balance. They participated in 39 sessions. The boys were told the group was a club. Arts and crafts were available to them as well as refreshments and games. Standard activity-type group materials were available including hammers, saws, screwdrivers, chisels, leather and lanyard material, wood, clay, copperfoil, model airplanes and boats, chess and checkers, and ping-pong. The meeting room was a renovated basement room in a staff residence cottage.

Some of the results included increased assertiveness on the part of the shy group members including reaching out to others, talking about their feelings, and becoming active in the sports and club activities of the institution. In general the group members became much more cooperative and socially sophisticated.

Games were used by Hinds and Roehlke (1970) as reinforc-

ing stimuli with groups of elementary school children from grades three, four, and five. Twenty children were involved in treatment and an equal number were used as controls. A learning theory model was applied in the group counseling to modify specific problem behaviors of the children. The groups met twice a week for 30–40 minutes each session over a period of 10 weeks. A male and female counselor were involved with each group and at least two male and two female children were included in each group. In addition to games, points, verbal approval, tokens, and video feedback were used as reinforcers.

The authors permitted games for the last 10 or 15 minutes of a session after the children had earned a certain number of points. The games were not described beyond being referred to as "cooperative" games.

Significant predicted behavioral changes were obtained in the treatment setting and they were also observed to have transferred to the classroom setting. Some of the changes included greater attention to classroom activities, less domination, less submissiveness, and greater participation in learning activities.

Hinds and Roehlke (1970) attempted to "maximize" conditions for reinforcement during counseling. They concluded that "One of the greatest advantages of group counseling is that it serves as a microlab for learning new behaviors" (p. 55). In addition the authors stated that

> Children in group modeling (role-playing) situations learn to discriminate effectively between appropriate new behaviors and inappropriate old behaviors. As each group member plays an appropriate role in the group situation, he receives reinforcement from the counselor. In addition, the presence and behaviors of peers provide important modeling cues, as well as additional reinforcement . . . . By providing the child with a model (or models) for the desired behavior, he is able to imitate and thus greatly increases the likelihood of receiving positive social reinforcement (p. 55).

The Life Career Game, a simulation device, has been adapted and used successfully in the group counseling of junior and senior high school students by Varenhorst (1968). Varenhorst described the application of the Game to low ability junior high school students. She claimed that the Life Career Game reduced the students' resistance to involvement and their avoidance of problem areas. Using a profile person or game character, the group member can hide behind the hypothetical game character. Varenhorst

contends that after the participants have played a few rounds of the Game, they are usually more acquainted with students in their group than they have ever been with any other peer group. She also believes that more can be accomplished in a much shorter length of time than in traditional groups. Other benefits of utilizing the Game in group counseling, according to Varenhorst, were that specific information had been taught; students had examined values; students had related in a meaningful way to a small group of peers—learning from and sharing with them; specific behavioral changes had been made such as staying in school when dropping out was being considered, talking to counselors, teachers, and parents for information, studying more, becoming more critical in their use of leisure time, and greater initiative had been exercised in personal decision-making.

Summary

The preadolescent (ages 9–13) is the subject group of this chapter. Group guidance and counseling procedures are described which are unique to this age group. Like the previous chapter, this chapter, when read in conjunction with Chapter two, is written to stand by itself. The chapter begins with a brief description of the preadolescent and includes three tables depicting the developmental tasks with corresponding coping behaviors based on the bio-socio-psychological position of Havighurst, as interpreted by Tryon and Lilienthal, the psychosocial position of Erikson, and the vocational position of Super, et al.

Group guidance is shown to relate to group counseling insofar as it serves the role of prevention of problems through the provision of accurate and timely information pertinent to the developmental needs of the preadolescent. The concept of gaming and simulation is stressed as appealing to the preadolescent's interests and thus potentially quite useful as a medium through which to present guidance information. Guidelines for constructing classroom simulation games are summarized as are selected illustrative research studies which utilize simulations and gaming.

Two types of group counseling for the preadolescent are outlined. Activity-interview group counseling incorporates aspects of activity group therapy *a la* Slavson and Ginott, plus interview group counseling. Activity group counseling is a modification of Slavson's activity group therapy. It emphasizes the activity or game as a part of the treatment procedure more so than does the com-

bined use of games followed by discussion, *viz.,* activity-interview group counseling. These methods are described as most appropriate for the preadolescent because he is game- and activity-oriented at this age level. A protocol of an activity-interview group is given as an illustration of this approach and the interactions are explained in accord with the developmental model including the learning principles operative in behavioral change as well as the core conditions *a la* Carkhuff.

The various types of games, simulations, and media utilized in the activity approaches are given and suggestions are made for their utilization within the total treatment program. Both sedentary and more physically active games are recommended.

A defense is provided for separating the sexes in the activity approaches to group counseling, and a rationale for selection and group composition is outlined. Essentially, the groups are homogeneous with regard to sex but heterogeneous with regard to problems of coping behaviors. The behavioral types for whom the activity group approaches are indicated are listed in this section.

Group size for optimum conditions is recommended at between five and seven depending on the severity of disturbance, appropriate models available for inclusion in the group, and counselor skills. Frequency, length, and duration of group treatment are all related to the same variables which are considered when determining the size of a preadolescent activity group. For closed groups, six months to one year of one session of 1½ hours to two sessions of 1½ hours per week are given as rough guides for the prospective practitioner of activity group approaches.

Since the activity group approaches call for settings both within the school and within the community, considerable emphasis has been placed on this section. Suggested media are also included in this section. Examples of the settings include swimming pools, athletic fields and courts, gymnasiums, conference rooms, parks, etc. Examples of media include arts and crafts, card and table games, simulation games, physical activities, and, of course, counselee verbal participation in the interview phase. The chapter is concluded with a presentation of research studies which illustrate how the various media have been implemented in activity-oriented group counseling approaches.

References

ABT, C. C. *Games for learning.* Occasional Paper #7, The social studies curriculum program. Cambridge, Mass.: Educational Services, Inc., 1966.

BARCLAY, J. R. Effecting behavior change in the elementary classroom: An exploratory study. *Journal of Counseling Psychology,* 1967, *14,* 240–247.

BLAKEMAN, J. D., & DAY, S. R. Activity group counseling. In G. M. Gazda (Ed.), *Theories and methods of group counseling in the schools.* Springfield, Ill.: Charles C. Thomas, 1969. Pp. 56–85.

CARKHUFF, R. R. *Helping and human relations.* Vol. 1 *Selection and training.* New York: Holt, Rinehart & Winston, 1969. (a)

CARKHUFF, R. R. *Helping and human relations.* Vol. 2 *Practice and research.* New York: Holt, Rinehart & Winston, 1969. (b)

CARLSON, E. *Learning through games.* Washington, D.C.: Public Affairs Press, 1969.

CHESLER, M., & FOX, R. *Role-playing methods in the classroom.* Chicago: Science Research Associates, 1965.

CRYSTAL, J. Roleplaying in a troubled class. Elementary School Journal, 1969. *69,* 169–179.

EPSTEIN, N. Activity group therapy. *International Journal of Group Psychotherapy,* 1960, *10,* 180–194.

ERIKSON, E. H. *Childhood and society.* New York: Norton, 1950.

ERIKSON, E. H. *Childhood and society.* (2nd ed.) New York: Norton, 1963.

GABRIEL, B. An experiment in group treatment. *American Journal of Orthopsychiatry,* 1939, *9,* 146–170.

GALKIN, J. The possibilities offered by the summer camp as a supplement to the child guidance center. *American Journal of Orthopsychiatry,* 1937, *7,* 474–483.

GAZDA, G. M. Group counseling: A functional approach. In G. M. Gazda (Ed.), *Basic approaches to group psychotherapy and group counseling.* Springfield, Ill.: Charles C. Thomas, 1968. Pp. 263–303.

GINOTT, H. G. *Group psychotherapy with children.* New York: McGraw-Hill, 1961.

GINOTT, H. G. Innovations in group psychotherapy with preadolescents. In G. M. Gazda (Ed.), *Innovations to group psychotherapy.* Springfield, Ill.: Charles C. Thomas, 1968. Pp. 272–294.

GUMP, P., & SUTTON-SMITH, B. Activity-setting and social interaction: A field study. *American Journal of Orthopsychiatry,* 1955, *25,* 755–760.

HANSEN, J. C., NILAND, T. M., & ZANI, L. P. Model reinforcement in group counseling with elementary school children. *Personnel and Guidance Journal,* 1969, *47,* 741–744.

HAVIGHURST, R. J. Developmental tasks and education. Chicago: University of Chicago Press, 1948.

HAVIGHURST, R. J. *Developmental tasks and education.* (2nd ed.) New York: Longmans, Green, 1952.

HAVIGHURST, R. J. *Human development and education.* New York: David McKay Co., 1953.

HINDS, W. C., & ROEHLKE, H. J. A learning theory approach to group counseling with elementary school children. *Journal of Counseling Psychology,* 1970, *17,* 49–55.

LILIENTHAL, J. W., & TRYON, C. Developmental Tasks: II Discussion of specific tasks and implications: In *Fostering mental health in our schools: 1950 Yearbook, ASCD.* Washington, D.C.: Association for Supervision and Curriculum Development, 1950. Pp. 90–128.

MORENO, J. L. *Psychodrama:* Vol. 1 *The principle of spontaneity,* New York: Beacon House, 1946.

NESBITT, W. A. *Simulation games for the social studies classroom.* Vol. 1, *New dimensions.* New York: Foreign Policy Assoc., 1968.

SHAFTEL, F. R. *Role-playing for social values.* Englewood Cliffs, New Jersey: Prentice-Hall, 1967.

SLAVSON, S. R. Differential methods of group therapy in relation to age levels. *Nervous Child,* 1945, *4,* 196–210.

SLAVSON, S. R. *Re-educating the delinquent.* New York: Harper & Brothers, 1954.

SLAVSON, S. R. Group psychotherapies. In J. L. McCarey (Ed.), *Six approaches to psychotherapy.* New York: Dryden Press, 1955. Pp. 129–178.

SLAVSON, S. R. *A textbook in analytic group psychotherapy.* New York: International Universities Press, 1964.

SUPER, D. E., CRITES, J., HUMMEL, R., MOSER, H., OVERSTREET, C. B., & WARNATH, C. *Vocational development: A framework for research.* New York: Bureau of Publications, Teachers College, Columbia University, 1957, Monograph No. 4.

TRYON, C., & LILIENTHAL, J. W. Developmental tasks: I The concept and its importance. In *Fostering mental health in our schools: 1950 Yearbook, ASCD.* Washington, D.C.: Association for Supervision and Curriculum Development, 1950. Pp. 77–89.

VARENHORST, B. B. Innovative tool for group counseling: The Life Career Game. *School Counselor,* 1968, *15,* 357–362.

VARENHORST, B. B. Information regarding the use of the Life Career Game in the Palo Alto Unified School District guidance program. Unpublished paper, n.d.

Suggested Readings

BEKER, J. The influence of school camping on the self-concepts and social relationships of sixth grade children. *Journal of Educational Psychology,* 1960, *51,* 352–356.

BLAKEMAN, J. D., & DAY, S. R. Activity group counseling. In G. M. Gazda (Ed.), *Theories and methods of group counseling in the schools.* Springfield, Ill.: Charles C. Thomas, 1969. Pp. 56–85.

BOOCOCK, S. S., & COLEMAN, J. S. Games with simulated environments in learning. *Sociology of Education,* 1966, *39,* 215–236.

BOOCOCK, S. S., & SCHILD, E. O. (Eds.), *Simulation games in learning.* Beverly Hills, Calif.: Sage Publications, 1969.

BULLOCK, L. M. Group guidance seminar designed for junior high school pupils. *School Counselor,* 1970, *17,* 174–177.

CARLSON, E. *Learning through games.* Washington, D.C.: Public Affairs Press, 1969.

CRYSTAL, J. Role-playing in a troubled class. *Elementary School Journal,* 1969, *69,* 169–179.

DURFEE, M. B. Use of ordinary office equipment in "play therapy." *American Journal of Orthopsychiatry,* 1942, *12,* 495–502.

EPSTEIN, N. Activity group therapy. *International Journal of Group Psychotherapy,* 1960, *10,* 180–194.

GAZDA, G. M., & FOLDS, J. H. *Group guidance: A critical incidents approach* Champaign, Ill.: Research Press (formerly Parkinson Div. Follett Educational Corp.), 1968.

GINOTT, H. G. *Group psychotherapy with children.* New York: McGraw-Hill, 1961.

GINOTT, H. G. Innovations in group psychotherapy with preadolescents. In G. M. Gazda (Ed.), *Innovations to group psychotherapy.* Springfield, Ill.: Charles C. Thomas, 1968. Pp. 272–294.

HANSEN, J. C., NILAND, T. M., & ZANI, L. P. Model reinforcement in group counseling with elementary school children. *Personnel and Guidance Journal,* 1969, *47,* 741–744.

HANSEN, L. S., & WIRGAN, O. Human relations training: A response to crisis. *School Counselor,* 1970, *17,* 253–257.

HINDS, W. C., & ROEHLKE, H. J. A learning theory approach to group counseling with elementary school children. *Journal of Counseling Psychology,* 1970, *17,* 49–55.

HOLT, J. *How children learn.* New York: Pitman Publishing Corp., 1967.

IRVIN, A. M. Regression in children's activity therapy group. *Smith College Studies of Social Work,* 1960, *31,* 22–37.

LIEBERMAN, F. Transition from latency to pre-puberty in girls: An activity group becomes an interview group. *International Journal of Group Psychotherapy,* 1964, *14,* 455–464.

MacLENNAN, B. W., & ROSEN, B. Female therapists in activity group psychotherapy with boys in latency. *International Journal of Group Psychotherapy,* 1963, *13,* 34–42.

MOORE, L. A developmental approach to group counseling with seventh graders. *School Counselor,* 1969, *16,* 272–276.

NESBITT, W. A. *Simulation games for the social studies classroom.* Vol. 1 *New dimensions.* New York: Foreign Policy Assoc., 1968.

RASER, J. R. *Simulation and society: An exploration of scientific gaming.* Boston: Allyn & Bacon, 1969.

ROSENTHAL, L. Limitations of activity group therapy: A case presentation. *International Journal of Group Psychotherapy,* 1957, *7,* 166–170.

SCHEIDLINGER, S. Three approaches with socially deprived latency-age children. *International Journal of Group Psychotherapy,* 1965, *15,* 434–445.

SIMULATION GAMES. New York: Western Publishing Co., Inc., School and Library Department. (brochure, n.d.).

SLAVSON, S. R. Differential methods of group therapy in relation to age levels. *Nervous Child,* 1945, *4,* 196–210.

STARK, G. K. A game theory in education. *School and Society,* 1968, *96,* 43–44.

WEBB, A. P. A group counseling approach to the acting-out preadolescent. *Psychology in the Schools,* 1964, *1,* 395–400.

Group Guidance Programs

A Teaching Program in Human Behavior and Mental Health

Publisher: Educational Research Council of America, Cleveland, Ohio.

Manual: Ojemann, R. H. *Developing a program for education in human behavior,* Cleveland, Ohio: Educational research Council of America, 1956.

Grade 4: *Book IV, Handbook for fourth grade teachers* (Revised Ed.)

Grade 5: *Book V, Handbook for fifth grade teachers* (Revised Ed.)

Grade 6: *Book VI, Handbook for sixth grade teachers* (Revised Ed.) *Learning on your own Series* (Sixth grade level).

Dimensions of Personality—A Mental Health Program.

Publisher: George A. Pflaum, Dayton, Ohio.

Grade 4: Limbacher, W. J. *Here I am,* (1969)

George A. Pflaum Publisher, Dayton, Ohio

Grade 5: *I'm not alone.*

Grade 6: *Becoming myself.*

National Forum Developmental Guidance Series

Publisher: American Guidance Services, Inc., Minneapolis, Minn.

Grade 5: *The people around us.*

Grade 6: *Seeing ourselves.*

Grade 7: *About growing up.*

Note: The publisher announced a 4th grade series for fall, 1969; however, it was not yet available when this text went to press.

Junior High School

Peters, D. L. *Homeroom guidance activities*. New York: Richards Rosen Press, 1967.

5 | Group Procedures for the Adolescent and Adult

Introduction

This chapter deals with group counseling and guidance for adolescents and adults beginning with age 13 through old age. Chapter four focused on the age group 9–13.

The inclusion of adolescents with adults in the application of group counseling and guidance may, at first glance, appear to be inconsistent. But when one considers the group medium (interview) which is utilized most frequently for these age groups, their concurrent treatment is observed to be theoretically sound. Unquestionably, the needs of the differing age groups will vary as illustrated in the developmental tasks and their appropriate coping behaviors outlined in Tables 5.1–5.9 which follow. The group leader is directed to these tables to familiarize himself with the developmental tasks and coping behaviors of various age groups within the adolescent-adult period. Consistent with Chapters three and four, Tables 5.1–5.9 include the bio-socio-psychological tasks and coping behaviors of Havighurst (1953) plus interpretations for late adolescence by Lilienthal and Tryon (1950) and Tryon and Lilienthal (1950), the psychosocial stages of Erikson (1950, 1963), and the vocational developmental stages of Super, et al., (1957, 1963).

The developmental tasks and coping behaviors of early adolescence, as interpreted by Tryon and Lilienthal (1950) and Lilien-

thal and Tryon (1950) are given in Chapter four and therefore are not repeated here. The reader is encouraged to review Tables 4.1–4.3 in Chapter four when he is planning to work with the child just entering adolescence. Also, Appendix A contains descriptions of appropriate and inappropriate behavior for children from infancy through age 15 which provides additional guidelines for the group leader.

TABLE 5.1

Bio-Socio-Psychological Developmental Tasks[a]
Late Adolescence: Age 15

Developmental Tasks	Coping Behaviors
1. Achieving an appropriate dependence-independence pattern	1. Establishing one's self as an independent individual in a mature way *Example:* The late adolescent wants to be treated like an adult. He evidences a need to deny his childhood and shows an amnesia for it. This is a period of reintegration that follows a period of disintegration in early adolescence. The late adolescent gives attention to civic responsibilities, explores seriously possible life vocations, models his parties after adults, etc. This task is defined quite differently for different social classes in the U.S. Upper- and middle-class parents exert pressure on their children to remain dependent by remaining emotionally, socially, and economically within the family until they finish college. Lower-class parents require their adolescent children to be independent financially as well as socially and emotionally; therefore lower-class children are compelled to move through this task more rapidly and to mature earlier than the upper- and middle-class adolescent.

[a](To avoid oversimplification and misunderstanding of the material shown in this table, the reader is directed to the ASCD 1950 Yearbook: *Fostering Mental Health in Our Schools* in which background material and a more complete rationale is given.)

From Tryon, C., & Lilienthal, J. W. Developmental Tasks: I. The concept and its importance. Association for Supervision and Curriculum Development, *Fostering mental health in our schools.* 1950 Yearbook. Washington, D.C.: Association for Supervision and Curriculum Development, 1950. Pp. 77–89. Copyright © 1950 by the Association for Supervision and Curriculum Development. Reproduced with permission.

From Lilienthal, J. W., & Tryon, C. Developmental tasks: II. Discussion of specific tasks and implications. Association for Supervision and Curriculum Development. *Fostering mental health in our schools.* 1950 Yearbook. Washington, D.C.: Association for Supervision and Curriculum Development, 1950. Pp. 90–128. Copyright © 1950 by the Association for Supervision and Curriculum Development. Reproduced with permission.

TABLE 5.1 *(continued)*

Developmental Tasks	Coping Behaviors
2. Achieving an appropriate giving-receiving pattern of affection	1. Building a strong mutual bond with a (possible) marriage partner *Example:* The definition of this task for a given individual is dependent upon what he has learned about love from his parents, siblings, and peers prior to this period. His heterosexual love relationships may reflect his way of securing love, his attitudes towards its permanence and his ability to share love. Successful completion of this task enables the person to establish a lasting and satisfying partnership in marriage.
3. Relating to changing social groups	1. Adopting an adult-patterned set of social values by learning a new peer code *Example:* Fitting into the social picture is now pursued in earnest. Cliques are formed by social class to reflect adult models. The parents and teachers are influential here as the late adolescent peer culture prepares the way for its members to move into mature adulthood.
4. Developing a conscience	1. Learning to verbalize contradictions in moral codes as well as discrepancies between principle and practice, and resolving these problems in a responsible manner *Example:* The late adolescent must be able to resolve problems of conscience, e.g., the fact that the peer group code frequently differs from that of the larger culture, and that there are inconsistencies within the peer code itself in regard to principle vs. practice. Successful completion of this task produces law-abiding citizens, whereas those who reject the moral code and defy social authority represent failures in task completion.
5. Learning one's psycho-socio-biological sex role	1. Exploring possibilities for a future mate and acquiring "desirability" *Example:* Very acceptable ways of exploring feasibility of a marriage partner are through dating and going steady. The "model" date is sought after through boys cultivating good manners, grooming, and poise and girls cultivating glamour and "sex appeal." 2. Choosing an occupation *Example:* Both males and females begin to seek relevancy in their schoolwork since they are preparing to make far-reaching vocational decisions. Some impatience with the school curriculum is frequently shown. Girls, in particular, must decide whether to seek advanced education and greater independence or accept a more dependent role of an early marriage. 3. Preparing to accept one's role in manhood or womanhood as a responsible citizen of the larger community

TABLE 5.1 *(continued)*

Developmental Tasks	Coping Behaviors
	Example: Idealism and a tendency to liberalism are the earmarks of the late adolescent. They show this in regard to social problems such as bad housing, lack of play space for children, etc. Well known adults who represent models to the late adolescent are identified with and imitated.
6. Accepting and adjusting to a changing body	1. Learning appropriate outlets for sexual drives *Example:* Acceptable sexual behavior varies considerably from one ethnic and religious group to another; however, adolescents need to learn the prerequisites of how to establish permanent and mutually satisfying sexual relations with members of the opposite sex.
7. Managing a changing body and learning new motor patterns	("After puberty the rate of bodily growth rapidly declines, and there seem to be no new tasks in this area at this stage of development. The late adolescent consolidates previous gains. He improves motor skills through exercise and practice and achieves as much body poise and grace as he probably ever will have" Lilienthal & Tryon, 1950, p. 115).
8. Learning to understand and control the physical world	("There are probably no developmental tasks in this area for the late adolescent, although at this time many individuals embark on scientific careers in which the major portion of their lives will be devoted to discovering better ways of understanding and controlling phenomena in the physical world" (1950, p. 118).
9. Developing an appropriate symbol system and conceptual abilities	1. Achieving the level of reasoning of which one is capable *Example:* During this period of development explanations by logical deduction and mechanical causality reach their peak, also progress is made in distinguishing between that which is possible and that which represents a dream.
10. Relating one's self to the cosmos	1. Formulating a workable belief and value system *Example:* The late adolescent must be able to deal with abstract problems of right and wrong, resolve discrepancies between what is voiced and what is practiced, resolve discrepancies between what can be empirically demonstrated and what cannot, and achieve a workable understanding of infinite truths and what they hold for him. In other words he must achieve some degree of comfort regarding his place in life and his beliefs about the hereafter.

TABLE 5.2

Bio-Socio-Psychological Developmental Tasks[a]
Early Adulthood: Ages 18–30

Developmental Tasks	Coping Behaviors

1. Selecting a mate	1. Rules vary from social class to social class as does degree of involvement by parents and relatives.
	   a. Primarily the task of young men and women in middle-class and lower-class circles.
	   b. Young men and women may seek assistance through courses in marriage and family life in high school and college.

2. Learning to live with a marriage partner	1. Learning to control and express one's feelings. 2. Achievement of biological sexual satisfaction.
3. Starting a family	1. Female must accept role of motherhood. 2. Male must accept wife's new role and his role of father. 3. Husband and wife must adjust to a reduced sexual life during pregnancy. 4. Middle-class prospective parents in particular must make psychological adjustment during first pregnancy, e.g., regarding amount and kind of medical care, regulation of working mother's work plan, and attitude of relatives toward the pregnancy. 5. Prospective mothers and fathers may participate in adult education courses directed to their needs.
4. Rearing children	1. Parents must meet the physical and emotional needs of the young child. 2. Parents must learn to adapt their daily and weekly schedules to the needs of the child.
5. Managing a home	1. Wife must be able to manage the house—cleaning and fixing meals. 2. Husband must share in the home management and must set up a plan to finance the home and furnishings.
6. Getting started in an occupation	1. Task is most difficult for middle-class male since success in his occupation is essential to holding his middle-class position. All other tasks are frequently subordinated to this one by the middle-class male.
7. Taking on civic responsibility	1. Most learn what is expected of them in civic organizations such as lodges, clubs, and churches. 2. Middle-class people must adapt to greater social pressure for civic participation than lower-class people. 3. Lower-class people must be prepared to participate in labor unions, churches, and fraternal orders, as well as in their immediate neighborhood.

[a]From Havighurst, R. J. *Human development and education.* New York: David McKay, Inc., 1953. Reproduced by permission.

TABLE 5.2 *(continued)*

Developmental Tasks	Coping Behaviors
	4. Upper-class people must adapt to and engage in civic responsibilities required of them because of their parents and/or society's expectations.
8. Finding a congenial social group	1. The young couple must be able to form a leisure-time pattern and find others to share it with.
	2. The young couple must be able to select among several alternative congenial groups to join.

TABLE 5.3

Bio-Socio-Psychological Developmental Tasks[a]
Middle Age: Ages 30–55

Developmental Tasks	Coping Behaviors
1. Achieving adult civic and social responsibility	1. Middle- and upper-class men must adjust to heavy professional or vocational demands on their time by civic and social groups. Working-class men must be able to participate in labor unions in their neighborhoods.
	2. Middle- and upper-class women must be able to fill the void of children leaving the home, e.g., through becoming active in civic organizations. Working-class women have few demands of this type placed on them.
2. Establishing and maintaining an economic standard of living	1. Middle-class men and women, especially, must maintain a satisfactory economic standard of living by: a. Planning expenditures and investments carefully. b. The man must place economic security of the family ahead of speculative ventures and he must enlist the rest of the family in making financial decisions. c. The wife and mother must learn to manage the family budget efficiently and enlist the children's aid in maintaining the home with a minimum of expense.
3. Assisting teen-age children to become responsible and happy adults	1. Parents must provide good models of father or mother, husband or wife, the good homemaker, and the good citizen.
	2. The middle-aged must be self-understanding to the degree that they can give freedom and guidance to their teenagers as well as nephews and nieces.
4. Developing adult leisure time activities	1. The middle-aged man or woman must abandon most strenuous forms of leisure time activities and develop leisure time activities that are meaningful and satisfying and that are applicable to middle- and old-age.

[a]From Havighurst, R. J. *Human development and education.* New York: David McKay, Inc., 1953. Reproduced by permission.

TABLE 5.3 *(continued)*

Developmental Tasks	Coping Behaviors
	2. The middle-aged man or woman must be prepared to take the action to achieve those life-long ambitions which may require a rather high degree of physical stamina and financial expenditures.
5. Relating oneself to one's spouse as a person	1. Wife must be ready to resume role as wife and husband to resume role as husband.
	2. Wife must provide support for husband's strenuous work efforts and also show affection and understanding and maintain her personal attractiveness and charm.
	3. Husband must be able to understand his wife's special psychological difficulties as she experiences the menopause. He must also maintain his attractiveness and attentiveness.
6. Accepting and adjusting to the physiological changes of middle age	1. Both males and females must accept the decline in physical activity as well as the aging of the body tissue which brings on significant changes in physical appearance.
	2. The female must understand and adjust to extremes in mood and sexual activity brought about through the menopause.
	3. Males must adjust to a gradually decreasing sexual activity.
7. Adjusting to aging parents	1. Middle-aged males and females must work out an affectionate but independent relationship with aging parents.

TABLE 5.4

Bio-Socio-Psychological Developmental Tasks[a]
Later Maturity: Ages 55–

Developmental Tasks	Coping Behaviors
1. Adjusting to decreasing physical strength and health	1. Ability to adjust to diminishing physical strength and limited physical activity such as induced by cardiovascular ailments and stiffness and/or weakness in the joints brought on through arthritis, etc.
2. Adjustment to retirement and reduced income	1. Capacity to adjust to increased leisure-time activity and part-time employment.
	2. Ability to adjust expenditures to reduced income.
3. Adjusting to death of spouse	1. Widows must learn to deal with business matters previously handled by the husband; they must also be prepared to move to smaller living quarters and/or to move in with relatives or old people's home. Perhaps most important widows must adjust to loneliness and/or remarriage.
	2. Widowers must be able to learn how to care for a house and to prepare food and clothing. Also,

[a]From Havighurst, R. J. *Human development and education.* New York: David McKay, Inc., 1953. Reproduced by permission.

TABLE 5.4 *(continued)*

Developmental Tasks	Coping Behaviors
	widowers must be prepared to deal with loneliness or remarriage. Widowers must be prepared to move in with children, relatives, or become a member of a larger community of older people by moving into an old people's home.
4. Establishing an explicit affiliation with one's age group	1. The aged person must learn to participate in an age-graded group once again, i.e., he must learn to adjust to fewer rewards from participating in middle-age groups and accept the rewards of another type from members of old-age groups. The middle-age groups are competitive and more status oriented whereas the old-age groups are oriented toward survival or maintaining the status quo.
5. Meeting social and civic obligations	1. Increasing numbers of old people continue to exert leadership in political and civic groups. Aged people must "keep abreast" of current affairs if they plan to remain active in political and community organizations.
6. Establishing satisfactory physical living arrangements	1. The aged person must be prepared to adapt to changing physical conditions such as smaller and less physically difficult dwellings, warmer climate, cooperative housing arrangements such as housing projects, old people's homes, or apartments within a larger home of a child or relative.

TABLE 5.5

Psychosocial Developmental Tasks[a]
Puberty and Adolescence

Developmental Task	Coping Behaviors
Identity vs. Role Confusion	Devotion is the basic strength and fidelity is the basic virtue during this stage. *Guidelines:* With puberty comes a rapid physiological change (revolution). Adolescents become concerned primarily with how others view them as compared to how they feel about themselves. The adolescent is seeking to connect the roles and skills developed earlier with current occupational prototypes. They are also searching for a new sense of continuity and sameness and for a sense of ego identity. Ego identity includes resolution of sexual identity as well as career identity. The adolescent's love is frequently an attempt to achieve some definition of his identity by projecting one's ego image on another, seeing it reflected and thus gradually clarified. The adolescent is characterized by his remarkable

[a]Based on Erikson, Erik H. *Childhood and Society.* New York: W. W. Norton & Company, Inc., 1950, and Erikson, E. H., *Childhood and Society,* Second Edition, Revised. New York: W. W. Norton & Company, Inc., 1963.

TABLE 5.5 *(continued)*

Developmental Task	Coping Behaviors
	clannishness, stereotypes, and his clique cruelty to the out-group. These behaviors represent attempts at identity solidification. (The adolescent's greatest danger at this stage is role confusion.) The adolescent mind is caught between the morality learned by the child and the ethics to be developed by the adult. The adolescent has an ideological mind and outlook toward society. He is eager to be affirmed by his peers and simultaneously to be confirmed by rituals, creeds, and programs which define what is evil.

TABLE 5.6

Psychosocial Developmental Tasks[a]
Young Adulthood

Developmental Task	Coping Behavior
Intimacy vs. Isolation	Affiliation is the basic strength and love is the greatest virtue during this stage. *Guidelines:* With the passing of puberty and the adolescent's search for identity comes his need for intimacy in terms of concrete partnerships and affiliations which require ego strength sufficient to abide by such commitments. The individual is ready for true genitality during this stage of development including mutuality of orgasm with a loved partner of the opposite sex for the purpose of procreation with its attendant responsibilities. Avoidance of contact leads to isolation or failure to commit to intimacy. Severe "character-problems" are the result of this psychopathology.

[a]Reprinted from *Childhood and Society,* Revised, Second Edition by Erik H. Erikson. By permission of W. W. Norton & Company, Inc. Copyright 1950 © 1963 by W. W. Norton & Company, Inc.

TABLE 5.7

Psychosocial Developmental Tasks[a]
Adulthood

Developmental Task	Coping Behaviors
Generativity vs. Stagnation	Production is the greatest strength and care "for the creatures of this world" is the greatest virtue for this stage of development. *Guidelines:* This stage of development requires the ability to lose oneself in the meeting of bodies and

[a]Based on Erikson, Erik H. *Childhood and Society.* New York: W. W. Norton & Company, Inc., 1950, and Erikson, E. H. *Childhood and Society,* Second Edition, Revised. New York: W. W. Norton & Company, Inc., 1963.

TABLE 5.7 *(continued)*

Developmental Task	Coping Behaviors
	minds—an essential stage on the psychosexual as well as on the psychosocial schedule. In addition to generativity, productivity and creativity are expected during this stage. "Where such enrichment fails altogether, regression to an obsessive need for pseudo-intimacy takes place, often with a sense of stagnation and personal impoverishment." (Erikson, 1963, p. 267).

TABLE 5.8

Psychosocial Developmental Tasks[a]
Maturity

Developmental Task	Coping Behavior
Ego Integrity vs. Despair	Renunciation is the greatest strength and wisdom is the greatest virtue of this developmental stage. *Guidelines:* "Ego integrity implies an emotional followership as well as acceptance of the responsibility of leadership" (Erikson, 1963, p. 269). It is characterized by: (1) . . . the ego's accrued assurance of its proclivity for order and meaning"; (2) ". . . postnarcissistic love of the human ego—not of the self—as an experience which conveys some world order and spiritual sense, no matter how dearly paid for"; (3) ". . . the acceptance of one's one and only life cycle . . . that had to be and . . . permitted of no substitutions: . . . a new and different love of one's parents"; (4) ". . . comradeship with the ordering ways of distant times and different pursuits, . . . expressed in simple products and sayings of such times and pursuits"; (5) [readiness] ". . . to the dignity of his own life style against all physical and economic threats," and (6) a ". . . style of integrity developed by his culture or civilization [which] thus becomes the 'patrimony of his soul', the seal of his moral paternity of himself. . . . In such final consolidation, death loses its sting" (Erikson, 1963, p. 268). The lack or loss of this accrued ego integration is signified by fear of death: the one and only life cycle is not accepted as the ultimate of life. Despair expresses the feeling that the time is now short, too short for the attempt to start another life and to try out alternate roads to integrity. Disgust hides despair . . . (Erikson, 1963, pp. 268–269).

[a]Based on Erikson, Erik H. *Childhood and Society.* New York: W. W. Norton & Company, Inc., 1950, and Erikson, E. H. *Childhood and Society,* Second Edition, Revised. New York: W. W. Norton & Company, Inc., 1963.

TABLE 5.9

Vocational Developmental Tasks[a] (Stages)
Adolescents and Adults

Vocational Developmental Tasks	Coping Behaviors
Crystallizing a Vocational Preference—Tentative Substage (Ages 14–18)	*Guidelines:* The teen-ager is expected to begin to develop his ideas as to fields and levels of work appropriate for him and which will prepare him to make tentative choices in regard to type of education and training he will need at least in a partially specified occupation—primarily a cognitive process. *Example:* Choice of a commercial curriculum in high school is considered a crystallization attempt which still allows numerous specific business choices later or even abandonment of the commercial field altogether for semiskilled work.
Specifying a Vocational Preference—Transition Substage (Ages 18–21)	*Guidelines:* The older adolescent is expected to convert his generalized choice into a specific choice and to make a final commitment through entering a specialized educational program or by taking a job designed to serve as an entry into a chosen field—best handled cognitively. *Example:* The job-seeking high school senior is expected to express a preference, to specify what kind of job he wants; the college sophomore is expected to specify his major field of study; and the graduating college senior is expected to select a specific job or graduate education.
Implementing a Vocational Preference—Transition and Trial Early Substages (Ages 18–25)	*Guidelines:* The young adult is expected to convert his vocational preference into a reality—to implement his choice. (Implementation at a low level can occur without having been preceded by specification since motor behavior is more central to the concept than verbalization.) *Example:* The implementation stage is exemplified by application to admission to engineering school, beginning the premedical course, or taking a job as a mechanic's helper.
Stabilizing in a Vocation—Trial (Late) and Stabilization Substage of the Establishment Life Stage (Ages 21–30)	*Guidelines:* The young adult is expected to settle down in a job compatible with his abilities, interests, and aspirations—to pursue self-realization. (A certain amount of trial and error in the process of choosing a job to settle down in is expected.) *Example:* The young adult chooses an occupational field in which he may change positions (jobs) and/or employers—the coping behavior is obtaining a stable job.

[a]Super, D. E., "Vocational Development in Adolescence and Early Adulthood: Tasks and Behaviors." Pp. 79–95 in *Career Development: Self-Concept Theory.* New York: College Entrance Examination Board, 1963. Adapted with permission of the publisher.

TABLE 5.9 *(continued)*

Vocational Developmental Tasks	Coping Behaviors
Consolidating Status and Advancing in a Vocation —Advanced Substage of the Establishment Life Stage (Ages 30–45)	*Guidelines:* The man or woman is expected to get firmly established in the occupation in which he has found a satisfactory slot, to consolidate his/her position, broaden and deepen his/her position to increase satisfaction and to insure its continued occupancy with greater security and comfort. (The relevant coping behaviors are both instrumental and verbal.) *Example:* Persons tend to establish a career pattern through different routes: (1) stable-conventional (stabilized after some trial); (2) unstable (alternately stable and upset with a new trial leading to later stabilization); or (3) multiple career (changes without stabilization in any occupation). (Consolidation tends to be well underway by age 35.)

Life Stages[b]	Coping Behaviors[b]
Maintenance (Ages 45–64)	*Guidelines:* The concern is holding onto one's place in the world of work—continuation along established lines.
Decline (Ages 65 on) Deceleration (65–70)	*Guidelines:* Pace of work slackens, duties and roles are shifted, or the nature of work is changed to accommodate declining capacities. Many men turn to part-time jobs to replace previous full-time occupations.
Retirement (71 on)	*Guidelines:* With many, complete cessation of occupation occurs and the individual becomes more of an observer rather than participant.

[b]Reprinted with the permission of the publisher from *Vocational development: A framework for research* by D. Super, J. Crites, R. Hummel, H. Moser, P. Overstreet, & C. Warnath, New York: Teachers College Press, Copyright, 1957.

Group Guidance

Adolescents (Junior and Senior High School Students)

Group guidance is an economical and effective way to provide information of a personal-social-vocational-educational nature. Since the purpose of group guidance is to serve the cause of prevention of problems, any media or means which enhances the imparting of information that is necessary for making appropriate life decisions is acceptable. The adolescent and adult can utilize a multitude of means for receiving guidance-type information but, especially for the adolescent, an organized and systematic means

for providing him with timely and accurate information is necessary.

In an earlier publication (Gazda & Folds, 1968), a systematic means for providing group guidance to the junior and senior high school student was developed. There are typically three different means employed for providing group guidance in the secondary school: (1) group guidance classes (which are usually organized through the homeroom), (2) units within academic courses (usually in the social studies core and the language arts core), and (3) credit courses (such as psychology, occupations, and "problems"). All three procedures are appropriate and should be used conjointly; however, to insure that some systematic and organized group guidance program is available to all students, the group guidance class which meets once a week or every other week is recommended as the primary group guidance procedure.

As in any other learning experience wherein the classroom setting must be the prime source of contact between student and teacher, the student is more receptive to learning if the information which is being dispensed is *relevant* and *timely.* Group guidance classes can and must be geared to the student's interests and needs. Thus the student himself should be involved in securing and presenting to the class guidance information that is relevant to the majority of other students. This information, if accurate and timely, can frequently be used by the student in making decisions and solving problems before they become debilitating. Thus the information is provided at critical periods ("critical incidents" or developmental levels) of a student's life. Such incidents or periods are called *critical* because they tend to occur with amazing regularity at certain ages and prior to or immediately following certain crucial experiences which the school provides.

By anticipating educational, social, vocational, and personal concerns in the developmental process and by preparing to meet the needs generated, the teacher or counselor who is responsible for group guidance can provide meaningful learning experiences which can facilitate understanding and decision-making as well as develop positive regard for self and others.

In *Group Guidance: A Critical Incidents Approach,* Folds and I developed 20 units around critical incidents which were subsumed under three parts: Orientation, Personal Development, and Educational and Vocational Planning. In this approach the teacher or counselor serves as the resource person and assists the students (in classes of approximately 30) plan each group session. Pupil panels, role-playing, and buzz groups are the key in-

gredients through which the information is dispensed, although the imparting of guidance information through such means as school assemblies, using invited experts, and audio-visual media are consistent with the "critical incidents" or developmental model.

If the group guidance presentations are kept short, to the point, moving and impactful, and if the leader is alert to schedule new topics or units when a previous unit or topic has been exhausted, neither students nor group guidance leaders will experience apathy, boredom, or indifference. Instead they will be excited and motivated to encounter additional meaningful experiences.

A number of conditions set natural limits to what should be attempted in large group guidance classes. The large size, for example, makes the development of intimacy and cohesiveness (necessary for preservation of confidentiality) extremely difficult; therefore the goals for a guidance class *should* be limited to *transmitting accurate and relevant information* of the type previously described, rather than attempting any type of depth exploration of feelings leading to a direct attempt at attitudinal or behavioral modification.

Adolescents and Adults (College and University Students)

For the college or university student there is little chance under current organizational structures for a systematically organized group guidance program such as described for the junior and senior high school student. Orientation of freshmen students is one of the few organized group guidance programs remaining on college and university campuses. Courses in human relations and/or interpersonal communications could fill the group guidance void. Student activity fees are, however, being added to institutional support for establishment and maintenance of counseling centers, infirmaries, speakers bureaus, etc., which do provide educational-vocational-personal-social kinds of information for college and university students on a demand basis. Student personnel workers in higher education should be in a position to encourage the extension and improvement of these programs which can provide accurate and timely information and serve the cause of prevention of problems.

Adolescents and Adults (Individuals not Engaged in Formal Studies)

For the adolescent and adult who is not pursuing formal education beyond high school, group guidance-type information is still nec-

essary. The mass media are perhaps the best source of this kind of information; however, unless the adolescent or adult has previously learned how to appraise the information received through the mass media, he may act on information which is only partially accurate or misleading. Adult education programs hold considerable promise for developing and expanding to fill this void for the adult who no longer has direct access to schools and colleges.

Business and industrial concerns, and local, state, and federal governments usually have in-service education and training programs that occasionally provide information useful in making career decisions and in problem solving which also serve the cause of prevention; nevertheless, much remains to be done by way of group guidance for the employed adolescent or adult and especially for the retired adult. Specialists in group procedures can provide leadership in this realm of group guidance.

Group Counseling

The typical adolescent and adult have achieved a stage in their development wherein the most natural and efficient medium through which they communicate is through the use of the language—verbalizing. Thus, with this age group *interview group counseling* is the preferred mode of treatment. An overview of the theoretical rationale that applies to all age groups discussed in this text is given in Chapter two. In this chapter more specific applications of the overall position will be given.

The group setting, the nature of each counselee, e.g., his needs, levels of expectation, and ability to become involved in the helping process, and the person of the group counselor with his qualities for helping must be integrated into a model or paradigm for counseling within the group setting. The group setting may be viewed as a potential asset or liability. If the healthy elements within each counselee can be elicited and focused constructively in helping the other group members, then the presence of several individuals maximizes the chance for help. If, however, the unhealthy elements in each individual predominate, the group could be a source of deterioration for each member. Obviously, then, the type of counselees selected for a group will be a significant factor in determining the potential for success or failure. Secondly, what the group counselor can bring to the group by way of his ability to lay a foundation for helping is of primary importance in determining whether counselees grow or deteriorate.

One might assume that when groups are perfectly balanced, there would be very little need for a group leader. Since we are still a long way from being able to set up counseling groups where a perfect or near perfect balance exists, the group leader must be the force that manages the group so as to elicit the best from each member.

I take the position that counselees as individuals and the group as a whole go through recognizable stages or phases during the treatment or helping process, and the group leader is in the position to control the pace and the development of the stages of helping. Carkhuff (1969b) has succinctly illustrated in Part A of Figure 5.1 the counselor conditions and their systematic application in helping. I have added to this chart the counselee's and group reactions to these conditions in Part B. The three Carkhuff stages of Exploration-Understanding-Action are consistent with my first three stages of group development (Exploratory, Transition, and Action). The Termination Stage (my fourth and final stage) is not included in the Carkhuff paradigm but in no way does it appear to be inconsistent with it.

Small voluntary groups which are not organized as counseling groups, per se, but rather as "interest" or discussion (guidance-type) groups do not require the same careful balancing as do counseling groups. These groups also do not go through all the stages of development as do the counseling groups unless (and this sometimes occurs) the group makes a decision in the course of their meetings to explore in depth personally relevant concerns. Some guidance-type groups which are organized to discuss results of their test data, college admissions requirements, military obligations, etc., develop into counseling groups. A similar occurrence often results from parent groups organized originally as child-study groups.

Exploratory Stage

During this initial stage the group members engage in a process of getting acquainted, learning the ground rules, and establishing their roles and functions in the group. This stage represents the beginning of building a facilitative base a la Carkhuff (1969 a, b) for the more action-oriented later phases.

During this phase the counselor sets the stage by his careful employment of the core conditions of empathy, respect, concreteness, and genuineness. Carkhuff (1969b) points to empathy as " . . . the key ingredient in the establishment of a viable communicating process" (p. 96). He also reminds us that " . . . mini-

FIGURE 5.1

COUNSELOR OFFERED CONDITIONS FOR THERAPEUTIC CHANGE (PART A)ᵃ	Phase I (Downward or Inward Phase of Self-Exploration) — Initial Stage of Individual Dimensions	Intermediary Stages of Individual Dimensions	Phase II (Upward or Outward Phase of Emergent Directionality and Action) — Final Stage of Individual Dimensions
EMPATHY	Level 3 (interchangeability)	Levels 4 and 5 (additive responses)	Levels 4 and 5 (emphasizing periodic feedback only)
RESPECT	Level 3 (unconditionality)	Level 4 (positive regard)	Levels 4 and 5 (regard and conditionality)
CONCRETENESS	Levels 3 and above (specificity of exploration)	De-emphasized (abstract exploration)	Levels 4 and 5 (specificity of direction)
GENUINENESS	Level 3 (absence of ingenuineness)	Levels 4 and 5 (self-disclosure and spontaneity)	Levels 4 and 5 (spontaneity)
CONFRONTATION		Level 3 (general and open)	Levels 4 and 5 (directionful)
IMMEDIACY		Level 3 (general and open)	Levels 4 and 5 (directionful)
GROUP (COUNSELEE) STAGES IN THERAPEUTIC CHANGE (PART B)	Stage 1 Exploratory	Stage 2 Transition	Stage 3 Action / Stage 4 Termination

ᵃFrom Chapter 7 from *Helping and human relations: A primer for lay and professional helpers.* Vol. 2. *Practice and research,* by Robert R. Carkhuff. Copyright © 1969 by Holt, Rinehart and Winston, Inc. Reprinted by permission of Holt, Rinehart and Winston, Inc., New York.

mally facilitative levels of genuineness provide the context within which all other helping communications may take place" (p. 96). The absence of inauthentic responses rather than the presence of high levels of authenticity is crucial in the Exploratory Stage. By "minimally facilitative" levels Carkhuff means different things for different dimensions. In terms of empathy, the counselor conveys at least an interchangeable level of understanding. In other words, he conveys to the counselees that he has understood them at the level that the counselees wish to be understood at the moment— no more and no less.

By respecting and accepting what the counselees are communicating about themselves, the counselor conveys that he is being non-evaluative or, as Carkhuff prefers "unconditional," and the counselees thus recognize that they will not be hurt, punished or destroyed for expressing themselves as they experience themselves.

Concreteness as a minimally facilitative level in conjunction with empathy serves to sharpen the understanding of the counselee's problems for both the counselor and counselee. Carkhuff (1969b) points up the importance of the counselee increasing his degree of concreteness in the exploratory phase of his problem solving since it serves to clarify the affective and intellective feedback. And thus it highlights the areas of counselee functioning about which the counselor can do something. It also concretizes areas of dysfunctioning for the counselees and provides hope that they will be able to do this some day themselves.

In the early stage of helping, Carkhuff specifies two critical functions served by the helper (counselor): "(1) the helper does not impede the helpee's development of himself and his problem in any respect; and (2) the helper has an opportunity to assess the helpee's level of development" (1969b, p. 97). (Refer to the protocol following the Termination Stage which illustrates the group leader's and members' attempts to build a facilitative base.)

Transition Stage

The Transition Stage of group development (interview group counseling in this instance) is consistent with Carkhuff's Intermediary Stage (see Figure 5.1). The Transition Stage occurs because the counselees have begun to sense the strength and acceptance of the group counselor—his positive regard for them.

During this group stage of development the counselor increases his levels of genuineness, empathy, and respect. That is to say, he becomes increasingly genuine in his expression of *positive* feelings toward the counselees and is unlikely to communicate

his negative feelings toward them. He also, for the first time, uses *self-disclosure* as a model for the counselees to follow.

The counselor's empathic communications are increasingly probing and dynamic as he assists the counselees in understanding themselves at deeper and deeper levels, particularly in those areas of their lives which are dysfunctional and where understanding is lacking. Carkhuff tells how the respect dimension is included in this phase as follows: "There are aspects of the helpee that elicit positive regard from the helper, and he freely and genuinely communicates his respect to the helpee" (1969b, p. 98).

As the counselor becomes more fully himself so do the counselees and this frees all parties to be more real, honest, and genuine. In this regard, and for the first time, the more directional and action-oriented dimensions of confrontation and immediacy are introduced at minimally facilitative levels—that is in a tentative manner as exemplified through simply raising questions about behavioral discrepancies and interrelationships rather than giving directions for modifying behavioral discrepancies. Carkhuff summarizes this stage of helping, which I see as synonymous with the Transition Stage of group development, as follows:

> *Thus, whereas the early stages of helping function to enable the helpee to make himself known in his own way, the intermediary stages take on the characteristic of tentative helper initiative and directionality. The development of the helper's directionality does not function to the exclusion of the helpee's development of his own directionality. Rather it is internally directed within the helping process, its probes and reinforcements serving to give directionality to the helpee's own efforts to come to understand himself at deeper levels in areas which he is not now functioning effectively . . . (1969, pp. 98–99).*[1]

(See also the protocol following the Termination Stage which illustrates the various phases in the movement of a given individual treated within a counseling group.)

Action Stage

The dimensions of confrontation and immediacy (see Figure 5.1) coupled with high levels of genuineness, are crucial to this phase of helping. The group counselor is freely and fully himself insofar as his doing so is helpful to the counselees. However, in being himself, the counselor is less likely to be self-disclosing.

[1] From *Helping and human relations: A primer for lay and professional helpers.* Vol. 2. *Practice and research* by Robert R. Carkhuff. Copyright © 1969 by Holt, Rinehart and Winston, Inc. Reprinted by permission of Holt, Rinehart and Winston, Inc., New York.

As the counselor and counselees consider various actions that might be taken by counselees which would be conducive to their problem resolution, the counselor may confront the counselees with discrepancies in counselee behavior that may preclude constructive resolution. The counselor also interprets his experiencing of the counselees' attitudes and behavior toward him (immediacy) and others in the group in terms of how he feels personally about the act(s) and how he views them in the overall resolution of counselee problems. In other words, he translates what is going on in the "here and now" for the counselees in such a way that they might utilize the experience in taking appropriate action in their behalf outside the group itself.

In the later phases of the Action Stage, the dimension of respect becomes more closely intertwined with genuineness and, according to Carkhuff, "along with positive regard directed toward self-constructive helpee behaviors the helper also generates negative regard toward self-destructive helpee activities" (1969b, p. 100).

Empathy during the Action Stage serves to provide periodic feedback on level of understanding, whereas concreteness is now once again necessary at high levels as it is employed to analyze the pros and cons and to consider the alternative plans of action available to the counselees. (See also the protocol following the Termination Stage which is used to illustrate the various phases of counselee development in a group setting.) Carkhuff concludes that the counselor (helper) . . . *will not accept the helpee at less than he can be. He will employ all of his resources in differentially reinforcing the helpee in order to enable him, in turn, to employ all of his resources in searching for the highest levels of productivity and creativity within himself"* (1969b, p. 100).

The Exploration, Transition, and Action Stages of group development discussed above are, in my evaluation, synonymous with the Carkhuff phases of helping as outlined in Figure 5.1; therefore I have chosen to incorporate his findings and explanations into my developmental approach of the *interview-type* with adolescents and adults. I have, however, included a Termination Stage which Carkhuff does not have in his model.

Termination Stage

A definitive Termination Stage is present only in closed groups. In a closed group with a preset termination date, group members usually begin to taper off in self-disclosure and press for last-minute help from the counselor and group members. Particularly

evident is their need to tell how much the group means to them. Frequently efforts are made for a group reunion at some specific future date. Another common practice is for the group members to ask for frank feedback from every other member in a kind of "going around" procedure.

In open groups with members terminating at different times, there is no group stage of termination although each individual separately experiences something of its equivalent. That is he, much as the group as a whole in closed groups, will make attempts to continue the sessions beyond the time that the group can continue to be helpful to him, and he will also usually seek some kind of closing feedback from the group as well as commitments to future contacts or meetings.

The group counselor is careful to observe the degree of regression in individual group members during the last three or four group sessions. The approaching loss of a supportive peer group may reinforce tendencies for some to deteriorate slightly as they contemplate this loss. If anyone shows significant deterioration, the counselor may wish to continue working with the individual on a one-to-one basis until such time that the counselee can make a reasonable transition. In other words, the counselor must be prepared to help a group member as long as it seems necessary. An alternative would be a mutually agreed upon referral.

I think that Carkhuff's (1969b) following statement succinctly concludes this section:

> *In summary the early stages of the helping dimensions enable the helpee to make himself known, the intermediary stages to allow the helper to give the helping process internal direction. The later stage of helping emphasizes a shared, highly interactional process in which both the helper and the helpee concentrate upon the interrelationship of the internal and external worlds of the helpee and the resolution of his areas of dysfunctioning within and between these worlds (pp. 101).*[2]

Protocol: Illustrative of the Application of the Carkhuff Model to Interview Group Counseling

The following protocol was taken from a group session very early in the life of a group. The protocol illustrates the application of the core conditions of Carkhuff (1969a, b) to a problem introduced by

[2]From *Helping and human relations: A primer for lay and professional helpers.* Vol. 2. *Practice and research* by Robert R. Carkhuff. Copyright © 1969 by Holt, Rinehart and Winston, Inc. Reprinted by permission of Holt, Rinehart and Winston, Inc., New York.

a group member in *interview group counseling.* Since there was no facilitative base built with the counselee, the group counselor and members were careful to begin with interchangeable responses, especially of empathy. The interaction covered only ten minutes of group time and yet led to a decision that the counselee felt was necessary and appropriate.

The counselee was in her mid-twenties. The group was composed of male and female members from their early twenties to their late fifties. Each statement is numbered to permit easy identification.

Protocol

Counselee: (1) Everytime the phone rings my heart jumps. I stay worried all the time.

Counselor: (1) You're really pretty sure then that you're going to get some bad news everytime the phone rings.

Counselee: (2) Yes, it seems like that I just wait to hear some upsetting news from home.

Group Member A (female): (1) Something then is going on at home than makes you think that something bad is going to happen?

Counselee: (3) Yes, my sister is ill and they're trying to find out what's wrong with her but they tell me that they don't know exactly what it is yet. I feel like maybe I should be there instead of 84 miles away, living my own life.

Counselor: (2) You feel kind of guilty that in this time of crisis in your family that you're not there to help out.

Analysis

Counselee: (1) Stimulus 1 was the counselee's initial statement of her problem.

Counselor: (1) Response 1 by the group counselor was an attempt to convey an interchangeable response of empathy in that the basic concern of the counselee was communicated regarding the problem at hand.

Counselee: (2) The counselee response showed that she felt understood at least at a minimal (three *a la* Carkhuff, 1969a, b) level.

Group Member A (female): (1) The group member simply gave another interchangeable level of response conveying understanding at the level the counselee was communicating. Now the counselor and Group Member A had both begun to build a facilitative base with the counselee.

Counselee: (3) At this point the counselee feels it is safe to be more concrete or specific about her problem.

Counselor: (2) Here the counselor detects guilt expressed by the counselee and he responds to it seeking to move to a level beyond

Protocol	**Analysis**
	what the counselee is revealing explicitly—a 4 level *a la* Carkhuff (1969a, b).
Counselee: (4) Yes, it seems like that every time they've needed me, that I was either away at school or not available. This really has me upset!	*Counselee:* (4) The counselee confirms the feeling of guilt and tells why she feels that way.
Group Member B (male): (1) It is not the first time that they couldn't depend on you to be around? You've been away quite a bit sometimes.	*Group Member B (male):* (1) Another group member responds. He attempts to give an interchangeable-level response, but his choice of words could be perceived as confrontive by the counselee.
Counselee: (5) Yes. Maybe it wouldn't affect me so badly if this were the first crisis, but it seems like its just been one a minute in the last five years, and I'm really feeling guilty. I'm married now, but I still feel like I have commitments to Mom and Dad.	*Counselee:* (5) The counselee does not misread group member B's response but uses it to expand on her reason for her feeling of guilt; therefore his response was slightly better than a level 3— perhaps a 3.5 or 4 in terms of a gross or overall response on the Carkhuff dimensions.
Counselor: (3) You feel that during these five years away from home you weren't doing enough to help your Mom and Dad. Now you are married and you're in less position to help them than you were before.	*Counselor:* (3) Here the counselor re-enters the interaction and tries to identify the conflict that he perceives regarding the counselee's married state and the dual commitments it introduced. He was trying to go beyond an interchangeable response to get at a source of counselee conflict.
Counselee: (6) Yes. This is it, and then this is the point that confuses me. They wanted me to go away to school and get an education and get a good job. But then being away from home and getting a good education caused me not to be there when they needed me. Now, I've got a good education and am working and I feel like I should be there with them.	*Counselee:* (6) The counselee feels understood and so introduces another source of her conflict and confusion.
Counselor: (4) After they sacrificed for you, you stayed away and now you feel like you	*Counselor:* (4) Now the counselor shows how well he understands by being concrete and specific

Protocol	**Analysis**
owe them something in return, but you haven't been able to pay them back in some way or other.	about the source of her conflict and feeling of guilt.
Counselee: (7) I guess that's getting to the point. Just marrying and getting your own life, job, house—just how much can you participate in family situations when you are out of school, out of the house, without really feeling like you are giving them less than you really should?	*Counselee:* (7) Counselee senses that the counselor is very closely in tune with her. It is a little threatening, perhaps since she comes back trying somehow to justify her current position.
Group Member C (male): (1) You just wish you knew what was a fair return to them (interrupted here by counselee response)	*Group Member C:* (1) Group member C picks up the counselee's struggle over what is fair on her part. He helps her concretize her conflict while still feeling accepted unconditionally.
Counselee: (8) Yes.	*Counselee:* (8) Counselee feels the accuracy of group member C's response and interrupts him with a "Yes."
Group Member C (male): (2) . . . after you're married, and what married people owe their parents.	*Group Member C:* (2) Group member C simply finishes what he intended to say.
Counselee: (9) Yes, especially after they've made sacrifices for me.	*Counselee:* (9) Counselee goes back to counselor's use of the word "sacrifice" in his fourth response. She accepts the fact that her parents did sacrifice for her.
Counselor: (5) I get the feeling that you feel that you do need to do more than you have done.	*Counselor:* (5) At this point the counselor makes the decision to move the counselee into more action-levels and introduces for the first time a degree of *conditionality*. Heretofore, as the base was being built, all counselor and other helpee counselee responses were unconditional.
Counselee: (10) Yes, but then on the other hand, I'm wondering if I really should.	*Counselee:* (10) The conditionality is sensed by the counselee and she backtracks slightly as she seeks to justify not doing anything about her guilt feelings—not taking action.

Protocol

Counselor: (6) Sometimes you think you should, and other times you don't know what a fair return is.

Counselee: (11) Yes, so if I could just work out this problem of not being so—so I wouldn't be so concerned with what's going on at home. If it just wouldn't occupy my mind so much. It really is upsetting me! It seems if I could adjust to the fact that Mom and Dad and my sister have a life, Jack (husband of counselee) and I have a life, and we can just do so much and then function normally.

Group Member D (female): (1) Somehow if you can just get settled in your own mind that there has to be this separation and that you can feel comfortable about whether you've been fair to your parents.

Counselee: (12) Do you think that it's normal to worry about a sister that is sick and ill, and is it normal to the point that you think about it 80% of the time and you really spend your time moping and wondering if something is deadly wrong with her? I just don't know what will become of me, nor would I know how to help Mom and Daddy.

Group Member C (male): (3) You really don't think it's normal to spend that much time worrying about her. You're also feeling quite a bit of guilt about her illness and the fact that you can't do more for her and your parents.

Analysis

Counselor: (6) The counselor senses the threat felt by the counselee and temporarily moves back to an interchangeable response (unconditionality).

Counselee: (11) The counselee points up (concretizes) the essence of her conflict once more.

Group Member D (female): Group member D gives an interchangeable-level response showing empathy and unconditionality.

Counselee: (12) Here the counselee is moving to action by asking if she is normal having the feelings that she does have. She is also indicating a readiness for conditionality on the part of the helpers.

Group Member C (male): (3) The group member interprets the counselee's earlier responses as meaning that the counselee felt her concerns to be at the abnormal level. He also aims for a four-level response by an interpretation of guilt feelings over the counselee's sister's illness and then he comes back to her concern with her parents at an interchangeable level.

Protocol

Counselee: (13) That's why I'm coming and asking for help, because I don't know whether or not it's normal or not. I kind of feel it is normal, since I do have close ties, and I really do love them —love her and my family. But then I don't have guilt feelings about her illness, 'cause this is something that I did not have anything to do with. I do have a guilt feeling about whether or not I really did help them (parents) enough, or if I'm committing myself to home (when I say home, I mean to Mom and Dad and family) as much as I should. That is the essence of my problem. And then it seems like that because I do have these guilt feelings, and it stays on my mind . . . like I'm always wondering about if something is going to happen. If it is, I say well I should be there. Then if I were there, I wonder how much I really could do.

Counselor: (7) What could you do? You're kind of torn between the feeling that you need to be there on the one hand, and realistically if you were there, you couldn't do anything anyway to change your sister's health, but you might in some way be a comfort to your parents.

Counselee: (14) Yes. Now what are your views on this?

Counselor: (8) I guess all I can tell you Marilyn, is what I hear you telling me—that you're pretty miserable right now the way things are, and it is not getting any better, and that you need to take some kind of action to feel better about this relationship between you and your parents, that

Analysis

Counselee: (13) Group member C's response forces the counselee to be more explicit in her feelings toward her sister; otherwise, she reiterates what she has been saying.

Counselor: (7) The counselor simply tries to communicate at an interchangeable level the nature of her feelings and conflict.

Counselee: (14) Counselee senses her base with the counselor and risks action or a counselor conditional response.

Counselor: (8) The counselor, not prepared to give specific advice, tries to respond by summarizing for the counselee the over-riding message that he had been receiving throughout the short interaction with the confidence that the counselee could translate

Protocol	Analysis
you need to do something more than you have done. I don't know what's possible, but that is what I heard you telling me—that you feel like you owe more than you've been giving them back.	the message to specific action. Here the counselor showed respect for the counselee's potential for arriving at specific behavioral responses.
Counselee: (15) I do feel that I have to do more. I guess now my next move must be to talk to my husband about my feeling and make plans to do something more for my parents but which will be acceptable to him.	*Counselee:* (15) The counselor was on target and this was confirmed by the counselee's response. Something that was not known heretofore, the husband's role, was introduced and apparently this was as far as the group could take the counselee until she took the action she herself decided upon.

Selection and Group Composition

Selection and group composition has been treated rather thoroughly in Chapter two. Since this section of Chapter two is most relevant for the adolescent and adult age group, I refer the reader to a review of the section: *Counselee Selection and Group Composition—General Guidelines.*

My purpose at this point is to call attention to some special problem areas of group composition as it applies to adolescents and adults. I have found that one should be careful not to mix high school freshmen and sophomores with juniors and seniors. Occasionally there can be groupings across more than two grade levels, but this arrangement should be made with care. Within the college age population there is less of a problem in mixing lower and upper division students than there is in the high school setting; however, undergraduates are not usually easily absorbed into counseling groups of graduate students.

Outside of a school or college setting, I have worked successfully with age ranges of over 40 years. Increasingly though, the generation gap has made it somewhat difficult to include the young adult of college age with adults over 30 years of age. Careful screening should be given if exceptions are to be made where the generation gap exists since the primary goal is to provide each individual with co-helpers and models that would best facilitate him in his problem resolution. If the general problem for the group

members concerns the generation gap itself, then the group should be constituted with young as well as older members to provide the opportunity to work out such differences in a therapeutic climate.

Of course, we should look to our developmental tasks and coping behaviors model as a gross indicator of the type of problems that a person might be experiencing in this age group. Once having classified the nature of counselee X's problem, *viz.*, absence of an appropriate coping behavior, we can be in a position to select a person of approximately the same age (counselee Y) yet one who has developed a successful coping behavior for the specific task of counselee X. In like fashion we would try to find another counselee who can model for counselee Y, etc. Matching for purposes of providing at least one good model other than the counselor should be the goal of the group counselor. Selecting two counselees for the same group who are having similar coping problems would be consistent with my position just as long as there is at least one person in the group who could model appropriate coping behavior in the task area wherein the other one is deficient.

In addition to selecting counselees on the basis of their inadequate or inappropriate coping behavior for a specific developmental task, the pretesting of each prospective counselee on the Carkhuff indexes of Discrimination and Communication would provide the counselor with levels of counselee functioning on these two dimensions. Since these indices are loaded on the verbal dimension, they would be especially appropriate for use in predicting a counselee's potential in *interview* group counseling. Carkhuff (1969a, b) has shown that the Communication Index, in particular, is a very good predictor of the ease or difficulty with which a person can be trained systematically in *human relations* skills. These skills are essentially the ability to implement the core dimensions in relating to others.

Carkhuff (1969a, b) has emphasized that high level (helpful) responses beget high levels. Thus, if a counselee can communicate at rather high levels in terms of his ability to be concrete or specific about the nature of his problems; if he can self-disclose in depth (high levels); and if he can be genuine as he talks about his troubles, he is in a better position to be heard in depth (helped) by the counselor and other counselees. In other words if he self-discloses genuinely and concretely, the counselor and other counselees are more likely to respond with high levels of the core dimensions of empathy, respect, warmth, concreteness, genuine-

ness, appropriate self-disclosure, confrontation, and immediacy. And, conversely, if a counselee can discriminate at relatively high levels and can communicate at helpful levels as shown on the gross measure of communication, he is likely to be a good counselee and model for other counselees. The higher the communication level of the total group of counselees and counselor the better the opportunity for the group to receive help and to receive it most efficiently.

Group Setting

The settings for interview group counseling will vary with the age group involved. For the high school and college age groups, a comfortable conference room for seating eight to ten individuals is all that is required. The chairs should be comfortable for both males and females. As a rule, the group should not sit around a table since the table frequently is a barrier to closeness and the resultant opportunity for healthy intimacy. If the room has a rug on the floor, the group may even choose to spend part of the time sitting on the floor as they become more informal and comfortable with each other. Especially important is the necessity for complete privacy and freedom from interruptions.

The setting for adult groups may range, depending on the purpose of the group, from a room in a clinic or industrial setting to a room in a home for the aged. In all cases the room should be large enough to accommodate eight to ten individuals and the chairs should possess the degree of comfort necessary for the physical condition of the counselee—usually padded or upholstered chairs or couches which can be arranged in a circle. Tables provide the group with an initial feeling of security but their ultimate effect is to serve as a barrier and therefore usually should not be included. A rug on the floor makes the room more adaptable to sitting on the floor if the group prefers—especially in the case of marathons.

With the advent of the video tape recorder came theoretical models such as Stoller's (1968) focused feedback which is compatible with the developmental model outlined in this text. The room for interview group counseling, therefore, should include space and electrical outlets for a video tape recorder and camera and also for an audio tape recorder which is standard equipment.

Ideally, the setting for interview group counseling should have a small ante room adjacent to it and also a bathroom so that it

could easily be adapted for a marathon session. The marathon approach is also compatible with the framework of the developmental model.

Group Size

Size alone as it effects outcome in a therapy (counseling) group is a limited and rather unproductive viewpoint. According to Goldstein, et al., " . . . group size as an influence in psychotherapy becomes meaningful only when viewed as an interactional variable" (1966, p. 339). In defense of the above quotation, Goldstein, et al., surveyed the group dynamics research in terms of the effects of group size on *member interaction, leadership and intermember relations.* Although they caution the direct application of their findings to therapy (counseling) groups, we can be guided somewhat by the findings from the group dynamics literature until we have carefully researched studies of the effects of group size on counselees in group counseling.

In terms of *member interaction,* the results of the Goldstein, et al., review of the literature appear to be exemplified and summarized best by a study of Bales and Borgatta (1955). They studied the interaction effect of problem-solving groups as they increased in size from two to seven. They found that the rate of giving information and suggestions increased with the increase of group size, whereas the rates of asking for opinions and showing agreement decreased. Goldstein, et al. (1966, p. 340) hypothesized that the reason for such interactional changes was that as size increased, there would be a tendency toward a more mechanical method of introducing information, less sensitive exploration of the viewpoints of others, and more direct attempts to control others and reach a solution—all of which are associated with the increasing constriction of time available per member.

When *leadership* is studied as an interacting variable with group size, the findings of Goldstein, et al., in their review of group dynamics research, are that as size increases, more and more of the members address the leader directly and the group becomes more leader-centered as he, in turn, begins to address the group as a whole. There is a corresponding increasing acceptance by group members of leader control and fewer opportunities remain for individual leadership and initiative of group members to emerge.

Intermember relations seem to be quite directly affected by

group size. The summary of research on this variable by Goldstein, et al. (1966) shows that small groups provide the best opportunity for interaction among all members and the greatest opportunity for the development of group cohesion—an important element in the success of a counseling group (see Chapter two). In problem-solving groups, Goldstein, et al., found that even-numbered groups seem to be characterized by more disagreements than odd-sized groups and that groups of five are most frequently reported as harmonious problem-solving groups.

One must reiterate the danger of making extrapolations of the research findings on group size of task- and problem-solving groups to counseling and therapy groups; nevertheless, the research *suggests* that we should construct counseling groups based on the knowledge that groups of approximately five to ten provide optimum limits within which we can best function. Odd-sized groups may produce less disagreement (since an even-split-polarization is not possible). If our proposed counseling group is to contain reticent members, keeping the group small has an advantage of improving their opportunities for participation and at the same time the disadvantage of introducing greater initial threat to a person who may have thought he could hide in a group. Keeping the group small, for example five, also could be important in giving the leader control over one or two rather aggressive individuals.

My clinical experience has led me to the development of a rule-of-thumb for group size which is based on the type of counselee in the group and the duration and frequency of group sessions possible. If the duration and frequency is short, such as three months, I prefer small groups of five to seven since this allows for greater intensity of interaction and greater opportunity for growth. If I have from three to six months or a year, I prefer groups of seven to ten. (With groups running beyond six months one must allow for attrition, for various reasons, of one or two members; therefore it would be prudent to begin with at least seven members—other considerations such as degree of disturbance of counselees taken into account.)

Nature of counselees' problems or degree of disturbance and duration and frequency of group sessions have a direct bearing on the size of a counseling group. Also, as a rule, the smaller the group, the more frequently it meets, and the longer it meets, the greater the opportunity for intensity of group involvement and growth.

Frequency, Length, and Duration of Group Sessions

As stated in the above section on group size, the frequency of the group sessions and also the duration of the counseling sessions is directly related to the intensity of group involvement and growth. But, in addition to group size, frequency and duration of the group sessions cannot be considered apart from nature of counselees' problems or degree of disturbance, and also whether or not a group is open or closed, i.e., continues to admit new members as old members complete their treatment (open), or retains all its original members until some agreed-upon termination date (closed). The more severe the counselees' problems, in general, the more frequently and the longer duration they would meet.

In educational settings, the quarter, semester, and academic school year are natural division points which must be considered in composing groups. The group counselor, therefore, can be guided somewhat by the likelihood that his group composition might change radically at any one of these division points and thus choose to set termination dates around them. In this regard a quarter arrangement would call for at least two group sessions interspersed during a week, whereas a semester arrangement might call for one session per week of approximately one and one half to two hours and the same would be true for an academic school year. Where I am faced with a short duration for treatment, I have used one or more marathon sessions in addition to the weekly group sessions to intensify the group involvement and potential for growth.

Media

The primary media employed in *interview* group counseling are, as the name implies, counselee and counselor talk—verbal communication. Of course, this is only complete when nonverbal behaviors are observed in conjunction with verbal communications. Any media, however, which enhance communication and lead to increased self-understanding of counselees and improved interpersonal communication, are suitable for use in interview group counseling.

Focused Feedback (Stoller, 1968) utilizing the video tape recorder is recommended as an auxiliary medium to be employed in

interview group counseling. When it is employed the counselor, co-counselor or group member who is operating the camera and VTR must be selective in focusing on both discrepant and non-discrepant feedback. In other words, the decision to view and play back a certain segment or interaction must be made on the basis of whether or not the interaction helps the counselee(s) understand wherein they are incongruent with themselves and thus punish (discourage) or, if congruent, reinforce (reward) their responses.

The VTR adds extraneous elements to a group and is not recommended for general application to interview group counseling until the counselor has had practice using the equipment and is very comfortable with it. An audio tape recorder can also be used in a group in much the same manner as the VTR; however, it lacks the quality of visual cues that are often very revealing to the counselees and group counselor. The use of GSR in groups has been recommended in a previous work (Gazda, 1968) and it has been used successfully in a pilot study in individual counseling. (Michels, Gazda, & Wiggins, in press).

Selected Illustrative Research Studies of Interview Group Counseling

The most prevalent form of group counseling consists of many variations of interview group counseling—almost to the point that many use group counseling synonymously with interview group counseling. A comprehensive review of group counseling research (primarily of the interview type) is given in Chapter seven; therefore, all that I shall attempt here is to cite and briefly to report on the results of research in which I, myself, utilized some variation of the model described in this chapter.

Two of three groups of parents who were counseled by the interview method (Gazda & Ohlsen, 1966) significantly increased in acceptance of self and others. Other indications of positive change included one person reaching the decision of an important job change—leading to a life-style change for him. A second male began to assume the role of head of the household and to show greater confidence in himself in his occupation which paid off in significant material benefits. One couple improved their marriage relationship which resulted in their daughter's giving up an unhealthy withdrawal into reading. And still another couple improved their understanding and handling of their son to the

extent that it resulted in the elimination of his asthma attacks and improved his school attendance.

A group of practicing group counselors who participated in seven weeks of group counseling significantly increased in their assumption of the roles of Information Giver, Aggressor, Interpreter, and Nonparticipant. It was hypothesized that the increase in Information Giver, Aggressor, and Interpreter roles represented a positive indication of increased self-confidence and that the increase in the Nonparticipant role was an artifact of members preparing themselves for the termination of the group (Gazda & Bonney, 1965).

Ahearn (1968) used the Hill Interaction Matrix, Form G, to study the interaction of a group of counselors who participated in nine months of group counseling with me as their counselor. He found that the group moved to significant levels of therapeutic interaction on the Hill matrix.

In a near replication of the Ahearn study, Sisson (1970) used the same Hill matrix to study the levels of therapeutic interaction achieved by a group of psychiatry residents who participated in nine months of group counseling with me as their counselor. The residents reached even greater levels of therapeutic interaction than did the school counselors in the Ahearn study.

At the time of this writing no objective research has been made of my efforts to employ the Carkhuff (1969a, b) model to my group counseling. However, I personally believe that it has given me much more direction in what I am doing and that I am more effective and efficient. The sample protocol in this chapter is representative of my application of the Carkhuff model to my own developmental concepts of interview group counseling.

Summary

Group counseling and guidance for the adolescent and adult is the subject of this chapter. Consistent with Chapters three and four, this chapter also focuses on a specific age group, *viz.*, ages 13 to old age and it also includes tables of developmental tasks and coping behaviors expected of this age group. The developmental tasks and coping behaviors are based on three independent positions: the bio-socio-psychological position of Havighurst (some areas of which were taken from the interpretations of Tryon and Lilienthal), the psychosocial position of Erikson, and the vocational position of Super, et al.

The recommended procedure for the implementation of group guidance in the junior and senior high schools is based on the hypothesis that these students require accurate and timely information to make appropriate life decisions. The most economical and efficient means is through regularly scheduled group guidance classes, equivalent to one period a week or every other week throughout the school life of the student. The topics included in the guidance classes are those areas, "critical incidents," which the student is facing and for which he needs accurate information. The topics can be organized around three major areas: Orientation, Personal Development, and Educational and Vocational Planning. The text, *Group Guidance: A Critical Incidents Approach* by Gazda and Folds (1968) is cited for further reference to this approach to group guidance.

For the college and university student, the current practices by Student Personnel Services divisions are cited. These include speeches by experts on topics from effects of drugs on drug users to vocational opportunities—offered by various groups as they tour college campuses recruiting personnel. A system currently used very infrequently, i.e., classes in human relations, is recommended as the basic method to provide guidance for the college and university student.

Interview group counseling is the form of counseling which is the most suitable to the adolescent and adult. Within this form variations such as marathons and focused feedback can be adapted to strengthen the treatment program. Interview group counseling, as detailed in this chapter, emphasizes both relationship and behavioral principles. Carkhuff's paradigm is the one which is most consistent with my current position for counseling via the interview medium. The systematic and cumulative application of the core conditions *a la* Carkhuff, of empathy, respect, warmth, concreteness, genuineness, appropriate self-disclosure, confrontation, and immediacy is consistent with the group stages or phases of development which I have postulated. These are Exploratory, Transitional, Action, and Termination. Their relationship to Carkhuff's model is described and also illustrated through the use of a protocol taken from one of my group counseling sessions.

Consistent with Chapters three and four, I have included for the age group of adolescents and adults treated in this chapter sections on Selection and Group Composition, Group Setting, Group Size, Frequency and Duration of Group Sessions, Media, and Selected Illustrative Research Studies. Selection and group

composition as it pertains to interview group counseling is treated rather extensively in Chapter two, but special problem areas are highlighted in this chapter. The concepts of role balancing and the provision of models for each group participant are the key elements stressed for proper selection and group composition. Locating inadequate coping behaviors of prospective group members is a guideline also recommended to the group counselor for his selection procedure.

The recommended setting for interview group counseling is a conference-type room with comfortable chairs and a rug on the floor (for sitting on the floor when appropriate) capable of seating ten people comfortably in a circle. The setting should be such as to guarantee privacy and freedom from interruptions. Also, it should include adjacent bathroom facilities and a small dining area which would be suitable for adapting to a marathon session. Space and electrical outlets suitable for video taping and playback are recommended facilities.

Group size for interview group counseling ranges from 5 to 10; however, optimum size is dependent on member interaction, leadership, and intermember relations. Odd-numbered groups seem to be least subject to polarization, according to group dynamics research reports and therefore groups of 5, 7, or 9 would be preferred over groups of 6, 8, or 10.

As a general rule, the severity of the counselees' problems will determine the frequency and duration of treatment. The more frequent a group meets and the longer the sessions (up to about two hours), the more rapid the development of group cohesiveness and positive therapeutic results. Closed groups of a quarter, a semester or even an entire academic year are quite feasible in educational settings, whereas open groups with no specified group termination date are more practical for clinical settings. Marathon group sessions are recommended to be interspersed to increase the intensity of group involvement as the time limits suggest.

The media most utilized in interview group counseling is, of course, counselee and counselor verbalizations. Non-verbal expressions are basic to full communication and, therefore, the group counselor must be proficient in reading non-verbal messages or expressive movements. The use of a video tape recorder with feedback of significant group and individual member interactions and non-verbal expressions is recommended for use in a group counseling setting. Group members or co-counselors can operate the T.V. camera and VTR.

The chapter closes with the citing of four illustrative research studies based on interview counseling groups for which I served

as the counselor. The results generally support *my* use of the developmental model and other criteria which I have outlined in this chapter.

References

AHEARN, T. R. Interaction process analysis of extended group counseling with prospective counselors. Unpublished doctoral dissertation, University of Georgia, 1968.

BALES, B. F., & BORGATTA, E. F. Size of group as a factor in the interaction profile. In A. P. Hare, E. F. Borgatta, & R. F. Bales (Eds.), *Small groups: Studies in social interaction*. New York: Alfred A. Knopf, 1955. Pp. 396–413.

CARKHUFF, R. R. *Helping and human relations*. Vol. 1, *Selection and training*. New York: Holt, Rinehart & Winston, 1969. (a)

CARKHUFF, R. R. *Helping and human relations*. Vol. 2. *Practice and research*. New York: Holt, Rinehart & Winston, 1969. (b)

ERIKSON, E. H. *Childhood and society*. New York: Norton, 1950.

ERIKSON, E. H. *Childhood and society*. (2nd ed.) New York: Norton, 1963.

GAZDA, G. M. Group counseling: A functional approach. In G. M. Gazda (Ed.), *Basic approaches to group psychotherapy and group counseling*. Springfield, Ill.: Charles C. Thomas, 1968. Pp. 263–303.

GAZDA, G. M., & BONNEY, W. C. Effects of group counseling on role behavior of counselors in training. *Counselor Education and Supervision*. 1965, *4*, 191–197.

GAZDA, G. M., & OHLSEN, M. M. Group counseling: A means of parent education. *Adult Leadership*, 1966, *14*, 231ff.

GAZDA, G. M., & FOLDS, J. H. *Group guidance: A critical incidents approach*. Chicago: Parkinson Div., Follett Educational Corp., 1968.

GOLDSTEIN, A. P., HELLER, K., & SECHREST, L. B. *Psychotherapy and the psychology of behavior*. New York: Wiley, 1966.

HAVIGHURST, R. J. *Human development and education. New York:* David McKay, 1953.

LILIENTHAL, J. W., & TRYON, C. Developmental tasks: II. Discussion of specific tasks and implications. In *Fostering mental health in our schools: 1950 Yearbook, ASCD*. Washington, D.C. Association for Supervision and Curriculum Development, 1950. Pp. 90–128.

MICHELS, T. J., GAZDA, G. M., & WIGGINS, S. Instrumentation (GSR) and its effects on counselor responses. *Counselor Education and Supervision* (in press).

SISSON, P. J. Process analysis of extended group counseling with psychiatry residents. Unpublished doctoral dissertation, University of Georgia, 1970.

STOLLER, F. H. Focused feedback with video tape: Extending the group's function. In G. M. Gazda (Ed.), *Innovations to group psychotherapy*. Springfield, Ill.: Charles C. Thomas, 1968. Pp. 207–255.

SUPER, D. E., CRITES, J., HUMMEL, R., MOSER, H., OVERSTREET, C. B., & WARNATH, C. *Vocational development: A framework for research*. New York: Bureau of Publications, Teachers College, Columbia University, 1957, Monograph No. 4.

SUPER, D. E., STARISHEVSKY, R., MATLIN, N., & JORDAAN, J. P. *Career development: Self-concept theory*. New York: College Entrance Examination Board, 1963.

TRYON, C., & LILIENTHAL, J. W. Developmental tasks: I. Concept and its importance. In *Fostering mental health in our schools: 1950 Yearbook, ASCD*. Washington, D.C.: Association for Supervision and Curriculum Development, 1950. Pp. 77–89.

Suggested Readings

ANDERSON, A. R., & JOHNSON, D. L. Using group procedures to improve human relations in the school social system. *School Counselor*, 1968, *15*, 334–342.

BRAMMER, L. M. Eclecticism revisited. *Personnel and Guidance Journal,* 1969, *48,* 192–197.

CARKHUFF, R. R. *Helping and human relations.* Vol. 1. *Selection and training.* New York: Holt, Rinehart & Winston, 1969. (a)

CARKHUFF, R. R. *Helping and human relations.* Vol. 2. *Practice and research.* New York: Holt, Rinehart & Winston, 1969. (b)

CARKHUFF, R. R., & BERENSON, B. G. *Beyond counseling and therapy.* New York: Holt, Rinehart & Winston, 1967.

DICKENSON, W. A., & TRUAX, C. B. Group counseling with college under-achievers. *Personnel and Guidance Journal,* 1966, *45,* 243–247.

DREGER, R. M. Aristotle, Linnaeus, and Lewin, or the place of classification in the evaluative-therapeutic process. *Journal of General Psychology,* 1968, *78,* 41–59.

ERIKSON, E. H. *Childhood and society.* (2nd ed.) New York: Norton, 1963.

GAZDA, G. M. (Ed.) *Basic approaches to group psychotherapy and group counseling.* Springfield, Ill.: Charles C. Thomas, 1968.

GAZDA, G. M. (Ed.) *Innovations to group psychotherapy.* Springfield, Ill.: Charles C. Thomas, 1968.

GAZDA, G. M. (Ed.) *Theories and methods of group counseling in the schools.* Springfield, Ill.: Charles C. Thomas, 1969.

GAZDA, G. M., & FOLDS, J. H. *Group guidance: A critical incidents approach.* Champaign, Ill.: Research Press (formerly Parkinson Div., Follett Educational Corp.), 1968.

GILLILAND, B. E. Small group counseling with Negro adolescents in a public high school. *Journal of Counseling Psychology,* 1968, *15,* 147–152.

GOLDSTEIN, A. P., HELLER, K., & SECHREST, L. B. *Psychotherapy and the psychology of behavior.* New York: Wiley, 1966.

GROUP PROCEDURES IN COUNSELING AND GUIDANCE: Special issue. *School Counselor,* May 1968, *15,* (5).

GROUPS IN GUIDANCE: Special issue. *Personnel and Guidance Journal,* April, 1971 (in press).

HAVIGHURST, R. J. *Human development and education.* New York: David McKay, 1953.

JOHNSON, J. J. The hippy as a developmental task. *Adolescence,* 1969, *4,* 36–42.

KAHN, M. D. The adolescent struggle with identity as a force in psychotherapy. *Adolescence,* 1968, *3,* 395–424.

KRAFT, I. A. Some special considerations in adolescent group psychotherapy. *International Journal of Group Psychotherapy,* 1961, *11,* 196–203.

KRUMBOLTZ, J. D., & THORESEN, C. E. The effect of behavioral counseling in group and individual settings on information-seeking behavior. *Journal of Counseling Psychology,* 1964, *11,* 324–333.

KRUMBOLTZ, J. D., & THORESEN, C. E. (Eds.) *Behavioral counseling: Cases and techniques.* New York: Holt, Rinehart & Winston, 1969.

LILIENTHAL, J. W., & TRYON, C. Developmental tasks: II. Discussion of specific tasks and implications. In *Fostering mental health in our schools: 1950 Yearbook, ASCD.* Washington, D.C.: Association for Supervision and Curriculum Development, 1950. Pp. 90–128.

MacLENNAN, B. W., & FELSENFELD, N. *Group counseling and psychotherapy with adolescents.* New York: Columbia University Press, 1968.

McGEE, T. F. Some basic considerations in crisis intervention. *Community Mental Health Journal,* 1968, *4,* 319–325.

MURO, J. J., & FREEMAN, S. L. *Readings in group counseling.* Scranton, Pa.: International Textbook Co., 1968.

PAUL, G. L., & SHANNON, D. T. Treatment of anxiety through systematic desensitization in therapy groups. *Journal of Abnormal Psychology,* 1966, *71,* 124–135.

SOMMER, R. Small group ecology. *Psychological Bulletin,* 1967, *66,* 145–152.

SPIELBERGER, C. D., WEITZ, H., & DENNY, P. J. Group counseling and the aca-

demic performance of anxious college freshmen. *Journal of Counseling Psychology,* 1962, *9,* 195–204.

SUPER, D. E., CRITES, J., HUMMEL, R., MOSER, H., OVERSTREET, C. B., & WARNATH, C. *Vocational development: A framework for research.* New York: Bureau of Publications, Teachers College, Columbia University, 1957. Monograph No. 4.

SUPER, D. E., STARISHEVSKY, R., MATLIN, N., & JORDAAN, J. P. *Career development: Self-concept theory.* New York: College Entrance Examination Board, 1963.

TRUAX, C. B., & CARKHUFF, R. R. *Toward effective counseling and psychotherapy.* Chicago: Aldine, 1967.

TRYON, C., & LILIENTHAL, J. W. Developmental tasks: I. Concept and its importance. In *Fostering mental health in our schools: 1950 Yearbook, ASCD.* Washington, D.C.: Association for Supervision and Curriculum Development, 1950. Pp. 77–89.

VRIEND, T. J. High-performing inner-city adolescents assist low-performing peers in counseling groups. *Personnel and Guidance Journal,* 1969, *47,* 897–904.

ZILLER, R. Toward a theory of open and closed groups. *Psychological Bulletin,* 1965, *64,* 164–182.

Group Guidance Programs

Grades 9–12: Belka, M. F. (Ed.) *Being and becoming: An action approach to group guidance.* Milwaukee, Wisc.:
The Bruce Co., 1966.
Grade   9: *Encounter,* Book I (1966)
Grade 10: *Identity,* Book II (1967)
Grade 11: *Involvement,* Book III (1968)
Grade 12: *Commitment,* Book IV (in press)

Grades 7–12: Gazda, G. M., & Folds, J. H. *Group guidance: A critical incidents approach.* Champaign, Ill.: Research Press, 1968.

National Forum Developmental Guidance Series

Publisher: American Guidance Services, Inc., Minneapolis, Minn.
Grade 7: *About growing up.*
Grade 8: *Being teen-agers.*
Grades 8–10: *Our school life.*
Grades 9–12: *Discovering myself.*
              Planning my future.
Grades 10–12: *Toward adult living.*

Grades 9–12: Shertzer, B., & Knowles, R. T. *Teachers guide to group vocational guidance.* Cambridge, Mass.: Bellman Publishing Co., 1964.

Grades 9–12: Wrenn, C. G., & Schwartzrock, S. P. *Planned group guidance.* Minneapolis: American Guidance Service, 1961.

6 | Training as a Preferred Mode of Group Treatment[1]

Several areas of parallel work converge upon the concept of training as a preferred mode of treatment. These areas include research growing out of the client-centered orientation and extensions to systematic training of counselors and therapists based upon the research findings. In addition, the behavior modification approaches often involve variations of systematic training in desensitization or assertive behavior. Finally, "sensitivity training," while it is not training at all, has established the need for training in human relationships.

In reverse order, sensitivity training, although it has served to call attention to the need for full and intense human relationships (Schein & Bennis, 1961), it has not been able to fill the need. Its apparent success has been due more to humanity's desperate and unfulfilled needs than to its demonstration of tangible evidence of effectiveness (Carkhuff, 1970a).

More important movements in terms of their substantive contributions are the behavior modification approaches which include variations of the themes of instrumental and classical conditioning (Krasner & Ullmann, 1965; Ullmann & Krasner, 1965; Wolpe, 1958). Depending upon the orientation, the same behavior may be modified by different approaches. Thus, for example,

[1]This chapter and Appendix C were prepared by Robert R. Carkhuff, Ph.D., Director, Center for Human Relations and Community Affairs, American International College, Springfield, Massachusetts. For the most complete understanding of this chapter, study Appendix C also.

anxiety-evoking stimuli such as the situation of talking before a group or asserting oneself with other people may be affected by different strategies: on the one hand, we might shape behavior by the successive reinforcement of small segments of desired behavior; on the other hand, we might counter-condition or de-sensitize an individual to the stimuli (Carkhuff, 1969b). The distinctive contributions of the behavior modification approaches have been their systematic methodologies and their resultant ability to demonstrate tangible evidence of behavior change and its sustenance, after relatively short periods of treatment, when compared to other more vague and amorphous therapeutic treatment approaches (Carkhuff & Berenson, 1967).

Perhaps the most important development contributing to the concept of training as a preferred mode of treatment has been the research growing initially out of the client-centered orientation and the eclectic extensions of this work. When Rogers was able to identify what were for him "the necessary and sufficient conditions of therapeutic personality change" and others were able to research these conditions with pathological as well as relatively non-pathological populations (Rogers, et al., 1967), important implications for training emerged. "If we are able," our reasoning went, "to identify the effective ingredients in therapeutic personality change, then we should be able to train people to be able to demonstrate these characteristics" (Carkhuff & Berenson, 1967; Truax & Carkhuff, 1967). Training programs beginning with a heavy experiential orientation relying implicitly on modeling—implicitly because Rogers denied it as a source of learning—gave way gradually to more systematic programs in which first the discrimination of the scales employed to assess therapeutic ingredients and then the communication of these ingredients were stressed (Carkhuff, 1969a, b).

In addition to the transformations from experiential counseling to systematic training, other changes that would make a traditional non-directivist roll over on a couch were instituted. Most significant of these changes were the conditional, action-oriented, and initiative dimensions that were added to the nurturant, facilitative, and responsive dimensions. In effect, the helping process and the helper were put back together with both responsive (traditionally mother) and initiative (traditionally father) responses in the repertoire. Moreover, the evidence was conclusive. *Systematic training in helping and human relations skills was far more effective than any and all other training and treatment control programs* (Carkhuff, 1969a, b).

It was only a short step from systematically training helpers to training helpees systematically. That is, it made more sense to train helpers directly, and they in turn to train helpees directly than to train helpers to provide experiential counseling for the helpees. In this context, the concept of training as a preferred mode of treatment was developed and applications were initiated.

Group Processes as a Preferred Mode of Treatment

At the same time as these developments in training emerged, group processes (Gazda, 1968) emerged as a potential preferred mode of treatment in their own right. In this regard several propositions have been forwarded.

Proposition I. The core of functioning or dysfunctioning (health or psychopathology) is interpersonal.

The assumption here is that interpersonal processes reflect intrapersonal dynamics or, conversely, that what is going on within the individual is manifested in what goes on between individuals. In any event people are institutionalized in one way or another for what goes on between rather than within individuals.

Proposition II. The core of the helping process (learning or relearning) is interpersonal.

Constructive interpersonal learning experiences constitute the corrective antidote for destructive interpersonal learning experiences. Again, the conditions of constructive interpersonal experiences are the inverse of those that led to the development of difficulties in living in the first place. In individual counseling the helper is the helpee's most significant source of new learning in this regard, for he alone offers the prospect of integrating the modeling, the experiential, and the didactic sources of learning.

Proposition III. Group processes are the preferred mode of working with difficulties in interpersonal functioning.

We can do anything in group treatment that we can do in individual treatment—and more. Since groups are inherently interpersonal, they offer the helpee the means not only to relate to the helper and himself with the helper's guidance but also to relate to other members of the group and to the group as a whole. Group processes offer the prospect for the greatest amount of learning for the greatest number of people at one time. (Carkhuff, 1969b, p. 130).

Again, it was another short step from group treatment to

group training. In short, we can do anything in group training that we can do in group treatment—and more. Group training in interpersonal skills strikes at the heart of most difficulties in living. Systematic group training in interpersonal skills affords a means of implementing the necessary learning in progressive gradations of experience which insure the success of the learning. In making explicit use of all sources of learning—the experiential, the didactic, and the modeling—systematic group training in interpersonal skills provides the most effective, economical, and efficient means of achieving the individual growth of the largest number of persons.

It is to be emphasized that the key throughout all group helping processes is the level of functioning of the leader. Those leaders who are functioning at the highest levels—physically in terms of their energy level, emotionally in terms of their interpersonal relationships, and intellectually in terms of their creativity —both within and without the group processes, will effect the greatest changes in the group members.

Standard Programs for Group Training

Before reviewing applications in group training it is important to view a standard training program in interpersonal skills for groups. It is to be emphasized that this is but one program in the emotional-interpersonal sphere. Variations from this basic program can be designed to meet specific program needs such as training professional counselors in the skills necessary to work with delinquents or training neuropsychiatric patients in the skills necessary to get out and stay out of the hospital. In addition, the emotional-interpersonal program should be accompanied by systematic training programs in the physical (development of exercise program to improve cardio-vascular functioning, etc.) and intellectual (development of intellectual journal entries into effective, working cosmology) realms (Carkhuff, 1970a).

The training model described in the following pages is not complete in every detail but all the guidelines essential to effective training are included. A more detailed outline can be found in the Instructor's Manual, Carkhuff (1971).

Preliminary Training

Preliminary training focuses exclusively on the discrimination and communication of empathy, the key helping ingredient. In the

context of a program conducted by two experienced trainers offering the helper-trainees high levels of these dimensions, the trainees participate in a systematic sequence of human relations training. The same scales which have been related to helpee gains in studies of helping are employed in training. Thus, employing five-point scales, the trainees first learn to discriminate levels of empathic understanding as, for example, in stage 2 of the Instructor's Manual:

Discrimination of helper empathy (3): Introduction
    a| Focus upon feeling only.
    b| *Interchangeable understanding (level 3)*
       1| Judgment of level 3 is made on basis of whether helper could have said what helpee said in terms of feeling and helpee could have said what helper said.
       2| Need helpee-helper or two-response sequence to make judgment.
    c| *Additive and subtractive understanding.*
       1| Judgment of 1 and 2 or 4 and 5 is made on basis of effects upon the helpee, i.e., does the helper's response enable the helpee to go on to a deeper level of self-exploration and/or self-understanding?
       2| Need helpee-helper-helpee or three-response sequence to make judgment.
       3| Judgment of levels 4 and 5 reflects additive nature of helper response, i.e., it enables helpee to go on.
       4| Judgment of levels 1 and 2 reflects subtractive nature of helper response, i.e., it holds helpee back.

The trainees practice listening to tapes and rating responses from 1 (worst) to 5 (best). The immediate goal of preliminary communication training, in turn, is to establish an interchangeable base of communication (level 3) in which the helper-trainee accurately expresses the feeling and personal meaning which the helpee has expressed. At first, the trainees respond to taped material and then they are organized for empathy communication training within the group as follows, as for example in stage 3:

Communication of interchangeable empathy: Group practice
    a| *Classwork:*
       1| Set up trainees in helpee-helper roles.

2| Helpee makes single expression.

3| Helpee attempts to deal with personally relevant material.

4| Helper listens for minimum of 30 seconds.

5| Helper makes single response to helpee expression.

6| Helper attempts to formulate interchangeable response in terms of feeling and meaning.

7| Helper begins response with "you feel . . ." indicating responsive mode.

Example: "You feel sad (happy, angry)."

8| Group rates helper on whether response is interchangeable (level 3) or not.

With the development of an interchangeable base of communication continuing as the goal, the communication process is gradually constructed in a step-by-step training sequence. Thus, as for example in stage 4, the previous practice is expanded:

Communication of interchangeable empathy: Advanced group practice:

1| Set up trainees in helpee-helper roles.

2| Helpee makes 2 expressions:

(a) initial expression, (b) responds to helper's response.

3| Helper makes 1 response.

4| Helper follows previous program.

5| Other trainees write down their responses to helpee and discuss.

6| Group rates helper response.

Finally, the communication process is gradually built up until it is allowed to flow in an interactional sequence as for example in stage 6:

Communication of empathy: On-going group practice:

A| *Classwork:*

1| Trainees in helpee-helper roles are allowed to practice extended communication.

a| Extended sequence of no less than 6 exchanges between helper and helpee.

b| Helper continues to focus upon an interchangeable level of empathy.

2| Helper's set is emphasized:

a| Helper relates to helpee's expressions of helpee's experience.

b| Helper does not attend to problem solution.

c| Helper responds to person—not problem.

3| Group rates helper on modal level of empathy, that is the level at which the helper is functioning most of the time.

4| Group rates helpee on modal level of self-exploration.

Advanced Training

Those trainees who have demonstrated the highest level of functioning on the basis of the results of preliminary training are selected for advanced training. Advanced training emphasizes the skills necessary (a) to be an effective teacher-helper and (b) to train others to be effective teacher-helpers. It includes training in the previously described dimensions and the development of effective courses of action. For example, after the trainees have been introduced to the remainder of the responsive dimensions (respect and concreteness) in a manner similar to that described for empathy in preliminary training, the trainees are then introduced to communications initated by the helper as for example in stage 10:

Communication of additive understanding: Group practice
A| *Classwork:*
1| Trainees function in helpee-helper roles.
2| Set up roles for making a minimum of 6 interchangeable responses before trying for additive response.
3| Make additive response, i.e., "What this all adds up to for me . . ." or "What I hear you saying is . . .", etc.
4| Rate helper on level of understanding in the following manner:
a| Rate the modal level of attempted interchangeable responses.
b| Rate the level of the additive response.
5| Rate the helpee on the level of self-exploration in the following manner:
a| Rate the modal level of helpee self-exploration as the helper attempted interchangeable responses.
b| Rate the level of helpee self-exploration in response to the helper's additive response.

6| Each member of the group formulates in writing his own additive response to the helpee.

   a| Following rating, each member offers his additive response to the helpee as if he were counseling the helpee.

      (1) The group member-helper formulates the response in such a manner that the helpee can respond to the helper's response.

      (2) The helpee assesses the effectiveness of the helper's response.

      (3) The remaining group members assess the effectiveness of the helper's response.

   b| The group member-helper's additive response will be dependent in part upon how well the original helper laid the interchangeable base of communication.

7| *Steps 1–6 of stage 10 will be repeated as necessary.*

   a| After demonstrating the ability to lay an interchangeable base of communication, stage 10 becomes the most significant aspect of helping.

      (1) The effectiveness of depth reflections or moderate interpretations are contingent upon practice of this stage.

      (2) The development of effective courses of action predicated upon the helpee's depth of self-understanding are contingent upon practice of this phase.

   b| Step 6 of stage 10 becomes particularly critical to the helpee's personal development.

      (1) As the helpee presents personally relevant material it becomes more critical that he receive the most effective responses.

      (2) The group members are a resource for effective responses and serve, in effect, as consulting helpers.

   c| As step 6 of stage 10 is repeated the flow of communication between group member-helper and helpee can be extended.

      (1) Effective helper responses can be allowed to develop into an extensive helping interaction.

      (2) In this manner the helpee makes maximum strides toward personal understanding in preparation for the development of his own personal courses of action.

    d| The trainer has the responsibility for himself or some group member-helper putting together all of the responses which have been helpful for the helpee.

Following this phase, individual pairing and practice in helpee-helper interactions is emphasized and the initiative dimensions of genuineness, confrontation, and immediacy are introduced in a manner similar to the responsive dimensions. In addition, the most advanced trainees are selected to function as trainers to supervise the helpee-helper interactions. Thus, concurrent with the development of the helping process, the trainees are initiated into the experience of trainers of others. Next, the concept of the development of courses of action is introduced and implemented as for example in stage 17:

Development of courses of action: Introduction and Practice
    1| Definition and description of problem area(s).
    2| Definition and description of direction and/or goal(s) dictated by the problem area(s).
    3| Analysis of the critical dimensions of these directions and/or goals.
    4| Consideration of the advantages and disadvantages of the alternative courses.
    5| Development of physical, emotional-interpersonal, and intellectual programs for achieving that course with the most advantages and fewest disadvantages in terms of ultimate success in goal achievement.
    6| Development of progressive gradations of the programs involved.
    7| *Classwork:* Continue to practice extended communication.
      a| Helper develops courses of action for helpee.
      b| Helpee develops courses of action for self.

Finally, emphasis is placed upon putting it all together in helping as, for example, in stage 18:

Putting it all together

1| *The stages of development in helping: Practice*

   a| *Individual work:*

     (1) The goals of helping for the helpee

       (a) First goal: Helpee self-exploration

       (b) Second goal: Helpee self-understanding

       (c) Third goal: Helpee action

     (2) Helper activities in achieving these goals:

       (a) First activity: Respond to the helpee with inter-changeable understanding

       (b) Second activity: Additive understanding and initiative dimensions

       (c) Third activity: Development of courses of action

     (3) Practice putting complete helping process together in helper-helpee pairs (1 complete session)

   b| *Classwork:* Helpers and helpees pair off

     (1) Helpees practice being selves at earlier crisis point in lives.

     (2) Helper and helpee develop course of action for helpee.

2| *The stages of development in helping: Advanced practice*

   a| Same as stage 18 with the exception of the reversal of helper-helpee roles.

3| *Training in human relations skills: An overview*

   a| An overview of the helping process

   b| An overview of training techniques

(See Appendix C for the protocol of a demonstration training session.)

Applications in Group Training

The history of training as a preferred mode of group treatment has its roots in group training of lay as well as professional helpers. Thus, in addition to training credentialed counselors and therapists, teachers, hospital attendants and nurses, dormitory counselors, and community volunteers have been successfully trained in groups by systematic methods (Carkhuff, 1969a).

    A natural extension of this work was to develop the concept

of functional professionals (Carkhuff, 1970a). Persons indigenous to the communities being serviced were systematically selected and systematically trained for paid positions involving the treatment, training, and teaching of other members of the community. Accordingly, two levels of benefits accrued to the functional professionals: (1) the personal benefits in terms of therapeutic change and more effective levels of functioning which occurred and (2) the vocational benefits in terms of having a rewarding and fulfilling job that was of service to the community. The results indicated the effectiveness of the functional professionals. It was concluded that all selected and trained functional professionals proved functional. It was hypothesized that some credentialed professionals are also functional.

Perhaps the first program employing training directly as a preferred mode of group treatment involved training parents of emotionally disturbed children and comparing the results to those of traditional parental counseling (Carkhuff & Bierman, 1970). While the original intention was to train parents in the interpersonal skills needed to live more effectively with each other as well as with their children, the greatest concentration of effort was upon the parents' interrelationships. Aside from the pre- and post-testing, their children were brought in only once for a practice session. The results reflected this emphasis. Significant changes occurred in the relationship between parents but not between the parents and their children. Follow-up studies, emphasizing direct training in parent-child relations, are currently underway. *It should be emphasized that the training was much more effective in effecting gains in interpersonal functioning (a level or more above the parental counseling groups) than the traditional groups conducted by high-level functioning as well as moderate and low-level functioning therapists.*

An even more direct form of training as a preferred mode of group treatment was conducted in training neuropsychiatric inpatients in the interpersonal and other skills necessary to be discharged from and remain out of the hospital. Pierce and Drasgow (1969) employed systematic human relations training with a group of chronic psychiatric patients who were not otherwise being seen in treatment. The patients were compared with patients in four different control groups who were receiving drugs, individual therapy, group therapy or all three forms of treatment. The results were again overwhelmingly in favor of training when compared to the different forms of treatment. The training group members demonstrated significant improvement and were found to be

functioning at significantly higher levels interpersonally following treatment (more than a level higher) than the members of the other groups. In addition, follow-up research indicated that the training group members got out and stayed out of the hospital with greater frequency than the control group members. With the replication of these results with other psychiatric populations (Vitalo, 1969), group training, it appears, has emerged as a potential if not the preferred mode of group treatment.

As a consequence, a pilot clinic built around interpersonal training was introduced (Carkhuff, 1970a). Families that were falling apart were put back together. New family constellations were developed. For example, families without fathers and with inadequate mothers were assigned regular meetings with trained "fathers" and "mothers." These trainers set up programs teaching the families to live more effectively with themselves and with each other. In some instances, the program became interracial, with white and black families integrated under a new black father-trainer and a new black mother-trainer. At other levels, training programs were set up specifically for homogenous groups: fathers with similar problems, mothers of families without fathers, and children of different sexes and at different developmental levels. In all, the program met with a high degree of success as a new approach to large scale action as well as individual helping.

Other examples of applications in group training abound. For example, many of the helping programs of the functional professionals involved training as a preferred mode of group treatment. Thus, systematically selected and trained functional professionals conducted new careers training programs transforming former welfare recipients into social welfare casework technicians (Carkhuff & Griffin, 1970b). In addition to the helping and human relations skills necessary for such employment, significant therapeutic change was accomplished and academic skills transmitted. This was all accomplished effectively.

In other programs, human relations specialists in the schools successfully trained parents and teachers as well as students in the skills necessary to communicate and live effectively with one another (Carkhuff, 1971; Carkhuff & Griffin, 1970b). Further, these human relations specialists led teams of counselors and teachers to teach systematically skills to ghetto children which were necessary to adjust to predominantly white schools. They demonstrated a high degree of success in this venture (Carkhuff, 1970b).

Still other examples of extensions of applications in group training are available. For example, in the area of relations between

races and between generations, training projects have been systematically conducted (Carkhuff & Banks, 1970). One such project involved black parents and white teachers. Viewing the racial relations problems in the broader context of human relations problems, each subgrouping was trained first to learn to communicate effectively with each other within the sub-groupings. Only then were they trained to communicate effectively with members of the other sub-grouping. Thus, black (white) adults worked first with black (white) adults and only upon successful completion of this stage did they move to work with other races and the younger generation. The most difficult and final stage, that of enabling the white teacher (black parent) to communicate effectively with the black child (white child) was accomplished with a high degree of success because success was built into the project by making movement to the next stage contingent upon satisfactory performance at the previous stage.

Indeed, the applications of training as a preferred mode of group treatment can be carried so far as to train the group to be able to devise their own training programs (Carkhuff, 1970a). Thus group members with common interests can be trained to define their problems and, accordingly, operationalize their goals in dimensions that are achievable. Following this, they can be trained to consider the advantages and disadvantages of the alternative courses of action available to achieve the goals. Finally, they can be trained to develop step-by-step programs involving progressive levels of reinforcing experiences which implement the courses of action and achieve the goals.

Summary and Conclusions

The potential benefits of systematic training as a preferred mode of group treatment can be analyzed in a systematic way. First, we may consider the unique contributions to helper as well as helpee of systematic approaches and, then, those of group processes. By unique contributions we mean simply those contributions to the helpee's change or gain over and above those accounted for by the helper's level of functioning on the critical responsive and initiative dimensions.

The unique contributions of systematic training approaches to the helpee may be summarized as follows (Carkhuff, 1969b): (1) systematic approaches provide the helpee with an understanding of the treatment process and his role in it; (2) systematic approaches provide the helpee with a concrete awareness of his

level of progress in the helping process; (3) systematic approaches provide the helpee with a useful knowledge of the history of the reinforcements that have created and sustained his symptoms; (4) systematic approaches provide the helpee with the knowledge that the helper is guided by helpee feedback insofar as it fits the helper's system; (5) systematic approaches provide the helpee with an opportunity to accelerate actively the treatment process; and (6) systematic approaches provide the helpee with the assurance that the treatment is "curing" what it sets out to cure.

In regard to the unique contributions to the helper, systematic training approaches accomplish the following: (1) they provide the helper with a system of well-defined procedures; (2) they provide the helper with a well-defined role; (3) they provide the helper with a high and extremely useful level of confidence in what he is doing and where he is going; (4) they provide the helper with a means to become meaningfully involved beyond the treatment hour; (5) they provide the helper with an opportunity to make translations from helping to life; (6) they encourage the helper to attend fully to nonverbal cues; and (7) they provide the helper with a specific behavioral base for understanding helpee behavior.

The limitations of systematic training approaches for both helpee and helper are primarily a function of the rigid employment of the programs. If the helper is not shaped by the feedback which he gets from the helpee concerning what is most effective for the helpee, and if he does not modify his treatment procedures accordingly, the program, as any, can be as harmful as it is helpful.

Concerning the unique contributions of group processes to the helpees the following advantages emerge (Carkhuff, 1969b): (1) each helpee has an opportunity to act out his characteristic behaviors; (2) each helpee has an opportunity to observe the characteristic behaviors of others; (3) each helpee has an opportunity to communicate directly with another person other than the helper; (4) each individual has an opportunity for dispensing with unsuccessful defenses and expressing himself freely in the context of a facilitative group atmosphere; (5) each helpee has an opportunity to share in the helper's clarification and interpretation of the behavior of another; (6) each helpee has an opportunity to try out new behaviors directly with others; (7) each helpee has an opportunity to have the experience of helping as well as being helped; (8) each helpee has an opportunity to be valued by more than one person; (9) each helpee has an opportunity to focus upon the generalities of experience within the group; and (10) each helpee has an opportunity to obtain a definition of social reality.

The advantages of group over individual processes for the

helper are also numerous: (1) the helper has an opportunity to observe directly the behaviors of the individual helpees; (2) the helper has a direct opportunity to facilitate communication between individual helpees; (3) the helper has an opportunity to create a facilitative group atmosphere within which each group member may come to serve as a helper; (4) the helper has an opportunity to focus directly upon the generalities in the group experience; (5) the helper has an opportunity to utilize his resources in such a way as to get a maximum return in human benefits for a minimum of investment of time and energy.

The limitations of group processes for helper and helpee are relatively few and revolve around the leader's rigid application of the group experience. These incidents can often be handled by different kinds of individual treatment that are offered concurrently with the group experience.

Together, systematic group training processes offer the most potent form of therapeutic treatment known to man. As an illustration, in the group context, systematic training provides a working structure within which the very deepest levels of therapy can take place. For example, stage 10 of training is perhaps the most critical phase of training for it accomplishes dual purposes: (1) it enables the trainees to develop their skills in the helper's role at the very highest levels; (2) it enables the trainees to understand themselves at the very highest levels as helpees in personally relevant areas of problem exploration. This modality of training provides the most potent form of treatment known to man because it provides the opportunity for the helpee to select from among the responses of multiple trained helpers and to interchange extensively with those helpers who are most effectively "tuned in" to the helpee's problem.

The number of unique benefits of systematic group training processes may be summarized as follows (Carkhuff, 1969b): (1) systematic group training is goal-directed and action-oriented; (2) systematic group training emphasizes group practice in the behavior which we wish to effect; (3) systematic group training leaves the group members with tangible and usable skills; (4) systematic group training promotes longer retention of learned skills; (5) systematic group training enables us to make systematic selection of group members; (6) systematic group training offers a built-in means for assessing the effectiveness of the program.

In summary, *treatment is what you do when you don't know what you're doing.* And you compound the ineffectiveness and inefficiency by treating the helpee individually.

Training is what you do when you know what you're doing. And you increase effectiveness and efficiency by treating helpees in groups. Training is truly a preferred mode of group treatment.

References

CARKHUFF, R. R. *Helping and human relations.* Vol. 1. *Selection and training.* New York: Holt, Rinehart & Winston, 1969. (a)

CARKHUFF, R. R. *Helping and human relations.* Vol. 2. *Practice and research.* New York: Holt, Rinehart & Winston, 1969. (b)

CARKHUFF, R. R. Principles of social action in training for new careers in human services. *Journal of Counseling Psychology,* in press, 1970. (a)

CARKHUFF, R. R. Development of effective courses of action for ghetto children. *Psychology in the Schools,* in press, 1970. (b)

CARKHUFF, R. R. *The development of human resources: Education, psychology, and social action.* New York: Holt, Rinehart & Winston, 1971.

CARKHUFF, R. R., & BERENSON, B. G. *Beyond counseling and therapy.* New York: Holt, Rinehart & Winston, 1967.

CARKHUFF, R. R., & BANKS, G. The effects of human relations training upon relations between races and generations. *Journal of Counseling Psychology,* in press, 1970.

CARKHUFF, R. R., & BIERMAN, R. The effects of human relations training upon parents of emotionally disturbed children. *Journal of Counseling Psychology,* in press, 1970.

CARKHUFF, R. R., & GRIFFIN, A. H. The selection and training of functional professionals for Concentrated Employment Programs. *Vocational Guidance Quarterly,* in press, 1970. (a)

CARKHUFF, R. R., & GRIFFIN, A. H. The selection and training of human relations specialists. *Journal of Counseling Psychology,* in press, 1970. (b)

GAZDA, G. M. *Innovations to group psychotherapy.* Springfield, Ill.: Charles C. Thomas, 1968.

KRASNER, L., & ULLMANN, L. *Research in behavior modification.* New York: Holt, Rinehart & Winston, 1965.

PIERCE, R., & DRASGOW, J. Teaching facilitative interpersonal functioning to neuropsychiatric inpatients. *Journal of Counseling Psychology,* 1969, *16,* 295–298.

ROGERS, C. R., GENDLIN, E., KIESLER, D., & TRUAX, C. B. *The therapeutic relationship and its impact.* Madison, Wisc: University of Wisconsin Press, 1967.

SCHEIN, E. H., & BENNIS, W. G. (Eds.) *Personal and organization change through group methods: The laboratory approach.* New York: Wiley, 1961.

TRUAX, C. B., & CARKHUFF, R. R. *Toward effective counseling and psychotherapy.* Chicago: Aldine, 1967.

ULLMANN, L., & KRASNER, L. *Case studies in behavior modification.* New York: Holt, Rinehart & Winston, 1965.

VITALO, R. The effects of training in interpersonal functioning upon psychiatric inpatients. In R. R. Carkhuff: *Helping and human relations.* Vol. 2. *Practice and research.* New York: Holt, Rinehart & Winston, 1969. P. 307.

WOLPE, J. *Psychotherapy by reciprocal inhibition.* Stanford, Calif.: Stanford University Press, 1958.

7 | Group Counseling Research

Introduction

My purpose in this chapter is to present the reader a first-hand account of the condition of research in group counseling, to point up the strengths and weaknesses, to suggest directions that must be taken to improve the quality of research and the resultant validity of the findings, and to illustrate how Developmental Group Counseling lends itself to research analysis. I purposely limited my study to *group counseling* research since that is the main concern of this text. I realize that there is a significant body of research that bears directly on group counseling, *viz.*, group guidance, group psychotherapy, and group dynamics. Others recently have made exhaustive surveys of these areas, especially group psychotherapy (Goldstein, et al., 1966) and group dynamics (McGrath & Altman, 1966).

In an earlier project (Gazda & Larsen, 1968) an exhaustive search of the group counseling research literature was attempted. All research articles that included group counseling or multiple counseling in their titles between 1938 and 1967 were abstracted according to nine criteria: (1) Purpose, (2) Type of Group, (3) Group Size, (4) Control (design), (5) Treatment and Process, (6) Instruments (for evaluation), (7) Test Statistics (employed), (8) Ex-

perimental Design, and (9) Criteria and Outcomes. There were 104 studies abstracted and analyzed in the above project. I have since updated this project for this chapter and included 41 additional studies from 1967 to 1970. Altogether 145 group counseling research studies have been abstracted and analyzed for this chapter. Although I attempted to make this survey exhaustive, I realize that I have overlooked many research articles in my survey either because they are in relatively obscure journals, or because I inadvertently overlooked some in the very visible journals. Nevertheless, I feel quite certain that my survey is *very representative of the group counseling research literature.*

In some respects group counseling research has escaped some of the problems highlighted in group psychotherapy literature (its predecessor). Goldstein, et al., (1966) made the following observation in their exhaustive survey of the group psychotherapy literature:

> *With only a few exceptions, the structure of contemporary group psychotherapy practice rests on a body of professional literature consisting overwhelmingly of anecdotal, case history, and related impressionistic reports .... Thus group psychotherapy literature as a whole has remained at the earliest and most primitive level of observation and inquiry (p. 319).*

In a rather exhaustive survey of the "small group field," McGrath and Altman (1966) pinpoint some of the problems in this broad field of group research that are applicable to group counseling research. In regard to general methodological problems facing this field they made the following observations:

> *There are several striking factors about research in the small group field, viewed in the collective, that have implications for methodology. One is the tremendous empirical vigor of the field, as indicated by the numbers of studies and the rate of their production. In the last three decades at least 2,500 small group studies have been conducted and reported, and the rate of production appears to be accelerating .... A second striking feature of small group research is that studies vary widely in rigor and methodological sophistication .... There is also variation in research settings ..., although most studies are done in the laboratory and relatively few are carried out in naturalistic settings (pp. 67–68).*
>
> *Another noticeable feature of small group research en masse is the tremendous diversity of terms, concepts, and operations which are used and the relative lack of replication.*

Replication studies are practically nonexistent in the field....
Clearly, we do not yet have a common, shared language in the
small group field; and the presence of a shared language is a
prerequisite for successful accumulation of knowledge (p. 68).

Perhaps the one area cited by McGrath and Altman that does not plague the group counseling research is the fact that most of it is done in natural settings and not in the laboratory, per se. The other problems cited by McGrath and Altman and Goldstein, et al., are relevant to group counseling research. What these surveys have shown for related fields of group work is applicable to group counseling research and, in fact, the nine criteria on which I have analyzed group counseling research are consistent with the areas of small group research which have also been identified by Goldstein, et al., and McGrath and Altman as well as by Anderson (1969) in his recent review of group counseling research. Each of these criteria is treated separately beginning with Nature of the Study.

Nature of the Study

This topic appeared to break down into four basic areas with some overlapping among the areas. Approximately 66 percent of the research studies were of the "outcome" variety with a few being "combinations" of outcome and process (2 percent). By outcome studies I mean research in which the effects of group counseling on certain specified behavioral and/or attitudinal variables was done and prepost or, at least, post-measures were taken. Eleven percent of the studies were process studies, i.e., studies of various types of interaction and dynamics within a counseling group.

The fourth area which serves to describe the nature of the studies might be called "comparison" studies. This group of studies included 21 percent of the research reported and various combinations such as individual versus group counseling, one type of group counseling versus another, group counseling plus some other treatment compared to still another treatment, and the like.

Type of Group

By far the majority of counseling groups are held in educational settings and with students of these educational institutions. Ap-

proximately equal numbers of studies are reported with combined undergraduate and graduate students as with combined high school and junior high school students.

These studies account for almost three fourths of all the studies surveyed. This finding is consistent with an earlier study (Gazda, Duncan, & Meadows, 1967) of the group and multiple counseling literature for the period January, 1960—spring, 1965.

A breakdown of college student groups showed that 28 percent of the total are undergraduates. The majority of this group consists of freshmen underachievers and a combination of other undergraduate groups in academic difficulty. Graduate student counseling groups represent 7 percent of the total with the majority of these being studies of group counseling with counselor candidates.

A look at the high school and junior high school groups revealed that the type of group studied most is freshmen underachievers. The other types of high school and junior high school groups can be best characterized as problem behavior and potential dropouts.

Group counseling research with kindergarten and elementary school-age children constitutes 8 percent of the total number of group counseling studies surveyed. These groups can best be characterized as behavioral problem-types and underachievers. The survey also revealed that half of the studies completed with kindergarten- and elementary-age school children have been done in the last three years, 1967–70, which suggests that with the increased interest and practice in elementary school guidance, there has been a concomitant increase in group counseling research with this age group.

A very significant observation gleaned from this survey of research in group counseling is the fact that most of the studies are concerned with remediation or rehabilitation, i.e., attempts to remedy a problem that has already developed. Very few studies have been designed with a view for *preventing* problems.

Of the remaining 20 percent of the studies, approximately 4 percent are group counseling with parents and teachers—mostly parent groups. These few studies are not truly prevention-oriented either, since the parent groups have been organized usually to assist in the rehabilitation process of their children. A developmental model for group counseling as described in this text can be used by group counselors to fill this void of group counseling for the cause of prevention.

A perusal of the approximately 15 percent of studies not yet

described shows that 2 to 3 percent are of mental patients and an equal percent are with inmates and mental retardates respectively. The remaining percentage is comprised of school dropouts, student nurses, and delinquent or pre-delinquent groups.

Group Size

Group size refers to the N's reported in each study, not the size of the counseling groups. The experimental samples ranged from a process study involving an N of three to an outcome study involving 266 experimental Ss—junior high school students one-half of whom were teacher-referred and the other half were self-referred for group counseling. The average experimental sample was 29. The largest total sample was 400, including both experimentals and controls.

With 29 as the average experimental group size it becomes apparent that the outcome studies of group counseling (process studies having even smaller N's) must be viewed with caution. Considering the fact that very few of the outcome studies were replicated, even more caution must be observed in interpreting the results. Nevertheless, a beginning has been made—usually by single investigators and frequently doctoral candidates who were doing a dissertation study—but if larger samples are to be obtained and with it greater credence in outcomes, substantial financial support must be forthcoming and/or investigators must begin to pool their efforts.

Controls

Of the studies surveyed, approximately 20 percent did not report the use of control groups or statistical controls. One might then question the inclusion of these "descriptive" studies in this summary of "research" of group and multiple counseling. They were included because they were read at professional meetings, accepted as dissertation studies and/or were published. Some descriptive studies, such as reported in Driver (1962) were not included in this report and many other descriptive studies were most likely rejected by journal editors suggesting a bias toward not reporting these studies. Although descriptive studies have their place in generating research hypotheses, the large number

being reported for group counseling suggests the relative infancy of research in group counseling.

Notwithstanding the above analysis, there is some reason for optimism because the majority (80 percent) of *outcome studies* which were analyzed did use controls. Approximately 45 percent reported a "random" assignment of controls, 20 percent "matched" controls, and the remainder of the studies using controls used statistical, or miscellaneous combinations of random and matched designs.

Approximately 80 percent of the outcome studies surveyed used some form of control group design. This fact would ordinarily generate some feeling of optimism regarding the quality of group counseling research; however, it is becoming increasingly apparent that our selection of control groups has been inadequate. For example, LeMay and Christensen (1968) followed up a control group and discovered that some control group members sought counseling help on their own and therefore were not legitimate controls.

Perhaps even more difficult to control is the condition reported by Carkhuff (1969a, b) that people who serve as controls seek help from lay helpers who may be functioning at higher levels of helping than the trained professionals from whom the experimental counselees are receiving treatment. This fact may account for the condition that Eysenck (1965), Levitt (1963), and Lewis (1965) found, i.e., that patients treated by psychotherapy do not, on the average, appear to improve more than their control counterparts.

When the kinds of data accumulated by Eysenck, Lewis, and Levitt are scrutinized, what also becomes apparent is that the experimental groups show a greater *variability* or *range* than do the control groups. This fact suggests that a counselee is more likely to be helped or more likely to be hurt when seeking help from a professional than when he seeks it from a lay person (Carkhuff, 1970). Thus, control designs which offer control groups must include follow-up of the control group members themselves to determine what kinds of help they seek, and also measures of counselor level of functioning to determine whether or not counselees can be *expected* to improve or deteriorate.

Treatment and/or Process

Since very few authors reported their theroretical orientations and the exact nature of the treatment process utilized in their research,

this summary is limited to a brief report of averages and ranges in terms of numbers and hours of group counseling sessions per group. Process variables are reported for the process studies.

The "treatment" can be described "on the average" as consisting of 16 group counseling sessions of one hour each week over approximately 16 weeks. However, the range was extensive: two sessions of behavioral-type group counseling to one year of group counseling of three-to-five sessions per week represent the range or "intensiveness" of the treatment. One study reported 60 sessions over a period of two years; two studies reported one class period per week over two school years, and another reported 50 sessions over a period of 9 months. These represent the most intensive types of treatment as well as the longest in duration of treatment.

The process studies consisted of role analysis, "client growth," topic, referent, and affect classification, counselor-client reinforcement, and phase development. The "client growth" studies utilized various topic or role analysis to appraise or speculate on client change.

The most frequent omissions from the studies reviewed were the lack of a clear statement of the counselor(s) theoretical orientation, a description of the treatment process and qualifications of the group counselor(s). Until these weaknesses are overcome, little by way of replication studies and comparisons among differing orientations can be accomplished. There has been a significant observable trend, however, within the last three years for the studies to contain more precise descriptions of the treatment process. This appears to be the result of the more frequent application of behavioral models to group counseling.

One is struck by the wide variation in duration and/or intensity of treatment. Perhaps group counseling will eventually become synonymous with short-term group treatment or merge with group therapy, and length of treatment will not be a differentiating factor of group counseling.

Instruments

"Instruments" refers to the means or measures for evaluating process or outcome variables. Since a wide range of evaluative instruments were utilized, only the most frequently employed measures will be reported here. Almost all studies reported the use of multiple instruments for measuring outcome and process.

The most popular means for evaluation was the grade-point-average (GPA). GPA was used in 25 percent of the studies analyzed. Twenty-five percent of the studies also reported the use of judges', teachers', and various supervisors' ratings of Ss. Thirteen percent of the studies utilized some variation of the self-report technique aside from self-report standardized personality tests. Questionnaires were used in 12 percent of the studies—usually the researcher's self-devised questionnaire. Interviews were used for evaluation purposes in 9 percent of the studies. Q sorts of various types were cited in 8 percent of the studies; 8 percent of the studies also cited the use of TAT-type instruments; 8 percent of the studies utilized the Bills Index of Adjustment and Values, and 8 percent used sociometric ratings. The California Psychological Inventory, sentence completion items, the Semantic Differential, and sociometric tests each were cited in 4 percent of the studies. Other instruments utilized in at least three studies were the Haggerty-Olson-Wickman Behavior Rating Scale, the Rotter Incomplete Sentence Blanks, the Taylor Manifest Anxiety Scale, the Brown-Holtzman Survey of Study Habits and the Allport-Vernon Study of Values.

The "shotgun" method, i.e., the use of several evaluation instruments for evaluating the research in group counseling appears to be the rule rather than the exception. In view of the infancy of this area of research this is to be expected as the experimenter attempts to glean the maximum from his hard-to-obtain data.

The Cohn (1967) report suggests that the use of multiple measures of group counseling should be encouraged because ". . . multiple measurement of a given concept increases the possibility of reliable measurement" (p. 17). The difference between what the Cohn report suggests and what is actually practiced is that his report suggests several means of evaluating or measuring a given concept, whereas in actual practice attempts are made to measure several different variables or concepts. It has been my goal in the abstracting of the group counseling research studies (Gazda, & Larsen, 1968) to provide the potential researcher with detailed abstracts so that he can analyze the effectiveness of the various instruments used and thus be in a better position to select the promising instruments to be utilized with specific populations for measuring specific variables.

The ways and means for measuring group counseling "process" variables included, for the most part, researcher-devised instruments to classify client-counselor roles, topics, affect, referents, content, nonverbal behavior, and the like. These process

scales usually employed some modification of the Bales Interaction Process Analysis instrument or the Hill Interaction Matrix and were based on the data obtained from on-the-spot group observations, typescripts, audio-tape recordings, and video-tape recordings. Only a beginning has been made in process research in group counseling.

Test Statistics

Approximately 35 different varieties of test statistics were employed by the authors of group counseling studies surveyed between 1938–1970. The most popular statistic was the *t*-test of mean differences. It was used in approximately 35 percent of the studies. Analysis of variance was close behind in popularity with approximately 25 percent usage and analysis of covariance was used in 10 percent of the studies. Descriptive statistics of many varieties was third in popularity being utilized in approximately 15 percent of the studies and closely behind it in popularity was the use of Chi square: 14 percent of the studies reported its use. Approximately 15 percent of the authors utilized some form of correlation in their research. The remaining test statistics were used no more than 3 percent of the time in the abstracted studies.

The Cohn (1967) report on research in group counseling recommends multivariate statistical methods as promising for group counseling research because of the many interacting process variables and complexity of goals in group counseling. Especially promising, according to the Cohn publication, is factor analysis. Although multivariate analysis was utilized in approximately 35 percent of the research studies surveyed, only two were described as factor analysis. Perhaps this represents the lag between what is recommended by the statistician and what the group counseling researcher is now doing, and this may be the reason the Cohn report recommends that the group counselor 'team-up' to form an interdisciplinary research team for investigating group counseling.

Experimental Design

Since this category requires some defining, definitions of various designs will be given, then the frequency of their use in the studies

which were surveyed will be cited. Brief reactions will be given at the conclusion of this topic in the summary.

In order to categorize the research design of the studies surveyed, the classificatory scheme developed by Campbell and Stanley (1963) was utilized. This scheme presents a summary of models of experimental and quasi-experimental designs most frequently used in educational research. Campbell and Stanley evaluated and described 16 designs and variations of these designs.

The purpose of following this outline of design models was an operational one. Attempts were made to determine which design most completely described a particular study—"outcome" studies were more readily classifiable by the scheme than were "process" studies. For this reason process studies were so identified and received no further classification.

The major research design models used were classified as Pre-Experimental Designs, True-Experimental Designs, Quasi-Experimental Designs, and Correlational and ExPost Facto Designs (Campbell & Stanley, 1963). The research models applicable to each of these major designs are included under each major design with the number of studies so classified.

The research design models are defined as follows:

Pre-Experimental Designs

One-Shot Case Study

This is a study in which a carefully studied single instance is compared with remembered or observed events. The inferences made are based on general expectations of what the behavior might have been had the treatment not occurred. The total absence of a control group and posttest observations are significant characteristics of this type study. (Three such studies were among those surveyed.)

One-Group Pretest-Posttest Design

This is a design in which both a pre- and a post-observation measure is used in the absence of a control group. (Eleven studies or about 8 percent were classified under this model.)

Static-Group Comparison

This design uses only post-treatment observations and the comparison is made between a group which has experienced the

treatment and one which has not. Randomization techniques are not employed in group selection. The purpose of the comparison is to establish the effect of the treatment. (Two studies were classified as Static Group Comparison.)

True-Experimental Designs

Pretest-Posttest Control Group Design

This design describes a model in which equivalent groups, as determined by randomization procedures, are used in the experiment. It incorporates many experimental and statistical variations into its model and offers control for all sources of internal validity and for some but not for all sources of external variation. (Eighty-seven studies or approximately 60 percent were classified under the Pretest-Posttest Control Group Design and its several variations.)

Solomon Four-Group Design

The high rank of this design in the hierarchy of research designs is attributable to its explicit consideration of factors influencing external validity. Since this design did not occur in the studies reviewed, the reader is referred to Campbell and Stanley (1963) for further description.

Posttest-Only Control Group Design

This is a design which employs group randomization and which controls for testing as the main effect but does not yield a measure of these effects. This design is internally valid, offers some external validity, and has numerous variations. It is preferable to the Pretest-Posttest Control Group Design when genuine randomness of assignment is assured. However, more powerful statistical tests are available for the Pretest-Posttest Control Group design and the availability of pretest scores in the Pretest-Posttest Control Group Design allows for the examination of interaction effects and for the more thorough generalization of the results. (Five studies were classified as Posttest-Only Control Group Design.)

Quasi-Experimental Designs

Equivalent Materials Design

This is a design in which groups which have received equivalent materials (treatments), purported to have enduring effects, are

compared with groups which have received different content (treatments). The sampling of materials is deemed essential to validity and any degree of proof of the treatment. (One study fit this classification or research model.)

Non-Equivalent Control Group Design

Both experimental and control groups have been administered a pretest and a posttest in this design. The groups of subjects used do not have pre-experimental sampling equivalence, but consist of naturally assembled groups which are available such as a classroom. In this design the treatment is randomly assigned and is under the control of the experimenter. Since many internal and external validity threats are controlled for in this design (Campbell & Stanley, 1963), it is meaningful for use when the employment of True Experimental Designs is impossible. Analysis of covariance particularly is considered to be applicable to this design. (Six studies were classified as fitting this design.)

Separate Sample Pretest-Posttest (No Control) Design

This design is applicable for use in situations where it is impossible to separate subgroups randomly for different experimental treatments. A type of experimental control is exercised by the random assignment of the *time* which subjects are to be observed. This design affords representative sampling of populations which have been specified prior to the experiments. (Three studies were classified as fitting this model.)

Other Designs

Descriptive-One Group Pretest-Posttest Study

This is a design or study which uses verbal description, rather than statistical procedures, to describe the differences observed between pretest and posttest scores for a single group of subjects. (Three of the studies surveyed were classified as fitting into this design.)

Descriptive-Simple Survey

This type of design or study describes the subject's responses and reactions after his exposure to the treatment. This type study cannot control for the direction of memory bias and the distortions which may have occurred. (Of the studies surveyed, eight could be classified as Descriptive-Simple Survey.)

Process Studies

The *Process Study* is a study which attempts to describe and/or explain what is happening in and during the treatment. This "on-going behavior" is the purpose of study. (Fifteen studies or 10 percent were classified as process studies.)

Summary—Experimental Designs

The summary of group counseling research regarding experimental designs is encouraging. Although the design itself does not guarantee quality research, it is an important first step toward achieving that goal. Approximately 70 percent of the outcome studies were classified as "True Experimental Designs," which, among other things, means that at least some form of control group was employed. An additional 10 percent also used some type of control group.

Criteria and Outcomes

Studies of Outcome

When the *outcome* research studies surveyed are examined, the conclusion is that some positive change or growth was reported in slightly more than half of the studies—that is not to say, however, that half of the variables tested showed positive change. The majority of positive changes were reported through descriptive means. They did not provide strong behavioral change indices and hence are not very convincing to the sophisticated researcher. Nevertheless, some objective outcome data show promise for group counseling. For example, about 50 percent of the studies utilizing GPA and/or academic achievement showed significant increases or improvement versus an equal number which showed no significant improvement. Self-concept improvement and related "self" variable changes were reported in approximately 20 percent of the studies. Other significant improvement was reported as decreased anxiety, improved family and peer relations, improved relationships with authority figures, improvement in work attitudes, improved behavior in school, improved school attendance, increased acceptance of others, increase in educational- and occupational-seeking behavior, improved sociometric choices, and improvement in reading.

In the "comparison" studies where individual counseling was

compared with the effectiveness of group counseling, the outcomes were about even where one was considered superior to the other. (Since 1967, fewer of these comparison studies have been done. This condition suggests greater acceptance of group counseling.) The review of the research indicated that the treatment most likely to produce growth is the conjoint application of group counseling and individual counseling.

Studies of Process

The process research in group counseling is in a stage of infancy. Only 15 studies were found in the literature between 1938 and 1970. Considerably more process research has been done with group psychotherapy, and therefore we must turn to that body of literature as well as the group dynamics literature for direction with this form of group research. When we look at the group counseling process literature, per se, we find only a few pilot studies. The only concerted effort made to investigate group counseling process was done at the University of Illinois. Eight of the 15 process studies originated at the University of Illinois under the direction of Merle Ohlsen. Few of the pilot studies done at the University of Illinois, however, produced statistically significant results in the predicted direction.

On the positive side in the Illinois studies, Katz, Ohlsen, and Proff (1959) found that a counseled group of adolescent underachievers was unproductive because of a symbiotic relationship detected between two leader-members. They also learned that the counselor was most effective in dealing with the symbiotic pair when he used *approach behavior, a la* Horney. In a related study, Cohn, Ohlsen, and Proff (1960) were able to identify and describe roles assumed by an unproductive group of adolescent underachievers, to reflect group progress via the roles assumed, and to use roles to compose a productive and nonproductive counseling group. Based on the same group of underachieving adolescents, Noble, Ohlsen, and Proff (1961) were able to devise an instrument with adequate reliability to categorize client and counselor verbal and nonverbal responses in a group setting.

On the negative side of the ledger of the Illinois studies, Wigell (1960) was unable to establish significant relationships between referent, affect, and topic and group change from the beginning to the end of counseling with underachieving adolescents. Carlson (1962), with the same group of underachievers, also was unable to show a statistically significant relationship between degree of success in group counseling and levels of

personality and between degree of success in group counseling and reduction in discrepancy of levels of personality between pre- and post-counseling.

Ohlsen and Johnson (1962) were unable to show a change in TAT protocols pre- and post-counseling for group counseled adolescent underachievers and group counseled prospective counselors. Ohlsen and Oelke (1962), using the same groups as Ohlsen and Johnson, were equally unsuccessful in showing a significant relationship between counselee growth and topic and affect expressed by the counselees. In a related study using audio and video taped sessions of the underachieving adolescents, Antenen (1964) was also unsuccessful in showing relationship between type of affect expressed and topics discussed.

McDaniel and Johnson (1962) used a counseled group of seventh graders to test the difference in philosophy between capable achievers and capable underachievers counseled in groups. In essence capable achievers and underachievers, when compared to control groups, reported less friction at home and expressed fewer problems with siblings, greater ease in studying, and a feeling of improvement in grades and citizenship marks. From typescript and tape analysis of group sessions, capable achievers described their parents as using corporal punishment and felt it was deserved versus parents of capable underachievers who did not use corporal punishment but rather revocation of privileges—and this was resented. Other differences showed that capable achievers worried about their nonconformist behavior reflecting on their families while underachieving capable achievers worried about it reflecting on themselves. Capable achievers did not blame the teachers for their difficulties whereas underachieving capable achievers did blame the teachers.

Analysis of audio taped group counseling sessions with adolescents by Bates (1966) produced seven recurring themes: My Vices; Outwitting the Adults; Problem Parents; My Brother, the Rat; My Public Image; Nobody Loves Me; and Let's Change the Rules. Other less frequently occurring themes were also isolated.

Foley and Bonney (1966) studied the group phases or stages followed by a counseled group of counselor trainees. The trainees did not follow the stages of group development hypothesized by Bonney; however, they did describe themselves positively in the beginning, negatively in the middle phase, and positively again near termination which was consistent with findings of others.

Thoresen and Krumboltz (1967) investigated the relationship between counselor reinforcement and model-reinforcement of information-seeking behavior outside the interview. They found

that there was a positive relationship between counselor-reinforcement and model-reinforcement behavior with vocational information-seeking behavior of counselees; that model-reinforcement Ss engaged in a significantly greater number of external information-seeking behaviors than did counselor-reinforcement Ss; and that there was no significant difference in counselees' ratings of helpfulness of individual or group counseling.

In a study similar to the Thoresen and Krumboltz study in its emphasis on behavioral conditioning, Kramer (1968) was able to condition members of a counseling group, composed of freshmen college students, to give more responses showing "responsibility," more "positive" responses, and more "questioning" responses than equivalent control groups counseled nondirectively. The counselors accomplished this result by responding with active verbal approval whenever a counselee made a response resembling any of the three chosen for reinforcement.

Ahearn (1968) and Sisson (1970) used the Hill Interaction Matrix, Form G, to study the dominant modes of interaction in a nine-month counseling group of counselor trainees and psychiatry residents, respectively. The same counselor counseled both groups and the patterns on the Hill Matrix were similar for both groups. Essentially, the groups started at rather high levels of therapeutic functioning and proceeded to still higher levels throughout the four quarters of counseling.

In general, the psychiatry resident group reached higher therapeutic levels of functioning than did the counselor trainees for the third and fourth quarters of counseling. All quarters in the Sisson study showed statistically significant differences for change across time moving from a lesser therapeutic functioning in the first two quarters to a greater therapeutic group functioning in the latter quarters, i.e., a heavy concentration of personal-speculative, relationship-speculative, personal-confrontive, and relationship-confrontive modes of interaction in the third and fourth quarters. These findings lend credence to the validity of the Hill Interaction Matrix, Form G, as an instrument for describing kinds or levels of therapeutic interaction across time or in the progress of a counseling group.

Conclusions

The basic conclusion is that group counseling research is still inconclusive. This is true for a number of reasons. There is much

variation in and inadequate control of the dependent variables or research criteria, group size, length and duration or intensity of treatment, type and quality of treatment, sophistication of research designs, instruments of evaluation, and test statistics. The outcome research, however, looks promising because of the number of studies (approximately half) that show *some* positive changes or growth in the Ss. Since a number of the studies reviewed were doctoral dissertations and one would expect rather careful control over these, it is not surprising that approximately 60 percent of the outcome studies utilized the Pretest-Posttest Control Group Design. This fact should not conceal the other evidence that the most favorable reported results came from simple, uncontrolled, therefore questionnable, descriptive "research" reports coupled with the likely possibility that studies showing nonsignificant results were not accepted for publication. Several areas require immediate attention. Some of these are cited below.

One of the more serious problems in need of resolution of outcome research in group counseling is that of defining explicitly experimental variables that are common to each group participant. Frequently when data are grouped, gains made by certain Ss are canceled out by other Ss who, to show positive change, may need to and perhaps actually do change in the opposite direction of another group member on a given variable.

Because outcome variables suitable for change through group counseling are frequently difficult to specify in advance, more replication studies need to be performed to make possible the isolation of these variables. The more heterogeneous the group, the more difficult the problem becomes—and yet for therapeutic reasons heterogeneous groups are frequently preferred.

The use of multiple criterion measures which are factor analyzed may be one means of detecting slight but significant changes in behavior and attitude. The APGA publication edited by Cohn (1967), which is the report of a research seminar on group counseling, outlines similar research needs and recommends the use of multivariate and factorial analysis-of-variance designs, discriminant functions, and a model referred to as the Markov Chain. These test statistics would be capable of application to designs controlling for internal and external validity simultaneously.

From another point of view, Carl Rogers (Hall, 1967) suggests that perhaps we should call a moratorium on "rigid scientific research" in the behavioral sciences and go back and do much more naturalistic observation to understand people, behavior, and dynamics. The Cohn report also recommends the use of "clin-

ical judgments" in the evaluation of outcome research; however, it recommends the use of several clinical judgments of the *same and differing* theoretical orientations to control for observation bias.

Before change variables can be defined and controlled, researchers must become more precise in describing a number of group variables such as age, sex, symptoms of clients, home environment, motivation for counseling, size of group, nature and goals of treatment, orientation and training of the group counselor, frequency and length of group sessions as well as duration of treatment, and a description of the dynamics and climate of the group. For further treatment of the problem of small group research, the reader is referred to the Cohn (1967) report, previously described, to Goldstein, et al., (1966), who have drawn upon the group dynamics and social psychological research to generate research hypotheses pertaining to group psychotherapy namely but also pertinent to group counseling research, and to McGrath and Altman (1966), who have studied and analyzed the entire field of small group research.

The developmental model which I have outlined in this text presents many opportunities for research in group counseling. Most of the questions that are unanswered regarding group counseling can be studied within the confines of the developmental model. The research literature, however, conveys very little guidance to the practitioner who must decide his position from among a number of competing theoretical positions.

I have taken the position that we must be guided in our practice by the developmental level of the counselee to be counseled. Therefore, we can test the validity of this proposition by using, for example, a highly verbal or interview-type approach versus a play and action-oriented approach for counseling the child from ages 5 to 9; we can use an interview and/or a strictly behavioral model versus an activity- or game-oriented model with the preadolescent; and with the adolescent and adult groups we can compare a variety of approaches with the one outlined in Chapter five, viz., an eclectic interview model using relationship (facilitation) and action dimensions *a la* Carkhuff.

In each of the specific age groups described within my developmental model I have stressed the relationship of a number of variables to the potential success of a counseling group. These variables include group selection and composition, group size, setting, media employed, leadership approaches utilized, frequency and length of group sessions, and duration of group treat-

ment. In addition to these variables, I have specified general ground rules for group orientation and functioning and I have outlined phases of group development in Chapter two. Any of these variables singly or in combination are grist for the reseɛrch mill of group counseling. Since these variables, however, woɪld often be difficult to isolate and study independently, the appliɔation of a multivariate research design seems much more appropriate for evaluating the effects of these variables on different types of counseling groups. Goldstein, et al. (1966) reached the same conclusion in their review of *group psychotherapy* research. They stated " . . . that research designs that focus on the siːnultaneous influence of two or more variables as they interact appɛ ar to correspond more realistically to the facts of group therapeutic life than do more simple, univariate designs" (p. 431).

In conclusion, I submit that a developmental approach to group counseling is based on as solid theoretical and research data as are currently available. Furthermore, it lends itself to further extensive research inquiries.

Summary

One hundred and forty-five group counseling research studies from 1938-1970 were analyzed to determine the status of group counseling research. Each of the research studies was abstracted on the basis of the following nine criteria: (1) Purpose, (2) Type of Group, (3) Group Size, (4) Control, (5) Treatment and Process, (6) Instruments, (7) Test Statistics, (8) Design, and (9) Criteria and Outcomes. Summaries for each of the nine criteria are presented in this chapter showing both the strength and weaknesses in the group counseling research literature.

The chief strengths revealed in the research studies to date are the large percentage (80 percent) of outcome studies using some control group design, and the fact that about half of the studies analyzed showed some significant positive change in the counselees. The more recent studies (within the last three years) also reflect a greater effort to define the nature of the treatment process employed and the specific behavioral indices to be modified by each treatment.

Many weaknesses in the group counseling research are evident. Some of the more serious ones include the need to define explicitly the experimental variables that are common to each group participant and the effects on outcome of the interacting

variables operating in a group setting such as age, sex, symptoms of counselees, motivation for counseling, size of group, type of leadership, frequency, length and durations of group treatment, setting, orientation and training of the group counselor, nature of the treatment, climate of the group, and group composition. Before we can tell what type of group counseling is best under which conditions for which types of counselees we will have to discover the interaction effects of the above group variables. The effects of many interacting variables will require the use of multivariate analysis which, to date, has been used very infrequently.

Perhaps the greatest weakness revealed in the group counseling research is not so much the research designs themselves as it is the nature of the group treated—the emphasis. Almost all the group counseling attempts were directed toward *rehabilitation* and very few of the studies were concerned with problem *prevention* through the early and systematic identification of potential problem behavior and the subsequent intervention or employment of group counseling. Since 16 sessions or approximately 16 hours is the average treatment time, the number of sessions and duration of treatment must be significantly increased.

Another serious weakness revealed is the fact that many of the studies reporting positive change through group counseling intervention were anecdotal or descriptive reports in which no control groups were used. If these results were discounted, fewer than half of the studies of group counseling would show positive change.

Since so few researchers carefully describe their theoretical orientation and treatment methodology, the group counseling research, like other small group research, suffers from a serious lack of replication studies and subsequent questionable cross validation. More replication studies, therefore, are needed.

The average sample size in group counseling research is 29. Therefore, larger studies, perhaps collaborative studies, must be initiated.

Control groups have not been adequately followed up in most counseling and psychotherapy research, including group counseling; therefore greater care in following control members must be exercised. In addition, the person in the role of helper (group counselor) must be rated regarding his ability to help if we are to make predictions of change through group counseling.

Still another limitation in group counseling research is the near absence of process studies. Of the fifteen process studies reviewed, few provided guidelines which group counselors could apply to their practice.

The chapter is concluded with a challenge to use a Developmental Approach to Group Counseling as described in this text as a model for researching the various effects of such variables as size, setting, type of leadership, group composition, etc., on counselee change. Finally, the Developmental model is presented as most applicable to problem prevention through group counseling.

References

AHEARN, T. R. An interaction process analysis of extended group counseling with prospective counselors. Unpublished doctoral dissertation, University of Georgia, 1968.

ANDERSON, A. R. Group counseling. In C. E. Thoresen (Ed.), *Review of Educational Research: Guidance and Counseling,* 1969, *39,* (2), 209–226.

ANTENEN, W. W. Change in topic and affect during group counseling: Its relationship to outcome of group counseling. Dissertation Abstracts, 1964, *24,* (12), 5185.

BATES, M. Themes in group counseling with adolescents. *Personnel and Guidance Journal,* 1966, *44,* 568–575.

CAMPBELL, D. T., & STANLEY, J. C. Experimental and quasi-experimental designs for research. In N. L. Gage (Ed.), *Handbook of research on teaching.* Chicago: Rand McNally, 1963. Pp. 171–246.

CARKHUFF, R. R. *Helping and human relations.* Vol. 1. *Selection and training.* New York: Holt, Rinehart & Winston, 1969. (a)

CARKHUFF, R. R. *Helping and human relations.* Vol. 2. *Practice and research.* New York: Holt, Rinehart & Winston, 1969. (b)

CARKHUFF, R. R. Systematic Human Relations Training. In G. M. Gazda & T. L. Porter (Eds.), *Proceedings of a symposium on training groups,* Athens, Ga.: College of Education, University of Georgia, 1970. Pp. 77–110.

CARLSON, W. A. The relationship between success in group counseling and discrepancy in levels of personality. *Dissertation Abstracts,* 1962, *22,* 3516–3517.

COHN, B., OHLSEN, M. M., & PROFF, F. C. Roles played by adolescents in an unproductive counseling group. *Personnel and Guidance Journal,* 1960, *38,* 724–731.

COHN, B. (Ed.) *Guidelines for future research on group counseling in the public school setting.* Washington, D.C.: American Personnel and Guidance Assoc., 1967.

DRIVER, H. I. *Counseling and learning through small-group discussion.* Madison, Wisc.: Monona Publications, 1962.

EYSENCK, H. J. The effects of psychotherapy. *International Journal of Psychiatry,* 1965, *1,* 99–178.

FOLEY, W. J., & BONNEY, W. C. A developmental model for counseling groups. *Personnel and Guidance Journal,* 1966, *33,* 576–580.

GAZDA, G. M., DUNCAN, J. A., & MEADOWS, M. E. Group counseling and group procedures—Report of a survey. *Counselor Education and Supervision,* 1967, *6,* 305–310.

GAZDA, G. M., & LARSEN, M. J. A comprehensive appraisal of group and multiple counseling research. *Journal of Research and Development in Education,* 1968, *1,* (2), 57–132.

GOLDSTEIN, A. P., HELLER, K., & SECHREST, L. B. *Psychotherapy and the psychology of behavior change.* New York: Wiley, 1966.

HALL, M. H. A conversation with the father of Rogerian therapy. *Psychology Today,* 1967, *1,* (7), 19ff.

KATZ, E., OHLSEN, M. M., & PROFF, F. C. An analysis of interpersonal behavior of adolescents in group counseling. *Journal of College Student Personnel,* 1959, *1,* 2–10.

KRAMER, H. C. Effects of conditioning several responses in a group setting. *Journal of Counseling Psychology,* 1968, *15,* 63–67.

LeMAY, M. L., & CHRISTENSEN, O. C. Uncontrollable nature of control groups. *Journal of Counseling Psychology,* 1968, *15,* 63–67.

LEVITT, E. E. Psychotherapy with children: A further evaluation. *Behavior Research and Therapy,* 1963, *1,* 45–51.

LEWIS, W. W. Continuity and intervention in emotional disturbance: A review. *Exceptional Children,* 1965, *31,* 465–475.

McDANIEL, H., & JOHNSON, B. A. Effects of group counseling on achievers and underachievers. *Journal of Secondary Education,* 1962, *37,* 136–139.

McGRATH, J. E., & ALTMAN, I. *Small group research.* New York: Holt, Rinehart & Winston, 1966.

NOBLE, F., OHLSEN, M. M., & PROFF, F. C. A method for quantification of psychotherapeutic interaction in counseling groups. *Journal of Counseling Psychology,* 1961 *8,* 54–61.

OHLSEN, M. M., & JOHNSON, H. Group counseling evaluated by blind analysis and projective technique. *Journal of Counseling Psychology,* 1962, *9,* 359.

OHLSEN, M. M., & OELKE, M. C. An evaluation of discussion topics in group counseling. *Journal of Clinical Psychology,* 1962, *18,* 317–322.

SISSON, P. J. An interaction process analysis of extended group counseling with psychiatry residents. Unpublished doctoral dissertation, University of Georgia, 1970.

THORESEN, C. E., & KRUMBOLTZ, J. D. Relationship of counselor reinforcement of selected responses to external behavior. *Journal of Counseling Psychology,* 1967, *14,* 140–144.

WIGELL, W. W. A content analysis of tape recordings of group counseling sessions with gifted underachieving ninth grade students. *Dissertation Abstracts,* 1960, *20,* 1466.

Suggested Readings

ANDERSON, A. R. Group counseling. In C. E. Thoresen (Ed.), *Review of Educational Research: Guidance and Counseling,* 1969, *39,* (2), 209–226.

CAMPBELL, D. T., & STANLEY, J. C. Experimental and quasi-experimental designs for research. In N. L. Gage (Ed.), *Handbook of research on teaching.* Chicago: Rand McNally, 1963. Pp. 171–246.

COHN, B. (Ed.) *Guidlines for future research on group counseling in the public school setting.* Washington, D.C.: American Personnel and Guidance Assoc., 1967.

DRIVER, H. I. *Counseling and learning through small-group discussion.* Madison, Wisc.: Monona Publications, 1962.

GAZDA, G. M., DUNCAN, J. A., & MEADOWS, M. E. Group counseling and group procedures—Report of a survey. *Counselor Education and Supervision,* 1967, *6,* 305–310.

GAZDA, G. M., & LARSEN, M. J. A comprehensive appraisal of group and multiple counseling research. *Journal of Research and Development in Education,* 1968, *1,* (2), 57–132.

GOLDSTEIN, A. P., HELLER, K., & SECHREST, L. B. *Psychotherapy and the psychology of behavior change.* New York: Wiley, 1966.

McGRATH, J. E., & ALTMAN, I. *small group research.* New York: Holt, Rinehart & Winston, 1966.

8 | Ethics and Professional Issues

Introduction

The explosion of interest in the field of group work during the decade of the 1960's, especially the latter half of that decade, has thrust upon numerous professional groups the problem of answering critics of the movement as well as contending with problems of ethical practices/behavior arising from the application of many new and relatively unresearched practices. As would be expected, when practice outruns research, questions of ethics arise.

Within the last two or three years of the 1960's, the popular press, which had heretofore promoted the group movement as a panacea for solving personal and social ills of our society, began to reverse the "rosey" picture it had been painting and numerous critical articles or "bad press" about the movement appeared. As this chapter is being written, the group movement is being attacked from all sides. If the respectable and helpful elements are to survive, the professional groups which are involved in its many uses must deal with the criticism.

Over ten years ago J. L. and Z. T. Moreno (1960) recognized the split emerging in the *group psychotherapy movement* between the medical and non-medical practitioners. They recommended then a set of professional standards which would be sufficiently broad in scope to include both medical and non-medical content

and expertise. Two years later J. L. Moreno (1962) wrote that "Two great problems are waiting for a solution: (1) the definition of professional standards of performance and skill and (2) a code of professional ethics" (p. 263–264). It seems that the problem facing group psychotherapy in the early 1960's is still with us in the early 1970's but it has been significantly increased with the addition of new group practices.

As a result of external and internal pressures on a variety of professional associations whose membership employ various group practices, these associations appointed various commissions, *ad hoc* committees, task forces, and the like to investigate the problems being reported. The American Psychiatric Association, the American Psychological Association, the American Personnel and Guidance Association, and the National Training Laboratory Institute are among the groups which have responded by appointing commissions and committees. Except for the standards published by NTL (*Standards for the Use of Laboratory Method,* 1969), and *Task Force Report 1: Encounter Groups and Psychiatry,* 1970, by the American Psychiatric Association, the recommendations or products of these committees and commissions are not yet available to their membership.

As a concerned educator and practitioner in the field of group work, I initiated in the fall of 1969 a survey of 1000 members of the American Personnel and Guidance Association who were active in the APGA Interest Group on Group Procedures. Subsequently, I was appointed chairman of an *ad hoc* committee of APGA by its President. This committee has been charged with investigating the ethical implications of group procedures which are relevant to the Association. The Committee has made an initial report and recommendations to the Association during the Association's Convention held in New Orleans, Louisiana in March, 1970.

Since very little objective information or data are available on the subject of unethical practices/behavior in the group work area, I have reported in the following pages those findings of my questionnaire survey that are especially relevant to the purpose of this text. The findings are summarized in a series of six tables and my interpretations of the data are given also.

Results of Questionnaire Survey of Ethical Practices/Behavior in Group Work

The *basic* purpose of the questionnaire was to attempt to establish the extent of unethical practice/behavior in the broad field of

group work. Each respondent was asked to report any violation of ethical practice/behavior that he had witnessed and/or had heard about from reliable sources. However, there were several additional purposes for the questionnaire.

First, there was an attempt to obtain information about the respondents so that they could be described in terms of their age, sex, degrees held, state and country of residence, work setting, group training, and professional affiliation(s). Secondly, the respondents were asked whether or not one should try to differentiate among group procedures, viz., group guidance, group counseling, group psychotherapy, T groups, sensitivity groups, and encounter groups. Thirdly, they were asked to specify the training/ education required for the leader of each of these six group procedures. They were also asked to describe the purpose of each of these six group procedures and the person served most appropriately by these groups.

Several other miscellaneous questions were asked of each respondent: (1) Who is responsible for punishing those whose practice and/or behavior in group procedures is unethical?, (2) Is new legislation needed to govern practitioners of group work? (If "yes," what type?), (3) Would you affiliate with a new division of the American Personnel and Guidance Association or the American Psychological Association if one were developed for professionals active in various types of group work?, and (4) What is your view of rectifying problems facing those practicing in the group procedures area?

In the following pages, I shall summarize the results of the questionnaire survey previously described, and I shall draw certain conclusions from the data. The data that I shall draw upon have been obtained from 164 usable questionnaire returns. The questionnaire was rather complex and for that reason, only the most highly motivated individuals completed and returned it. Table 8.1 supports this contention, in part at least, as indicated by the large percentage of doctoral level respondents. Golan (1969), however, has reported that the rate of return for surveys requesting actual incidents of ethical problems is only 15 percent. Since the questionnaire which was sent to the 1000 individuals in my survey did solicit information regarding specific cases of unethical practice/ behavior, my return rate is consistent with Golan's findings.

The typical respondent, based on data in Table 8.1, was a 42-year-old male with a doctorate degree who worked in a university setting. He was most likely a member of APGA and/or APA

TABLE 8.1

Description of Respondents

Age		Degree[a]	
Range	*Median*		
26–68	42	Ph.D. or Ed.D.	109
		M.Ed.	29
		M.A.	12
Sex		Sixth Year Certificate	7
		M.S.	6
Male: 125		Other	9
Female: 39			

Number of states represented   38
Number of countries represented: 2 (U.S.A. & Canada)

Work Setting		Training/Educational Institutions	
University	74	58 different institutions represented	
School	33	where respondents received degrees	
State institution	21		
Federal institution	7	*Supervised Experience*	
Public clinic	3	One course	53
Private clinic	2	Two or more courses	20
Other	24	None	91

Professional Affiliation[b]		Training Workshops	
American Personnel & Guidance Association	129	One session	61
American Psychological Association	60	Two sessions	33
American Group Psychotherapy Association	3	Three sessions	13
American Psychiatric Association	1	None	57
American Society of Group Psychotherapy and Psychodrama	1		
Others (Primarily Educational Associations)	47		

[a]Total does not equal 164 because some respondents held two degrees of equivalent levels.
[b]Total does not equal 164 because some individuals reported membership in more than one professional organization.

and was not extensively trained in group work. (In this age of group work, few people are extensively trained.)

Of the 164 respondents, only 20 reported violations of ethical practice/behavior; however, some of these individuals reported more than one incident. The following brief descriptions are illustrative of the types of unethical practices/behaviors reported:

> 1| A university professor who teaches introductory counseling courses was conducting encounter groups which students in these courses were required to attend. Several became upset but felt they had no recourse.

2| An unqualified student was reported to be leading fee paid encounter weekend groups.

3| A group leader was reported to be encouraging the use of drugs by participants.

4| Nude encounter groups with sexual experimentation were held for beginning teachers in a particular school system.

5| Under the pretense of a group marathon, a group leader permitted participants to be inflicted with abuse which created a situation resulting in psychotic decompensation for a participant.

6| A philosophy professor was reported to have attended a weekend marathon group at Esalen Institute and upon returning to his classroom initiated with his classes an encounter-type experience involving nude bathing and a baptismal-type rite in a campus stream.

7| Sensitivity training involving encounter experiences was conducted without safeguards for support or follow-up.

8| A sensitivity trainer working as a consultant to the Employment Security Commission held a training session and left town. A trainee of the group suffered an 'emotional breakdown' and had to be hospitalized.

9| A medical doctor (General Practitioner) untrained in group work was reported to be serving as a psychologist-hypnotist doing family group therapy.

10| An untrained probation officer claimed to be doing "amateur" group psychotherapy.

Without a careful investigation of the incidents reported as unethical practice/behavior, there is no way, of course, to be sure that the ten examples all represent unethical practice/behavior. Nevertheless, several *appear* to represent violations of ethics. Twenty reported incidents from 164 respondents do not appear to be a large number of incidents of violations of ethical practices/behaviors, but it is not so much the number of violations as it is the harm done to the participants as well as the damage done to the helping professions as a result of the 'bad press'. At the time of this writing, in 1970, the backlash against the "group movement" appears to be gaining momentum to the point that group practitioners have been reluctant in certain areas to speak of doing sensitivity training or basic encounter group work. Paradoxically, however, there are individuals, notably among the college student

population and the young and middle-aged adults (American Psychiatric Association, 1970), who increasingly are seeking these kinds of small group encounters.

Group Procedures: Professional Preparation for and Clientele Served

Three questions on the questionnaire were intended to solicit from the respondents their feelings regarding the need to differentiate among the following six group procedures: group guidance, group counseling, group psychotherapy, T groups, sensitivity groups, and encounter groups. In addition the respondents were asked to indicate how they would define the six group procedures if they did view them as being separate and distinct practices. Likewise, they were asked to describe the "essential professional preparation requirements" for each of the six group procedures.

The majority of respondents, 137 to be exact, did wish to differentiate among the six group procedures—especially with respect to the techniques used and the degree of participant involvement. Eighteen felt that there was no need to differentiate because "there was already enough confusion." Eight did not respond to the question and one was undecided.

When asked to differentiate among the six groups based on (a) the persons best helped by each, and (b) the purpose of each, a wide range of responses was given. Since the two procedures emphasized in this text are group guidance and group counseling, only those two will be summarized and analyzed in this chapter. Table 8.2 includes a summary of the most frequently occurring responses for *group guidance*. Although a large percentage of the respondents failed to answer these items, those who did were in high agreement concerning the *purpose of group guidance,* i.e., to provide/disseminate information. Also, there was high agreement on the *persons best served by group guidance,* viz., students and "normals." I concur with the respondents' answers on both issues. The fact that so many persons failed to give responses to these items may be indicative of the number who *are not familiar with widely accepted goals and practices* and the *clientele best served by it.*

From Table 8.3 one can conclude that, at least for those who provided an answer, there was considerable agreement as to the *purpose of group counseling* and the *clientele best served through group counseling.* The majority of those who answered viewed group counseling as a type of assistance offered to essentially

TABLE 8.2

Purpose of and Persons Best Served by Group Guidance

Purpose	N[a]	Persons Best Served	N[a]
1. Provide/disseminate information (type of information not specified):	54	1. Students	57
		2. Normals	20
Vocational-educational information	9	3. Everyone (general population)	12
Growth information	2	4. Miscellaneous:	
Orientation	2	Persons seeking educational & vocational guidance	3
2. Vocational-Educational assistance	4	Persons in need of information	3
3. Instruction-oriented	4	Persons seeking common information	2
4. Self-understanding	2	Counselors, teachers, administrators	1
5. Miscellaneous.		Persons in planning stages	1
Better understanding of the world	1	Persons with decision problems	1
Establish goals	1	Persons who have common needs	1
Feedback on behavior	1	Class groups & adults	1
Improve study skills	1	Those experiencing personal difficulties	1
Assist in decision-making	1	People in a new setting	1
Meet developmental tasks	1	Almost any group— particularly schools	1
Task-centered	1	5. No response	32
Help direct person	1		
Preventive and developmental	1		
6. No response	51		

[a]N equals only 137—the number who chose to differentiate among the different group procedures.

"normal" persons who were experiencing some problems in their day-to-day living. There were, of course, several variations of this basic position. Once again, I concur with the respondents' regarding the purpose of group counseling and the individuals best served through it; however, I would prefer a greater emphasis on the developmental and preventive application of group counseling.

Since approximately one-half of the questionnaire respondents failed to answer this part of the questionnaire, one can only speculate that those who failed to respond did not feel very confident with their understanding of group counseling. Thus, we see that many practitioners may have little to be guided by and perhaps as a result would be susceptible to unethical practice/behavior.

Table 8.4 contains a summary of the respondents' replies to the question: "What are the essential professional preparation requirements for practicing ... [group guidance and group counseling]?"

Table 8.4 shows the distinctions in training and professional

TABLE 8.3

Purpose of and Persons Best Served by Group Counseling

Purpose	N[a]	Persons Best Served	N[a]
1. Problem solving	16	1. Normal people with normal problems	31
2. Assistance with 'everyday' problems (normal concerns)	10	2. Student groups	9
3. Self-understanding	10	3. Everyone (anyone)	6
4. Personal adjustment	8	4. Persons with problems of interpersonal functioning	6
5. Self-actualization	5	5. General population	5
6. Personal development	5	6. Persons who need assistance with life adjustment problems	5
7. Behavioral change	4	7. People with common concerns	4
8. Decision-making	4	8. Neurotics	3
9. Communicate better	3	9. College students	3
10. Information-giving	3	10. Emotionally disturbed	2
11. Long-term treatment	3	11. Persons with problems	2
12. Personality change	3	12. Young children through adult age	2
13. Attitude change	3	13. Miscellaneous	20
14. Miscellaneous	15	14. No response	39
15. No response	45		

[a]N equals only 137—the number who chose to differentiate among the different group procedures.

TABLE 8.4

Essential Preparation Requirements

Group Guidance	N[a]	Group Counseling	N[a]
Master's degree	43	Master's degree	47
Courses in counseling	30	Courses in group procedures	20
Courses in group procedures	21	Practicum in group counseling	20
Courses in guidance	19	Courses in counseling	16
Master's degree in counseling	14	Group dynamics	12
Group dynamics	9	Courses in guidance	11
Supervised experience	7	Ph.D.	11
Practicum	7	Supervisory experience	10
Professional counselor	3	Internship	9
Miscellaneous	11	Supervised experience	8
No response	29	Courses in group counseling	6
		Experience in groups	6
		Group counseling experience	6
		Miscellaneous	16
		No Response	25

[a]N does not equal 164 because some respondents cited more than one requirement.

preparation that the respondents made between group guidance and group counseling. The basic difference is the specification of group counseling practicum and "courses in group counseling" for professional preparation in that area. There is also a greater emphasis on experience in groups and internship-type experiences for group counseling preparation.

Professional Considerations

Each respondent was asked to reply to the question: "Who is responsible for punishing those whose practices and/or behavior in group procedures is unethical?" Table 8.5 gives a résumé of the replies to this question.

TABLE 8.5

Groups Recommended for Policing Unethical Practices/Behavior

GROUP	N[a]
Professional organizations	72
APGA, APA	18
State Licensing Board	9
Peer group	6
Miscellaneous	3
No response	65

[a]The N does not total 164 because some respondents gave more than one response to the question.

Two distinct statistics are evident in Table 8.5. First, almost all the respondents expressed their opinion that some kind of *professional organization* should punish persons for unethical practices/behaviors in group procedures. Secondly, approximately two-fifths of the questionnaire respondents did not reply to this question. This phenomenon may indicate that a large number of group practitioners have not decided how the field should be policed. This observation is further strengthened by the responses to another questionnaire item: "Is new legislation needed to govern practitioners of group work? If "Yes," what type?"

The majority of respondents answered "No" to this question, i.e., 76 answered "No," while 55 answered "Yes," and 33 did not respond. Of those who answered "Yes," 31 chose to list the type of new legislation needed. Licensing and certification respectively were each recommended by seven respondents. National and state laws was a recommendation given by six, professional orga-

nizations was a recommendation given by five, and miscellaneous recommendations were given by six others. There is obviously no clear directive in these recommendations for new legislation to govern practitioners of group work.

A related question illuminates the issue a little further. Each questionnaire recipient was asked to respond to the following question: "What is your view for rectifying problems facing those practicing in the group procedures areas?" Table 8.6 gives a summary of the responses to this question. The most frequent recommendation appears to include *more and better* training programs for group practitioners. Also high on the list is the establishment of some type of certifying or accrediting agency which would be able to provide a list of certified group practitioners. A third area which ranked high in the recommendations is informing the public of pros and cons of various group procedures. The need for some kind of clarification of the various group procedures also is recognized and various recommendations are concerned with the related problem of clarifying ethical practices through a new "Code of Ethics for Group Practitioners" and/or interpretation of existing codes.

A final question concerned with professionalization within the field of group work was asked of the respondents. It was, "Would you affiliate with a new division of the American Personnel and

TABLE 8.6

Recommended Procedures for Alleviating Problems Facing the Group Work Field

Recommendation	N
Provide better training programs	18
Provide more training and supervision	17
Develop some form of certifying agency or board	16
Educate the public	12
Expose those who violate ethics	8
Standardize and/or clarify group terms, techniques, procedures, and goals	7
Improve selection procedures for trainees	6
Develop a new division of APGA	5
Develop a "Code of Ethics for Group Practitioners"	5
Develop some form of licensing	5
Express more concern from the professional groups	5
Coordinate standards and policing among professional groups	3
Show more responsible behavior as a professional	3
Develop screening procedures for prospective group participants	3
Self-policing by professional groups	3
Hold joint meetings among appropriate professional groups	3
Adhere to current ethical codes for professionals	2
Miscellaneous recommendations	14
No response	29

Guidance Association or the American Psychological Association if it were developed for professionals active in various types of group work?" There were 94 "Yes" responses for affiliation with *APGA* and 38 "No" responses. (This finding is the reverse of a similar poll taken [Gazda, Duncan, & Meadows, 1967] five years earlier.) Seventy-eight said "Yes" and 44 said "No" in regard to their willingness to affiliate with *APA*. Thirty-six persons did not respond to the question and some showed a willingness to join a new division of one or both professional groups.

Conclusions

The reported incidents which were considered as unethical practice/behavior by the respondents of the questionnaire survey chiefly involved T, sensitivity and/or encounter groups. These group practices, in particular, appear to be 'under fire' by the press and various professional association members. Lakin (1969), Shostrom (1969), Birnbaum (1969), and the American Psychiatric Association (1970) have addressed themselves to issues of concern raised by various methods and techniques particularly as they apply to these group procedures.

The majority of questionnaire respondents indicated that they felt there should be differentiation among the following group procedures: group guidance, group counseling, group psychotherapy, T groups, sensitivity groups, and encounter groups. Especially relevant to the purpose of this text are the distinctions reported between group guidance and group counseling. Group guidance was viewed accurately as a group procedure where the purpose was to impart or disseminate information (vocational, educational, personal, social) to normal individuals (primarily students), whereas the purpose of group counseling was viewed as *problem-solving* of a variety of concerns (personal, social, educational, emotional) besetting *normal* individuals (respondents emphasized student groups) in their day-to-day living.

The majority of respondents made accurate distinctions between group guidance and group counseling in terms of their purpose(s) and the clientele best served. The disconcerting fact is that almost half of the questionnaire respondents did not respond to this item, which leaves us to speculate that those "no responses" were the result of the individual's not knowing how to define these two group procedures.

The questionnaire survey produced responses which dem-

onstrated that the respondents viewed the professional preparation for group counseling and group guidance to be different in
certain areas of emphasis. Basically, they agreed on the requirement of a Master's degree-level of training with counseling and
guidance as the areas of emphasis. The major difference between
the requirements was the addition of a practicum in group counseling, coursework in group counseling, and greater emphasis
on group experience through group participation and through
supervision in internships. I concur with the differences in training emphasis suggested by the respondents; however, I believe
that if group guidance is limited to giving of information which is
pertinent to career and life decisions, some classroom *teachers*
and Master's degree-level *counselors* can perform this function
under the direction of Master's degree-trained *group specialists.*

The majority of respondents did not favor new legislation to
govern group practitioners. Their preference was for the current
professional associations to police their own membership. Furthermore, they recommended more and better training programs
for group practitioners and some type of central certifying or accrediting agency which, in addition to serving the accrediting
function, would publish a list of certified group practitioners.
These are recommendations with which I can concur and upon
which I shall elaborate in the following section.

Recommendations

Before the "professional" group practitioners can set forth criteria
for standards of practice and/or a code of ethics, they must first
come to an agreement on the goals or purposes and methodology
of various group procedures. Goldman (1962) made a significant
contribution when he differentiated among group guidance, group
counseling, and group psychotherapy on the basis of the content
and process of each. In Chapter one I have tried to clarify the
issue further by emphasizing the inter-relationships among these
three group procedures in terms of their emphasis or purpose, i.e.,
a preventive-remedial continuum. With the addition of many new
group procedures, e.g., the basic encounter groups, marathon
groups, and the changing emphasis of T and sensitivity groups,
the Goldman paradigm must be extended to include these basic
group procedures.

It would be ideal if associations such as the American Psychological Association, the American Personnel and Guidance Asso-

ciation, the National Training Laboratory Institute, the American Group Psychotherapy Association, the American Society of Group Psychotherapy and Psychodrama, and the American Psychiatric Association could send representatives to a national conference for the purpose of reaching some consensus on definitions of group practices, and subsequent setting of goals for each, training or competencies required for each, clientele to be served by each, and similar criteria which would lead to some mutual understandings among professionals of related disciplines and which would provide some guidelines for practitioners. If this kind of national conclave is not possible, each of the professional associations whose membership includes practitioners of group procedures should define these group practices and set up standards and ethics for group practitioners within their own membership. Until such time as these standards and code of ethics can be developed on a multi-discipline level or even a single association level, each professional association is obligated to provide interim guidelines for its membership. If necessary, and certain unique features of group treatment or practice suggest that it is, current standards and ethical codes should be revised to incorporate those features which are particularly relevant to group procedures. Some of the features which are unique to group practices and therefore should receive special attention in any set of standards or code of ethics include the following:

1| First, and perhaps the most unique feature of group work, is the fact that the group includes the clients or members who themselves serve as co-therapists, co-trainers, co-helpers, etc., but who are not professionals and are not guided by a professional code of ethics. This creates unique problems in dealing with confidentiality and privileged communication.

2| Working in a "helping relationship" with several individuals simultaneously requires, in my estimation, a special kind of security in the leader, a special understanding of small group processes, and a high level of sensitivity necessary to maintain some type of direction or control which can be used for the benefit of each individual in the group. Thus, standards for leaders must be set for the different levels of group work.

3| Non-verbal techniques of many varieties have been developed for use in group settings, yet little research evidence is available to tell us when they are most appropriately employed. Some direction must be given to

protect the group participant from physical contacts, e.g., Attack Therapy, and similar non-verbal methods which may be harmful to him.

4| Special consideration must be given to methods of grouping individuals for training and treatment. For example, the degree of risk involved in working with close associates such as superiors and subordinates may preclude the potential benefits of such a group if adequate safeguards are not established.

5| On a one-to-one basis, the professional helper has fewer problems of deciding when his assistance should terminate; however, members in group training or treatment progress at different rates. Therefore, when closed groups are set up the professional helper or trainer must assume responsibility for those group members who need further assistance even though a pre-set termination date had been agreed upon. Even when the professional helper or leader can safely terminate the group at a pre-set date, there is frequently a need for follow-up contacts of group participants individually and/or as a group. Frequently this has not been a responsibility assumed by the trainer or leader. There are ethical responsibilities here which must be clarified.

6| There remains much to be clarified in the area of *required* group counseling, group therapy, encounter group experiences, etc., for students or trainees. Especially questionable is the practice of placing students or trainees with classmates in a group led by the instructor for that course.

7| The group is potentially capable of exerting extreme pressures on a given member and the leader as well to conform to its norm. This facet of a group is potentially very helpful and equally potentially very harmful. Group leaders must be capable of resisting group pressures for the welfare of and protection of the individuality of a given participant. The use of the group norm as a pressure tactic must be clarified as it affects the autonomy of a given group member.

The National Training Laboratory Institute has published *Standards for the Use of Laboratory Method* which provides general guidelines for the NTL trainers and although it represents a commendable first step, greater specificity must be given in addition to the endorsement of *Ethical Standards of Psychologists* as

guidelines for NTL members. The seven points described above represent some of the issues to which NTL as well as other professional associations must address themselves.

While the various professional associations grapple with the problem of standards and ethics for group practitioners, the prospective group participant can be guided by Shostrom's (1969, pp. 38–39)[1] propositions for deciding whether or not a group and its leader would be beneficial or harmful to him. These propositions are summarized as follows:

1| Never respond to a newspaper ad.
2| Never participate in a group of fewer than a half-dozen members.
3| Never join an encounter group on impulse—as a fling, binge, or surrender to the unplanned.
4| Never participate in a group encounter with close associates, persons with whom you have professional or competitive social relations.
5| Never be overly impressed by beautiful or otherwise class-signaled surroundings or participants.
6| Never stay with a group that has a behavioral ax to grind—a group that seems to insist that everybody be a Renaissance mensch, or a devotee of *cinema verité* or a rightist, or leftist, or a cultural, intellectual, or sexual specialist.
7| Never participate in a group that lacks formal connection with a professional on whom you can check.

Summary

This chapter begins with a description of the explosion of interest in and practice of group work with the resultant lag between the development of standards for training and practice, and the development of a code for ethical practice and behavior. A questionnaire survey was used to fill in some gaps regarding the number of cases of unethical practice/behavior in group work and the respondents' recommendations for dealing with the problems raised both externally by the public media, and internally by professional association members. The data from the questionnaire were summarized, analyzed and made relevant to the problem of ethics and related professional issues in group work.

Conclusions were drawn from the questionnaire data, from

[1] From Shostrom, E. L. Group therapy: Let the buyer beware. *Psychology Today.* 1969, *2*, (12), 37–40. Reproduced by permission.

others who have addressed themselves to the problems, and from my own experiences in the group field. From these conclusions recommendations were listed for alleviating the problem. The chapter closes with a list of guidelines recommended to prospective group members to assist them in deciding whether or not they should enter into a group experience.

References

AMERICAN PSYCHIATRIC ASSOCIATION. *Task force report 1: Encounter groups and psychiatry.* Washington, D.C.: Author, 1970.

BIRNBAUM, M. Sense about sensitivity training. *Saturday Review,* Nov. 15, 1969 82-ff.

GAZDA, G. M., DUNCAN, J. A., & MEADOWS, M. E. Group counseling and group procedures—Report of a survey. *Counselor Education and Supervision,* 1967, *6,* 305–310.

GOLAN, S. E. Emerging areas of ethical concern. *American Psychologist,* 1969, *24,* 454–459.

LAKIN, M. Some ethical issues in sensitivity training. *American Psychologist,* 1969, *24,* 923–928.

MORENO, J. L., & MORENO, Z. T. An objective analysis of the group psychotherapy movement. *Group Psychotherapy,* 1960, *13,* 233–237.

MORENO, J. L., Common ground for all group psychotherapists. What is a group psychotherapist? *Group Psychotherapy,* 1962. *15,* 263–264.

NATIONAL TRAINING LABORATORY INSTITUTE. *Standards for the use of laboratory method.* Washington, D.C.: Author, 1969.

SHOSTROM, E. L. Group therapy: Let the buyer beware. *Psychology Today,* 1969, 2 (12), 37–40.

Suggested Readings

AMERICAN PERSONNEL AND GUIDANCE ASSOCIATION. *Ethical standards: American Personnel and Guidance Association.* Washington D.C.: Author, 1961.

AMERICAN PERSONNEL AND GUIDANCE ASSOCIATION. *Ethical standards casebook.* Washington, D.C.: Author, 1965.

AMERICAN PSYCHIATRIC ASSOCIATION. Task force report 1: *Encounter groups and psychiatry.* Washington, D.C.: Author, 1970.

AMERICAN PSYCHOLOGICAL ASSOCIATION. *Casebook on ethical standards of psychologists.* Washington, D.C.: Author, 1967.

BIRNBAUM, M. Sense about sensitivity training. *Saturday Review,* Nov. 15, 1969, 82-ff.

GAZDA, G. M., DUNCAN, J. A., & MEADOWS, M. E. Group counseling and group procedures—Report of a survey. *Counselor Education and Supervision,* 1967, *6,* 305–310.

GOLAN, S. E. Emerging areas of ethical concern. *American Psychologist, 1969, 24,* 454–459.

KELMAN, H. C. *A time to speak—On human values and social research.* San Francisco: Josey-Bass, 1968.

LAKIN, M. Some ethical issues in sensitivity training. *American Psychologist,* 1969, *24,* 923–928.

MORENO, J. L. Code of ethics for group psychotherapy and psychodrama: Relationship to the Hippocratic Oath. *Psychodrama and Group Psychotherapy Monograph* No. 31. Beacon, New York: Beacon House, 1962.

NATIONAL TRAINING LABORATORY INSTITUTE. *Standards for the use of laboratory method,* Washington, D.C.: Author, 1969.

SHOSTROM, E. L. Group therapy: Let the buyer beware. *Psychology Today,* 1969, 2 (12), 37–40.

Appendix A[1]

Developmental Schema Chart

THE TODDLER AND PRE-SCHOOL AGE (Under 5 Years)
Tasks in Process

CHILD

To reach physiologic plateaus (motor action, toilet training).

To differentiate self and secure sense of autonomy.

To tolerate separations from mother.

To develop conceptual understandings and "ethical" values.

To master instinctual psychologic impulses (oedipal, sexual, guilt, shame).

To assimilate and handle socialization and acculturation (aggression, relationships, activities, feelings).

To learn sex distinctions.

MOTHER

To promote training, habits and physiologic progression.

To aid in family and group socialization of child.

To encourage speech and other learning.

To reinforce child's sense of autonomy and identity.

To set a model for "ethical" conduct.

To delineate male and female roles.

Acceptable Behavioral Characteristics

CHILD

Gratification from exercise of neuromotor skills.

Investigative, imitative, imaginative play.

Actions somewhat modulated by

MOTHER

Is moderate and flexible in training.

Shows pleasure and praise for child's advances.

Encourages and participates with

[1]Senn, M. J. E., & Solnit, A. J. *Problems in child behavior and development. Philadelphia:* Lea & Febiger, 1968. Reproduced by permission.

Acceptable Behavioral Characteristics

CHILD

thought; memory good; animistic and original thinking.

Exercises autonomy with body (sphincter control, eating).

Feelings of dependence on mother and separation fears.

Behavior identification with parents, siblings, peers.

Learns speech for communication.

Awareness of own motives, beginnings of conscience.

Intense feelings of shame, guilt, joy, love, desire to please.

Internalized standards of "bad," "good"; beginning of reality testing.

Broader sex curiosity and differentiation.

Ambivalence towards dependence and independence.

Questions birth and death.

MOTHER

child in learning and in play.

Sets reasonable standards and controls.

Consistent in own behavior, conduct and ethics.

Provides emotional reassurance to child.

Promotes peer play and guided group activity.

Reinforces child's cognition of male and female roles.

Minimal Psychopathology

CHILD

Poor motor coordination.

Persistent speech problems (stammering, loss of words).

Timidity towards people and experiences.

Fears and night terrors.

Problems with eating, sleeping, elimination, toileting, weaning.

Irritability, crying, temper tantrums.

Partial return to infantile manners.

Inability to leave mother without panic.

Fear of strangers.

Breathholding spells.

Lack of interest in other children.

MOTHER

Premature, coercive or censuring training.

Exacting standards above child's ability to conform.

Transmits anxiety and apprehension.

Unaccepting of child's efforts; intolerant towards failures.

Over-reacts, over-protective, over-anxious.

Despondent, apathetic.

Extreme Psychopathology

CHILD

Extreme lethargy, passivity or hypermotility.

MOTHER

Severely coercive and punitive.

Totally critical and rejecting.

Extreme Psychopathology

CHILD

Little or no speech; non-communicative.

No response or relationship to people, symbiotic clinging to mother.

Somatic ills; vomiting, constipation, diarrhea, megacolon, rash, tics.

Autism, childhood psychosis.

Excessive enuresis, soiling, fears.

Completely infantile behavior.

Play inhibited and non-conceptualized; absence or excess of auto-erotic activity.

Obsessive-compulsive behavior; "ritual" bound mannerisms.

Impulsive destructive behavior.

MOTHER

Over-identification with or overly submissive to child.

Inability to accept child's sex; fosters opposite.

Substitutes child for spouse; sexual expression via child.

Severe repression of child's need for gratification.

Deprivation of all stimulations, freedoms and pleasures.

Extreme anger and displeasure with child.

Child assault and brutality.

Severe depression and withdrawal.

Developmental Schema Chart

SCHOOL AGE AND PRE-ADOLESCENCE (5 to 12 Years)
Tasks in Process

CHILD

To master greater physical prowess.

To further establish self identity and sex role.

To work towards greater independence from parents.

To become aware of world-at-large.

To develop peer and other relationships.

To acquire learning, new skills and a sense of industry.

PARENT(S)

To help child's emancipation from parents.

To reinforce self-identification and independence.

To provide positive pattern of social and sex role behavior.

To acclimatize child to world-at-large.

To facilitate learning, reasoning, communication and experiencing.

To promote wholesome moral and ethical values.

Acceptable Behavioral Characteristics

CHILD

General good health, greater body competence, acute sensory perception.

PARENT(S)

Ambivalent towards child's separation but encourage independence.

Acceptable Behavioral Characteristics

CHILD

Pride and self confidence; less dependence on parents.

Better impulse control.

Ambivalence re dependency, separation and new experiences.

Accepts own sex role; psychosexual expression in play and fantasy.

Equates parents with peers and other adults.

Aware of natural world (life, death, birth, science); subjective but realistic about world.

Competitive but well organized in play; enjoys peer interaction.

Regard for collective obedience to social laws, rules and fair play.

Explores environment; school and neighborhood basic to social-learning experience.

Cognition advancing; intuitive thinking advancing to concrete operational level; responds to learning.

Speech becomes reasoning and expressive tool; thinking still egocentric.

PARENT(S)

Mixed feelings about parent-surrogates but help child to accept them.

Encourage child to participate outside the home.

Set appropriate model of social and ethical behavior and standards.

Take pleasure in child's developing skills and abilities.

Understand and cope with child's behavior.

Find other gratifications in life (activity, employment).

Are supportive towards child as required.

Minimal Psychopathology

CHILD

Anxiety and oversensitivity to new experiences (school, relationships, separation).

Lack of attentiveness; learning difficulties, disinterest in learning.

Acting out; lying, stealing, temper outbursts; inappropriate social behavior.

Regressive behavior (wetting, soiling, crying, fears).

Appearance of compulsive mannerisms (tics, rituals).

PARENT(S)

Disinclination to separate from child; or prematurely hastening separation.

Signs of despondency, apathy, hostility.

Foster fears, dependence, apprehension.

Disinterested in or rejecting of child.

Overly critical and censuring; undermine child's confidence.

Minimal Psychopathology

CHILD

Somatic illness: eating and sleeping problems, aches, pains, digestive upsets.

Fear of illness and body injury.

Difficulties and rivalry with peers, siblings, adults; constant fighting.

Destructive tendencies strong; temper tantrums.

Inability or unwillingness to do things for self.

Moodiness and withdrawal; few friends or personal relationships.

PARENT(S)

Inconsistent in discipline or control; erratic in behavior.

Offer a restrictive, overly moralistic model.

Extreme Psychopathology

CHILD

Extreme withdrawal, apathy, depression, grief, self-destructive tendencies.

Complete failure to learn. Speech difficulty, especially stuttering.

Extreme and uncontrollable anti-social behavior (aggression, destruction, chronic lying, stealing, intentional cruelty to animals).

Severe obsessive-compulsive behavior (phobias, fantasies, rituals).

Inability to distinguish reality from fantasy.

Excessive sexual exhibitionism, eroticism, sexual assaults on others.

Extreme somatic illness; failure to thrive, anorexia, obesity, hypochrondriasis, abnormal menses.

Complete absence or deterioration of personal and peer relationships.

PARENT(S)

Extreme depression and withdrawal; rejection of child.

Intense hostility; aggression towards child.

Uncontrollable fears, anxieties, guilts.

Complete inability to function in family role.

Severe moralistic prohibition of child's independent strivings.

Developmental Schema Chart

PUBERTY AND EARLY ADOLESCENCE (12 to 15 Years)
Tasks in Process

CHILD

To come to terms with body changes.

To cope with sexual development and psychosexual drives.

To establish and confirm sense of identity.

To learn further re sex role.

To synthesize personality.

To struggle for independence and emancipation from family.

To incorporate learning to the gestalt of living.

PARENT(S)

To help child complete emancipation.

To provide support and understanding.

To limit child's behavior and set standards.

To offer favorable and appropriate environment for healthy development.

To recall own adolescent difficulties; to accept and respect the adolescent's differences or similarities to parents or others.

To relate to adolescents and adolescence with a constructive sense of humor.

Acceptable Behavioral Characteristics

CHILD

Heightened physical power, strength and coordination.

Occasional psychosomatic and somato-psychic disturbances.

Maturing sex characteristics and proclivities.

Review and resolution of oedipal conflicts.

Inconsistent, unpredictable and paradoxical behavior.

Exploration and experimentation with self and world.

Eagerness for peer approval and relationships.

Strong moral and ethical perceptions.

Cognitive development accelerated; deductive and inductive reasoning; operational thought.

PARENT(S)

Allow and encourage reasonable independence.

Set fair rules; are consistent.

Compassionate and understanding; firm but not punitive or derogatory.

Feel pleasure and pride; occasional guilt and disappointment.

Have other interests besides child.

Marital life fulfilled apart from child.

Occasional expression of intolerance, resentment, envy or anxiety about adolescent's development.

Acceptable Behavioral Characteristics

CHILD   PARENT(S)

Competitive in play; erratic
work-play patterns.

Better use of language and other
symbolic material.

Critical of self and others;
self-evaluative.

Highly ambivalent towards
parents.

Anxiety over loss of parental
nurturing.

Hostility to parents.

Verbal aggression.

Minimal Psychopathology

CHILD   PARENT(S)

Apprehensions, fears, guilt and   Sense of failure.
anxiety re sex, health, education.
                                   Disappointment greater than joy.
Defiant, negative, impulsive or
depressed behavior.   Indifference to child and family.

Frequent somatic or   Apathy and depression.
hypochondriacal complaints; or   Persistent intolerance of child.
denial of ordinary illnesses.
                                   Limited interests and self
Learning irregular or deficient.   expression.

Sexual preoccupation.   Loss of perspective about child's
                                   capacities.
Poor or absent personal
relationships with adults or peers. Occasional direct or vicarious
                                   reversion to adolescent impulses.
Immaturity or precocious
behavior; unchanging personality   Uncertainty about standards
and temperament.   regarding sexual behavior and
                                   deviant social or personal
Unwillingness to assume the   activity.
responsibility of greater
autonomy.

Inability to substitute or postpone
gratifications.

Extreme Psychopathology

CHILD   PARENT(S)

Complete withdrawal into self,   Severe depression and
extreme depression.   withdrawal.

Acts of delinquency, asceticism,   Complete rejection of child
ritualism, over-conformity.   and/or family.

Neuroses, especially phobias;   Inability to function in family role.
persistent anxiety, compulsions,

Extreme Phychopathology

CHILD

inhibitions or constrictive behavior.

Persistent hypochondriases.

Sex aberrations.

Somatic illness: anorexia, colitis, menstrual disorders.

Complete inability to socialize or work (learning, etc.)

Psychoses.

PARENT(S)

Rivalrous, competitive, destructive and abusive to child.

Abetting child's acting out of unacceptable sexual or aggressive impulses for vicarious reasons.

Perpetuation of incapacitating infantilism in the pre-adolescent.

Panic reactions to acceptable standards of sexual behavior, social activity and assertiveness.

Compulsive, obsessive or psychotic behavior.

Appendix B

Action Maze[1]

An action maze is a written description of an incident for analysis, followed by a list of alternative actions. Each action directs the learner to a new page which gives him the results of his action and a new set of alternatives from which he is to choose a new action. The results the learner receives after each step may give him additional information as well as giving a reaction to his action.

The action-maze technique incorporates several ideas from programmed instruction, but it is not programmed instruction as such. The uniqueness of the action maze makes it an ideal teaching device that could be used for a wide variety of "personal" problems within educational settings.

Jimmy Jones Action Maze

Introduction

This will be an experiment in a new way of thinking about your actions. It begins with a statement of a problem. The path down which you proceed in taking action can and will differ from that of others. There is no "one path" to follow—just as there is no "one path" in real life. But the path you move down will depend on your attitudes and actions at each point and you have a choice.

This booklet will be used differently from any you have seen in the past. Instead of looking at each page in sequence (page 1, 2, 3, 4, etc.), you will decide on page one what action you would

[1]This brief action maze was developed by Dr. Richard D. Jones, College of Education, University of Georgia, as an illustration of the type of exercises that can be applied to group guidance and counseling, especially for the preadolescent. Several pages of the maze in the illustration are shown on one printed page to conserve space; however, in an actual maze, a separate page would be required.

take and then turn to the page indicated under that choice. Other action choices will refer you to other pages back and forth in the booklet.

Please write down each page you turn to on the record sheet.

Jimmy Jones Action Maze

You are the parent of Jimmy Jones a nine-year-old boy who is in the fourth grade. Last year when your son was tested they said that he should be able to do above average school work. His grades, however, have not come up to your expectations. It is time for report cards and your son comes in and hands you his card. You notice that he has all C's except a D in cooperation and citizenship. When you ask about this your son states:

Turn to page 1

Page 1

"Gee, I do as well as any of my friends and besides nobody likes that teacher; she is too hard. She always gives us homework and it's no fun doing all that work."
What action would you take?

1. Call the teacher to talk over any problems your son was having.

Turn to page 5

2. Say: "Does she give you more homework than any of the other teachers?"

Turn to page 6

3. Say: "Well homework isn't supposed to be fun. Unless you bring up those grades I am going to have to keep you from going out so much, like the baseball practice and the Scouts."

Turn to page 8

4. Say: "You think that it is the teacher's fault that you aren't making good grades."

Turn to page 7

Page 2

Nowhere were you instructed to turn to this page. You are not following direction. Return to your previous page.

Page 3

Your son states, "It doesn't seem important to learn all those things the teacher wants us to learn. No one cares anyway, what's the use!"

1. Say: "It's hard to want to learn when no one cares."
Turn to page 11
2. Say: "I know that some of the things you learn don't seem important but in the long run you'll be glad you did well in school."
Turn to page 10

Page 4

The teacher states "No, what he needs is more interest because he can do the work."

Return to your previous page and make another choice.

Page 5

When you talk with the teacher she states, "Jimmy is a fair student but he could do much better. Everytime I try and get him to do more he says that I am not his parent. He really needs to see the value of education."

What action would you take?

1. Tell your son: "I am really disappointed in you. Unless you do better we will have to punish you."
Turn to page 8
2. Say to the teacher: "Do you think that we need to have a special tutor?"
Turn to page 4
3. Tell your son: "Son, you really need to see the importance of school. How can you get anywhere without a good education?"
Turn to page 10

Page 6

Your son states, "I don't know how much the other kids have to do."

Return to previous page and make another selection.

Page 7

Your son states, "I don't know, maybe it's part my fault too. I really don't like school too much."

1. Say: "What don't you like about school?"
Turn to page 3.
2. Say: "It is hard to put forth all your effort for something you don't like very much."
Turn to page 11.

Page 8

Your son states, "It isn't my fault and it's not fair to keep me from doing things. No one else's parents keep them in. You're not fair!"

What action would you take?

1. Say: "I am as fair as any parent and when your grades come up, you will be treated like others."

Turn to page 10.

2. Say: "You think that it's the teacher's fault that you aren't making good grades."

Turn to page 7.

Page 9

QUESTIONS FOR DISCUSSIONS

1. Does what you say or action that you take when you are faced with a problem determine what the outcome might be?

2. Who is really to blame for this problem?

3. Is there any difference in what Jimmy says on page 10 and 11? Why did he say what he said on these pages?

Page 10

Your son states, "Well, I'll try and do better."

END OF MAZE

(Start discussion questions)

Turn to page 9.

Page 11

Your son states, "Yes it really is, especially when not even my parents are really interested in what I do. All you worry about is the report card."

END OF MAZE

(Start discussion questions)

Turn to page 9.

Appendix C

Introduction to Training[1]

Explanation Given to the Demonstration Group

I would like to introduce something first that will help to operationalize what we are doing. I will try to operationalize this at two levels—one in more scientific terms, and one in more global terms that may be understandable to you.

I am going to draw a few things on the chalkboard. Basically what we are working with is what you could call a developmental model. The model is this: In very global terms, mother prepares the child for father *and* mother. I did not say mother prepares the child for father, but mother prepares the child for father *and* mother. This is the basic model with which we are working. This is the way of characterizing it in terms of traditional sorts of stereotypes. I am not talking about qualities of maleness or femaleness now. I am saying that basically mother, who is nurturant and nourishing and protective, prepares the child for a father who is directionful and action-oriented. The mother, later, at high levels, is still more nourishing and nurturant. Another way of looking at it is in terms of the responsive and initiative dimensions or facilitative and action-oriented dimensions.

What we are going to do is divide the activities of the helper and the helpee and we are going to divide the phases of the helping process. This top row will represent the activities of the helper, and this bottom row will represent the activities of the helpee (see Figure C.1). In the first phase we are suggesting that the goal of the helping process, the necessary goal without which the helping

[1]This presentation was made by Dr. Robert Carkhuff at the University of Georgia Symposium on Training Groups, January 20, 1970.

FIGURE C.1

*Schematic Representation of Helpee and Helper
Activities in Exploratory, Understanding
and Action Phases of Helping*

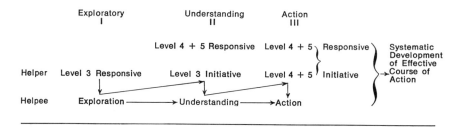

process cannot place, is self-exploration by the helper of himself, his feelings, his experiences, his problem areas. So down here we are saying that self-exploration is the *immediate* goal in the helping process.

How do you get to self-exploration? (Now I am talking to potential helpers and helpees, because you will be cast in both roles.) Well, the most effective way to get to self-exploration is to be responsive to the feelings and the experiences of the helpee. Therefore, we are talking about first being responsive to the helpee. Now we also find that during this period of self-exploration we are most effective when we respond to the helpee in terms of the feelings and experiences that he is expressing and do not go beyond them. In other words, we do not go into moderate interpretations or depth reflections or anything like that, initially. But we try to respond to the helpee at the level that he is expressing himself. We are taking him just at the level that he is expressing himself. A non-directive orientation, if you are familiar with it, is very helpful at this point. Unfortunately the nondirective approach does not go beyond this, but it is very helpful at this point.

What we are saying is that at level 3, on scales from 1 to 5, the helper is interchangeable in his understanding that he is communicating to the helpee. He is unconditional in the kind of positive regard that he is communicating. Operationally, this means that he is suspending his own feelings, his values, and his judgments that might have a potentially deliterious effect on the client. Okay, so initially our goal is going to be to achieve level 3 of the responsive dimensions. Today we are just going to focus on one dimension (empathy). Our goal initially is to be able to achieve level 3 of empathy. Now this would bring us to phase two. (Is this familiar to this group up here? Okay. I have just put a 3R up here, i.e., a 3 on the

responsive dimensions and an EX down here to show that it leads
to helpee exploration.)

The purpose of self-exploration is to help the client locate the
important pieces necessary for better self-understanding. When
he self-explores he gets a piece here, a piece there, and a piece
here. He cannot put the picture together, because if he could put
the picture together, he would not be there to see you. He gives
you the pieces, but he wants you to do something with them. He
will give you a lot of cues, telling you when he is ready for you
to do something with the pieces. At that point it is the helper's
responsibility to go to higher levels of empathic understanding, to
go to 4 and 5. At the same time when you go beyond the material
that an individual is giving you, you are also initiating. What you do
then is automatically start to introduce the initiative dimensions at
this point (see Figure C.1). (There is a point that I might make here.
It is a little didactic, but they go together. People who confront at
the highest levels are also those who are most understanding, empathic, etc. People who are most empathic are also most confront-
ing. They go together at the highest levels.)

Your goal or purpose is to move toward additive levels of empathy. We will try to do that here with this group. At the same time
that you move toward additive levels, you are automatically going
beyond the material that the helpee has given you and therefore
you automatically are starting to initiate from your own experiences. You are trying to put the picture together. The helpee gives
you the pieces in the exploration stage, and now you are trying to
help him put that picture together at whatever level he is, and at
whatever level you are. You are *starting* to try to help him put that
picture together. The purpose in all this is to help the client understand himself more fully, so that *he* can put the picture together, so
that *he* can put those pieces together. The goal then of the second
phase of helping (and you can measure this) is understanding—
helpee understanding.

Understanding has no purpose in and of itself if you do not
translate it into action or if you do not translate it into behavior.
We are saying then that the therapist has to do something else. He
has to initiate more fully himself, because his initiating on the basis
of his own experience provides a model for action. We are talking
here in this final stage about a helper who is functioning at both
levels 4 and 5 on both initiative dimensions and responsive dimensions (see Figure C.1). The function of the helper is to get the
helpee to act on his understanding of the problem that he explores.
One goes through three phases here: (1) the helper responds at

minimal levels so that the helpee will explore himself and thus the helper will be able to put the pieces together, because that is his expertise; (2) so that the helpee will be able to understand himself more deeply in order that the helper can start to initiate in terms of his own experience; and (3) thus enable the helpee to *act* upon his new understanding of himself. This cycle continues.

The only additional thing that I would add to what I have just described would be the development of courses of action which would be, under optimum conditions, jointly accomplished by helper and helpee. This is an ongoing kind of process because once I act, if I am the helpee, I open new areas of exploration; I learn new things about myself; I increase the effectiveness and the accuracy of my actions on the next action. Thus, *we have initiated an ongoing or lifelong kind of learning process.*

I said when I began that I was talking about a model where the helper prepared the child (and I am saying the analogy is between child and client) for father and mother—a full father and a full mother functioning at the highest levels of both responsive and initiative dimensions. The helper responds fully to the experience of the helpee and initiates fully in terms of the helper's own experience.

I think we have the group waiting up here and I would like the audience to save your questions until after the demonstration. Now we are going to deal with just one dimension. Of necessity the kind of thing that we are going to do here is going to be somewhat superficial.

Carkhuff, to the demonstration group: We are going to deal with one dimension today—empathy. We are going to try to define empathy. First we are going to try to define it in terms of our immediate goal. You will have to make this discrimination. Our immediate goal here is going to be for you to be able to make an interchangeable response with that of the helpee. Now it will be interchangeable not in terms of the content that the helpee is expressing, but in terms of the feeling. If you want, you can utilize the content of his message and you can integrate it with the feeling (we can define that too) and create what we call meaning complimenting the feeling. But initially we are just talking about the feeling. If, for example, the individual expresses something about his sadness (this is a superficial kind of statement that I am going to make now), you might say, "You feel sad." If you want to compliment that feeling with meaning, you might say, "You feel sad because she was the most important person in the world to you and now she's gone." In this way you have utilized the *content* of

his message to compliment the *feeling* with the personal meaning that it had for him.

Our first goal is to be able to make responses that are interchangeable. We are going to go through this now. If responses are not interchangeable, the helper is in some way subtractive or additive to the expressions of the helpee. He is subtracting from the feelings and the experiences that the helpee is expressing in not allowing the helpee to explore himself fully and in preventing him in some way from going on to explore this material more fully. And if the helper goes beyond what the helpee says, then it is in some way additive (see Figure C.2). We are going to operationalize these additive responses too. If the helper goes beyond the material, then he enables the helpee to go to deeper levels of exploration and deeper levels of understanding. *These are additive dimensions.*

FIGURE C.2

Operationalization of Levels of Empathy

Empathy Scale

Levels of functioning

5 + + (plus-plus)	
4 + (plus)	Additive to helpee's expression.
3 *Interchangeable in terms of feeling and meaning expressed by helpee*	
2 — (minus)	
1 — — (minus-minus)	Subtractive of helpee's expressions

Now I want to keep this in perspective. You remember on the previous chart (Figure C. 1) that I talked about the first phase being the development of this *interchangeable base.* I want to maintain the perspective that level 3 is nowhere; non-directive counseling is nowhere. It is what you do with the interchangeable base that makes your process effective. So even though our goal immediately is level 3, level 3 is still nowhere. It is just simply a good client-centered reflection, but you have not gone beyond it. Now is this clear to the group?

Now I am going to start to deal with you. I just want to get the background work out of the way. Here is what we are going to do then. We are going to go through about 4 or 5 phases out of what would be about a 20-phase sequence. Twenty phases is arbitrary, but what we are going to try to do is cut through some of them. We are not going to spend a lot of time on them. Ordinarily we might

spend several hours on the first phase, but we are not going to do that here today. We are going to establish simple kinds of goals—go around the group and in a fairly systematic way just to illustrate the procedure. But I will say this, as we go on I will gradually shift the burden over to you, because I would like to make a couple of points with training. I will ask you *initially* to deal with problems—to *roleplay* a problem—some kind of problem that maybe somebody brought to you. I will ask you *later* to deal with a *personally relevant* problem. It might be something that transpired right here in the group, but I do not want you to expose yourself unnecessarily. You be the guide of that and we can stop it at any point.

Here is our first task. We are going to pair off and have helper-helpee roles and we are going to go around the group and each one is going to have a responsibility for rating the helper as to whether or not he was interchangeable; that is all. That is the only discrimination we are going to make, initially. First the helpee is going to make a response, and the helper is going to make a response, and then the group is going to make a rating as to whether or not the response was interchangeable. That is our only responsibility.

Dave, would you roleplay some kind of problem for Bill? Bill will be the helper. Now you are just making one response, and you are not to respond to it. What we are going to do—here is our way of operationalizing it—is simply lay the responses side by side in terms of feeling and meaning, etc. We must answer this question for ourselves: "Could Bill have said what Dave said, and could Dave have said what Bill said?" Put the responses side by side and if we can say, "Yes, clearly one could have said what the other said," then we call them interchangeable and we rate it level 3. That is simply the discrimination operation. Now we are going to go through it and following it each of you will be asked to rate whether or not it was interchangeable. Okay?

Demonstration Protocol

Dave: Maybe we prefer to deal with something personally relevant. I'm feeling pretty anxious up here. We're in front of the whole group and I had to leave my defenses at the back door, with the doorkeeper, for the last two days.

Bill: Right now I'm frightened and would like to leave. Perhaps I'm scared, coming up here, having to be quite open.

Carkhuff: Okay. Dave broke the rule. The first rule that I gave him was to roleplay. But that's okay, because that's just for his own protection. He can talk about immediate and personally relevant feelings if he wants to. Dave talked about his feeling anxious and Bill said something like, "Right now I'm frightened." Bill, you even used the first person: "Right now *I'm* frightened and feel like *I'd* almost like to get out of here,"—something like that. Okay, now we're going to go around the group and rate this and then we'll ask Dave whether he felt that this was an interchangeable response. Brad?

Brad: Interchangeable up to a point. Dave at one point was talking about his being a doorman. He'd been out of it and this was responding to—you know we've had a facade about us—being part of the program. We've had to get in and be part of it. Bill responded up to that point interchangeably.

Carkhuff: Okay. You needn't elaborate it right now. If you can just rate it interchangeable or not, but if you want to comment on it you can.

Alice: Slightly less than interchangeable.

Carl: I thought it was less.

Ralph: That was my feeling too.

Carkhuff: Okay, the basic feeling words that each used were that you were *anxious* and his was that he was *frightened.* Go ahead Dave if you want to, comment on it.

Dave: In terms of what I was feeling, I didn't feel good about the response I made, and I think . . . .

Carkhuff: You feel a little more secure now?

Dave: Beautiful! I didn't feel good about his response, but I think initially I did. I was sort of reading it as accurate but he then sort of took it away from me and said, "I'd like to leave."

Carkhuff: Right. This is the way I experienced it—that *frightened* was okay. It was compatible. You could lay them side by side. Then, Bill, when you tried to compliment it with meaning, you started talking about Bill, not him. If you look at him you know he wants to stay here. One of the points that I want to make is for you to take in all behavioral clues. You know you've got to look at Dave here in front of you and don't just respond to the words. Okay? But even if you take the ratings here of the group, you got pretty good ratings for the first shot at it. You got pretty good ratings. By-and-large they averaged about 3. I think you hurt yourself a little bit by trying to go to the meaning.

Okay, I'm going to try to progress—add a little bit on each stage even before we get to the second phase. I'm going to try to keep this moving. I know there's a lot more discussion that could go on, but I'm going to try to keep this moving. What I'd like you to do now, Bill, is to turn around and be helpee. Brad you be helper. But I'd like you to get involved in a couple of rules now for me. I'd like you to listen for at least 30 seconds before responding. Now, Bill, you came right in there and it wasn't a bad response until you elaborated. But Brad, I'd like you to listen for at least 30 seconds before you respond. That's a very difficult task for most of us, but just listen until you feel like you've got the response right there. I'd like also that you phrase it in a reflective paradigm. I don't mind using first person, if you want to use that, but in some way communicate to this guy that you're responding to *his* experience—"You feel," or something like that. And the other thing is simply to focus on the feelings, the point which we made already. These are a couple of rules that I'm imposing on you now.

Bill: I'd like to stay within myself too. At this point that's most comfortable for me. I was quite anxious at having to break the ice and felt pretty stroked by you (Carkhuff) when you said, "That's still not too bad a response," because I was hurting a little bit. I wanted to make a good response.

Brad: Being yourself right here at this time is more meaningful. It's easier to do this and to be stroked by Dr. Carkhuff. And to be valued by these people out here in this group (audience) is very important.

Carkhuff: One reason I didn't want you initially to deal with so immediate an experience was because I wanted you to save them for later, but that's all right. We'll have new ones later! Okay, let's rate it—Ralph.

Ralph: I'd say it was sufficient.

Carkhuff: You rate it 3?

Ralph: Three.

Carkhuff: Carl?

Carl: Three or maybe a little lower. It was a good solid three, maybe a little lower.

Alice: A little less than 3.

Dave: A little less than 3.

Bill: I think you got very close to what I was feeling in terms of comfort. I feel much more at ease, and that's what I was trying to express. I was pretty uptight before, and put a lot of myself into

what I was trying to respond to. I don't feel that anymore. My anxiety level has dropped.

Brad: Mine is still up!

Bill: Yeah, I felt it!

Carkhuff: You didn't get rated by me yet! You sure shot beyond what we were calling for here, that's clear. There's a dimension that we deal with—the very last dimension—and we call it *immediacy.* I think that on the surface a level 3 response would have reflected the relief that you felt and so on, it doesn't go too far. You really took the ball to go all the way—you know—very immediate kinds of things that were going on, and that he was trying to tell you at different levels. You'd get a very high rating on immediacy and, I think, essentially an adequate rating on empathy. In other words, 3. You probably would get a much higher rating on immediacy. It was a complex response to rate, making it difficult from the beginning, because of how far you went with it. You didn't just use a simple, "You feel" paradigm. You took that ball and ran with it. You made it more difficult to rate. This is the point I'm making right now. I think it was essentially a good response to make to a helpee at this point.

All right, now I want to add another dimension as we go on. We're going to rate, but we're also going to formulate the kinds of interchangeable responses that we might make. Alice, you're going to be helper. You be helpee, Brad. But after you make your one response, we're going to formulate the kinds of interchangeable responses that we might make. I've talked about response repertoire before—you're going to have an opportunity to hear a series of other responses. You're going to hear a series of alternate responses that you might have incorporated. Okay? Let's have just one exchange again.

Brad: I'm going to stay with the immediate too. I've been questioning quite a bit—I think even from my coming here—my role and the way I've seen it here, being photographer, you know, looking through the keyhole etc. and not entering into the activities. And I've been questioning very strongly whether or not I did this as a defense mechanism or what other type of need I was trying to meet, or if it was just one of those things, you know—I was asked to do it. I think I can read a little bit more into it and I'm questioning: "Am I afraid to interact with this group?"

Alice: You sound like you feel a little unsure of yourself and that you question why you feel so unsure.

Carkhuff: Okay. Now let's go one round with the rating, and then we'll go one round with—try to keep track of the response which

you made—the response which you might have made. It was hard to hear her, but do the best you can. Carl, what would you rate?

Carl: Slightly less than 3.

Ralph: 2.

Dave: 3.

Bill: 3.

Brad: In empathy, possibly somewhat less than 3, but there was something about what she said that hit directly, so possibly 3 minus. There was another area there that . . . .

Carkhuff: Yeah, you were asking a lot of questions that (interrupted by Brad)

Brad: . . .that moved in and she just cut right through it and went straight to the heart of it.

Carkhuff: We didn't ask her to go beyond. There was other stuff there but we didn't ask her to go beyond. What kind of response might she formulate? It's kind of hard to formulate something more when you're really not sure which it is or something like that, which is what she did. And I think as such she formulated a more or less adequate response. You could have added some other kinds of words, but basically what they were communicating were things like: "You didn't know which way to look at your own behavior, or interpret it or . . . (interrupted by Brad)

Brad: And I am questioning it, like she said.

Carkhuff: Right. There are other things that she could have done, but she would have gone beyond and we are going to hold that for now. Okay, now let's formulate the kinds of responses that we might have made to Brad.

Carl: You feel a bit unsure about taking part, and you were questioning whether or not you should have actually accepted being part of the thing?

Ralph: You're really not sure what your role is in this whole business. Are you a part?

Dave: Brad sort of is saying, "Why was I placed in this position?" "What is it about me that people say, 'He'll do it'?" Questioning, it seems: "I'm a little more adequate than that as an individual."

Carkhuff: Okay, now you know you've gone beyond. You're shooting for an additive response here. You went quite a bit beyond what he said. You can shoot of course for an additive response very early, but the thing about that is if you do and you miss, you're subtractive. This is all I'm saying. I think you might

have stopped him a little bit when you got him thinking, but right now you went beyond it.

Bill: I heard you say that I have some question about my reasons or my motives of why I did or accepted the job that was given me. And perhaps I'm wondering why I would rather not have been involved or am I safe where I am and then I would have done that because I feel safe?

Carkhuff: Okay at this point I would like to emphasize the brevity of the response, too, that you can get yourself entangled. If you make a good response, leave it! Just like you had to end before: "Brad, you're really frightened," and leave it. If you find yourself making too long a response at this point it's probably because you missed and you're trying to 'recoup'. Brad, which of those alternate responses did you like best?

Brad: Bill's. I felt his was the closest. His was very close. Dave's was additive—some understanding, because I think my feelings were basically a projection of your (Dave's) feelings. I think that these two others had totally missed.

Carkhuff: Okay, now let me use this as an opportunity to introduce the next stage that we'll try to go through. What we really have to do is make a decision whether or not these responses would have enabled you to go on. Was, for example, Dave's response additive or subtractive? How can we find out?

Alice: By the helpee's next response.

Carkhuff: Right! That is what we're doing then, building on here in a sequence—a helpee-helper-helpee response sequence. Now we're going to allow it to roll, and we're going to add another response. That is, the helpee will be allowed to respond to the helper's response and you will also, as a group, rate and formulate your own responses. Again we're still shooting for level 3. We don't want to get beyond ourselves—it's easy to do. I'll make comments on this later. So, Alice, you're helpee. Carl, you are helper. Alice, you can respond to his response.

Alice: I have this problem. I had this big fight with my major professor and I'm kind of scared about what's going to happen to my career now. And I don't know what is going to come up next.

Carl: Do you feel that you might have taken a rash step and actually expressed the way you felt at the time?

Alice: Yeah, I think I might have gone too far in how I felt about the situation.

Carkhuff: Now that's all, Carl, you don't get a second shot at it! Okay. Ralph, do you want to rate it?

Ralph: A little below 3.

Carkhuff: Okay, now we have to make a decision. We're looking at the helpee's response to the helper's response. Now we're saying that that will allow us to make a determination of whether it is additive or subtractive. You're saying that it was subtractive. See if you can quantify that a little bit. In other words, was it level 2, 1, etc.?

Ralph: I don't think it was that subtractive.

Carkhuff: Okay, you're saying something like a 2?

Ralph: 2.5 probably.

Carkhuff: Okay, Brad?

Brad: I'd say the same, 2.5, because he repeated something to make sure he got it.

Bill: 3.

Dave: I felt it was a 3.

Carkhuff: Was what?

Dave: 3.

Alice: I thought he got pretty close, but I wasn't completely sure he understood everything I said.

Carkhuff: Did he understand *what* you said?

Alice: It was like the words came across, but I wasn't sure about all of the feeling.

Carkhuff: You said, "Gee I'm really worried about my career—I just had a big fight with my major professor." You said, Carl, that you (Alice) felt like you did the right thing by expressing yourself.

Carl: I felt that she might have gone too far in expressing herself, or something like that.

Carkhuff: Did you use the word right?

Dave: Rash.

Carkhuff: Oh, rash, okay. You feel that you may have gone too far in expressing yourself. I thought I heard you saying that you did the right thing, or something like that. Okay, you said *rash*. Okay, so what we have here in a group rating is something like about 2.5 or something like that where he got close but he didn't quite make it? Okay, I'll go along with that. I didn't hear—I heard it differently when I heard it, so I won't rate it this time. Okay, let's formulate our responses to Alice and, Alice, you can respond to them now. Dave?

Dave: Alice, you're wondering, this fight with your professor, this has really blown your career?

Carkhuff: If you feel like he's said something to you, you can respond to it.

Alice: Yes, I really feel it.

Carkhuff: Okay, Bill, I'm going to keep this moving as much as I can.

Bill: Alice, I hear you saying that you might have done something that is quite frightening to you in terms of your own dreams or goals.

Alice: That's exactly how I feel.

Brad: You had this fight and you feel somewhat jeopardized and you're having second questions as to whether or not this was the thing to do?

Alice: Yeah, I felt completely unprepared to meet him again.

Ralph: (As an aside, I was amazed at my own words used in the term—to blow it. I was going to say, "Well it sounds like you really blew it this time," and then he preempted me.)

Carkhuff: That's okay.

Alice: Of all the responses, I felt all of them were good. All hit the point but his (Brad's) was the closest—right on the spot.

Carkhuff: Okay, he got more to the feeling level because he put some of the feeling into words.

Alice: Yes, exactly.

Carkhuff: Your world was blown apart, okay? I want to keep it moving and I know I'm adding on to each stage as we go around, but I want to get something that could be fairly significant. Since we're doing so well as a group, let's move to an extended interaction. Let's let it roll a little bit now. You have responsibilities here to rate the *modal* level of empathy that Bill is communicating, that is, at what level is he at most frequently if we have half a dozen exchanges? Not his peak and not his depth, but at what level is he at most frequently?

Carkhuff: Now we're going to have an extended interaction. Carl, you're the helpee and Ralph you're the helper.

Carl: It gets to be rather frightening at times being away from my family.

Ralph: I don't really understand; would you tell me more about this being away?

Carl: I guess it is the idea of not being there as much as I might.

Ralph: You're not really sure what you have to sacrifice is worth what you're getting?

Carl: I'm sure that the sacrifice is worth it and I feel I'm doing the right thing; it's just the feeling that maybe being away creates anxiety at times. I don't think it's out of hand. It just creates a feeling.

Ralph: It would be a lot nicer if you could have your cake and eat it too?

Carl: Yeah, yeah. That isn't always possible.

Ralph: I'm not quite sure what you're questioning at this point—the value of what you're experiencing or . . . (Carl interrupted.)

Carl: I think the value of what I'm experiencing. I think it is well worth it. It's nothing more than just being away.

Ralph: Just plain old lonesomeness for the wife and kids?
Carl: Periodically, not constantly.

Ralph: About how periodic?

Carl: There's no way to measure it. It comes at times.

Ralph: I keep wanting to say you sound as though you miss the kids and you get kind of 'horny'.

Carl: I wouldn't go quite that far; it's just being away.

Carkhuff: Okay, we'll stop this here anyway. Let's hold it a minute and get some ratings. Dave?

Dave: I thought he was operating at 2 most of the time, and the last one was—may have been off the scale at the bottom—but about 1.5 to 2 most of the time.

Bill: I felt like Ralph was operating about 2, somewhere around there, but I have another feeling. I didn't feel like Carl was feeding into him. You know, this was my feeling. Carl, you were not giving to him. He was coming back at you for kinds of clarification and you were playing hard to get to. Now this is just a feeling I have.

Carkhuff: The helpee has to be helper too. The helpee has to help the helper along, so to speak—at least when we're doing this for demonstration.

Brad: I'm probably very unfair, but I felt that you were operating below 2, well below. And I think, basically, because a couple of us know Carl and I was able to hear what he was saying, and I had some feelings and you were completely missing them and asking him, "What are you talking about?" I knew what he was talking about, so everytime I'd hear what you were saying, I had to rate down. I was putting you at 1 basically all the way.

Alice: I felt the first couple of responses were about 2.5. They were pretty good with what he was working with. The last two, I thought, were pretty bad. They just missed it completely.

Carkhuff: Carl, would you take the mike and respond.

Carl: I think he started off getting close—2.5, 2.0. Then he began to reach, and I'll admit I wasn't helping him very much. But, you know, I felt that the responses that he gave didn't give me the possibility of continuing.

Carkhuff: Ralph, for one thing you broke the rule of just responding to his experiences and his feelings, and that got you off the track. You even threw a question in there. Then you made a real attempt to go to additive levels which I think is the critical element in doing this kind of thing. You have to assure yourself that you can lay this kind of interchangeable base before you can make that move to additive levels. Now you tried before with Brad, but you got some past history together and you were bringing some of your own in-terpretations of things that you've seen for a long time and all of that. The broader the interchangeable base of communication that you establish, the higher the probability is that when you make your move to additive levels you can do it. And that's why we're trying to get this base down here.

I'm going to—just to take it to this fourth level—trust you Dave with this and then you Ralph. I know we moved quickly. I'm well aware of that. We're going to try to take it to an additive level here. Dave, that means that you've got to be disciplined here in laying an interchangeable base—in really responding to Ralph's experi-ences. Ralph, deal with what you just went through, you know, the fact that you did get shot down. And Dave, I want you to do this: After you feel that these pieces are starting to fall in place and I don't care if you have six responses or eight, take what time you need; then make an additive response. I'll try to give you a para-digm for that, too—something like, "Ralph, what I really hear you saying is . . . " or "What this all adds up to for me is this." In other words, after you feel that these pieces are starting to fall into place, then you start to try to put it together. Now at this point we're just going to have the responsibility for rating him at two levels: (1) Did he lay that interchangeable base? (2) Did he make that additive response? That's all we're going to do now. Okay, Ralph.

Ralph: I really felt quite uncomfortable going around and getting shot down and then tried to run it through, and Bill was talking here a minute ago to figure out why it was necessarily important.

Dave: It's an uncomfortable feeling to have people to rate you on something that maybe you've done.

Ralph: Yeah, and I'm paranoid enough to feel as though I'm the

outsider of these six—that you people know each other at some level that I don't and that perhaps this is part of it.

Dave: So possibly being an outsider may have brought on more of the anxiety than what you wanted—made you feel a little more uncomfortable than what you wanted to feel?

Ralph: No, I guess it is more that I would and *do* feel sort of put upon. I got pretty desperate in the exchange with him and really wanted to say, "I give up because I can't pull anymore out." I guess you're the only one who made me feel like you understood this.

Dave: Somewhat like you worked as hard as you could and yet he wasn't really willing to help you.

Ralph: Yeah, I guess that's pretty close to it.

Dave: Maybe you're wondering why you were sort of left by yourself and the rest of the group couldn't have been made available to give you some help in this crisis situation.

Ralph: No, I think more than that I wondered why the hell I got into it for in the first place!

Dave: Why were you selected? Why did you get in? You questioned, "Why did I get in in the first place?"

Ralph: Why did I let myself get in?

Dave: What I think I hear you saying is, "Where am I in relation to the group? Everybody sort of knows each other. I sort of see myself as being an outsider and that you're feeling pretty damned uncomfortable about the whole experience."

Ralph: You bet your bippie!

Carkhuff: Okay, I'm going to go through the rules that I promised originally, and we're going to go around. Carl, will you rate whether or not he got to the interchangeable base and whether or not he was additive when he went to it.

Carl: I think yes to both. He established the base, and I think when he went to the additive level Ralph might have almost been to the point, you know, that we weren't here. So I think he made an additive response, and when he moved to the level it appeared that they were together.

Alice: Yes to both questions. Dave established a very good level and, of the additive responses I heard, most of them were plus.

Carkhuff: But you (Dave) really only made one, I hope, or tried one.

Brad: I feel that he reached the additive level and he added on at that point to give him (Ralph) something. But in the process of get-

ting there, he was sometimes at 3 and sometimes just below because you (Ralph) were still fighting. You (Ralph) still felt somewhat like an outsider, even though still in the group.

Bill: I would say a little below 3 on the base. I was wondering—I kept hearing hurt and anger, a hell of a lot of it. And I was wondering where this was going to be. I thought in terms of the base that the additive movement was there and good but I kept hearing this other you know and seeing it.

Ralph: I think maybe the anger—outright hostility which will subside probably day after tomorrow—was pretty basic and he (Dave) touched upon this. I would rate him slightly less than a 3. At this point I don't know whether that's accuracy or my own reaction to the whole business.

Carkhuff: I heard from most of the last three evaluations that you hit 3 a couple of times in laying the base, but you also fell below it and when you went to what you presented as an additive response you were probably just where you should have been in the beginning. In other words, that was about a 3 overall. It looked like a little more than what you started with. Ralph made some of the points here and the anger was there. As a matter of fact, at one or two points, Ralph, I felt like you were talking to some of the segments of the audience more than you were to Dave. I don't know if anybody else picked that up—you know, like you need some allies and it is because you do feel like you're up there alone and you would like to reach them out there in the audience. I did feel you were talking past Dave. Did you feel that, Dave?

Dave: I wasn't sure whether he was talking about here and now, you know, within this, or if he wasn't talking about two days hence.

Carkhuff: The other point I think, and this is an important point, is to relate it Ralph to Ralph. Now there are a lot of rules along the way, and I haven't gotten into them, but to relate it Ralph to Ralph is most critical. There's a basic question here, you know, "What is there about Ralph that he gets into these kinds of situations?" See? Ralph can ask that question about something: he can be hostile at Carl for not sharing, he can be hostile at me for using him up here, he can be hostile at you for not hearing his hostility, but the question that he has to ask himself is "What is there about me that I get into these kinds of situations?" And that's when you start moving to additive levels and start to push him to high levels of exploration and understanding.

I'm just going to try one more now. I'd like to add another

dimension here. Bill, you be helper and, as much as you can, stay to that reflective paradigm. I don't care if you use "I feel"; that's okay, but when you make your move let us know, like Dave did. I think Dave's got a nice technique, even if he didn't pick up some of the essential feeling. But when you make your move, Bill, let us know and we will try to do two things. We're going to rate you on whether you lay the base and whether you made it to the additive levels. But we're also going to formulate our own additive kinds of responses. Now this is going to be difficult, because you've got a lot of tasks here. How well we do, depends on how well you lay that base with him. In other words, you're helping to elicit that self-exploration that we have to work with. Okay? Go back to something immediate now so we can all work on it.

Dave: I felt the response that I gave to Bill was pretty high level. You know I thought, "Gee, that's a beauty, a number 5 all the way, you know." And I was feeling pretty good about it, particularly when you said—I'm not sure of the exact words, but I'll use mine—"You bet your bippie, man." And yet the feedback that I got from the group was good except for one group member who happens to be the leader. I was expecting more, you know, because I've heard so much about him and the model itself. I kind of felt hurt that it wasn't a 4 or 5.

Bill: I'm hearing you say several things. I'm hearing you say, "I kind of liked what I did and I feel pretty shitty right now because I asked for something and I got something else as a response which cancelled out the way I felt." And, "I'm still not too sure I wasn't right in there because I got a good response."

Dave: Yeah, I feel good about what you say, except I don't feel shitty. I kind of feel anxious about it; I feel a little sadness, a little unhappy.

Bill: "I'm (Dave) hurting right now about what just happened."

Dave: Yeah, I'm hurting too.

Bill: I hear you saying that "I'm in a lot of pain right now inside myself and the way I see myself as a counselor in what just took place."

Dave: Yeah, because it's pretty important, you know, that you feel good about yourself and about what you do, and particularly in relations with—any type of relationship with another person, that you want to be significant, you know. You want to make change, you want to effect it if at all possible—some change in them, because you know this is why we're here, man.

Bill: "It's very important to me (Dave) that I do a good job, and it

hurts a little bit to feel like I did a good job and be rated by some-one I feel significant as having done a bad job, and I'm questioning right now which way to go, what to do with myself, regroup."

Dave: Yeah, maybe sort of where I am in relation to the group and then more so in terms of him, (Carkhuff) you know: What am I basically? Regrouping, yeah. Maybe I'll have to take a little closer look. Maybe I'm not as good as I thought I was.

Bill: This experience has caused me to ask some deeper questions about myself and why I'm up here on this stage instead of a door-man.

Dave: Yeah, man.

Carkhuff: Bill, you know you were shooting for additive levels early. Are you going to give us something? Are you going to give us a punch line?

Dave: I'll try to move back in. I moved out on that.

Carkhuff: Yeah, you did.

Dave: I don't know whether I can.

Carkhuff: I'd like you to try.

Dave: Yeah, why am I on the stage here and maybe I should be a doorman. I'm more significant than that, you know.

Bill: "I've got more to give and I don't like being put down. I'm ready to make a positive move somehow in some way to get there."

Dave: Yeah, I feel good about that statement. That's all.

Bill: I feel like I'm going on. I feel like I have exhausted my re-sponses.

Carkhuff: I said you could have all the time you need, you know, but we'll stop it here. All right, let's give Bill an overall rating. Let's just give him an overall rating, because I think he broke all the rules anyway. Ralph what would you rate him as?

Ralph: 4.

Carkhuff: Carl?

Carl: Give him a 3.

Alice: 4.

Brad: 2.5

Dave: I felt real good about what he was giving me, both in terms of words and in terms of affect and in terms of eye contact. And yet at times I sort of felt, "Which way am I going?" But I thought he was tuned in.

Carkhuff: Bill puts out a whole lot, and even though he maybe

didn't capture what you were wrestling with, he put out enough to communicate to you that this guy is here to help you.

Dave: Right. He was hearing everything I was saying.

Carkhuff: I think your range got pretty wide and that made it a little more difficult. You started high, went down, came back up and went down a little bit, but overall you can do therapy. I think you've got to discipline yourself, Bill, to lay that interchangeable base. I know you don't want to. All you guys think you've got enough under your belt to just go right into it, but you lay that base and then that picture will start to fall together and it will be his. It will be more finely tuned with Dave, because you lost a lot of what Dave said originally. You made such a lengthy response, that following it, both of you guys were working with your own responses rather than his. It was at least twice the length of his initial introduction. Okay? But you can do it, but you've first got to learn that discipline, Bill. Let's formulate what kinds of additive responses that we might make. Brad, you begin. Dave you can respond to them if they are appropriate.

Brad: You had done a job and you had gotten a lot of reward out of Bill's last statement to you and this reward you know kind of jived right along with what you were feeling: "I (Dave) did a good job: I hit." And then you got angry with Dr. Carkhuff when he started cutting and saying that wasn't really additive, you know, and that you weren't always hitting 3 all the way along the line. It gets down to that point where I've (Dave) either got to question the model or I've got to question myself. You know, you've got to question yourself or the model. If the model is right and Dr. Carkhuff is the sole originator of this model, then you didn't quite live up to it. And yet you felt like you did, and so it brings about the question of either you can't accept the model or if you do accept the model you've got to accept some change that I (Dave) didn't quite do everything that I perceived I was doing at the time.

Dave: Almost like I'd rather reject the model than myself.

Brad: That's right.

Dave: And maybe that's why I used him rather than (Brad breaks in.)

Brad: I could feel the anger going—vibrating this way, anyway.

Alice: Dave, I hear you saying that you feel pretty disappointed with what's happened and that you take some stock in what Dr. Carkhuff has said. You're wondering what he saw in your responses that you didn't see. You'd like to be able to see that, but right now you just don't care.

Dave: Except for, "You don't care," I thought you were really tuned in. You were saying what I was feeling. It was almost like you were sitting right there as you were talking about it.

Carl: Dave, I hear you saying that you feel as though something pretty important to you is being tampered with, that is, your internal sense of judgment. Usually when you feel good about what you're doing it is usually good, (you felt good about what you did) and you're being told by a person whose model you liked and respected and thought a great deal about that you weren't so good. It becomes a choice now—your internal sense of judgment which has worked for a long time, and is usually right and the acceptance of a model. You just feel that what you've been using internally is more important.

Dave: Yeah, and you know this is what I've got to rely on, too. I can sort of take the model and build it in hopefully, but it is still me and if it fits I need to use it if it is going to help me be effective.

Ralph: Of course I had the contact with you when you were responding to me and the expression on your face was sort of, "Gee I'm doing this real well and I'm sort of happy that it is bouncing back and forth the way it is." And then (maybe I stepped off the line a little bit here) as I saw the two of you responding, I half facetiously thought to myself he (Dave) might have responded, "I'm not really sure that Bob Carkhuff understands the model."

Dave: And I'm on the spot again! For some reason, Ralph, I can't relate to that.

Ralph: In fact, I thought he was going to say this. I thought that was the direction you were going.

Dave: I'd have to say "no." I might have gotten there, but—you know, I feel bad—I think you heard what I said and you're trying to really feed me emotionally. I feel bad that I can't come back and say, "Gee you know I feel good about what you said." I wish I could.

Ralph: No, I wouldn't want to ruin a good average!

Dave: But you know, you come on like you want to help, that you are interested, that you're concerned, and I sort of feel bad that I can't relate to you now.

Carkhuff: You're copping out, Dave.

Dave: Am *I*?

Carkhuff: You are. He gave you an opportunity to come at him and you're copping out. Okay look, here's what I heard you saying: "Hey, I've been there; I've got good eyes and now you're asking me to use yours."

Dave: Yeah, that's true. And is it worth it? Are they better than mine?

Carkhuff: Your first question is, "Are they better than mine?" The second question is, "If they are, are they worth the price that I've got to pay?" Because, like Carl said, "I've done a whole lot with what I've got; I've gone a long way with it."

Dave: Yeah, there are a lot of other things involved. (Carkhuff breaks in.)

Carkhuff: No, no, no, just deal with this!

Dave: Yeah, and it is hard for me to separate them, really.

Carkhuff: Just deal with this now.

Dave: I feel like I'm right on the spot.

Carkhuff: Three times now.

Dave: Three times—well I'm asking myself and I've tried to incorporate this—you know, I like it, it suits my life style, but is it better than what I've done? Does it have any meaning to me as a person? Do *you* believe in it?

Carkhuff: Now that's not what I hear you saying. What I hear you saying is that I've gone a long way. I've been able to measure men, and I've gone a long way and I've developed a damn smooth technique and I haven't put it all the way out there. I'll never put it all the way out there. Never, Dave!

Dave: Am I willing to take the risk to expose myself in front of 650 people?

Carkhuff: It's between you and me now. It's got nothing to do with them now.

Dave: Yeah, I think I am. It's worth the price. I'm questioning it. I think it's worth the price. I don't know.

Carkhuff: You haven't answered that yet. You haven't answered that question yet.

Dave: I'm not sure I can answer it.

Carkhuff: Well if you can't answer it now you can never answer it.

Dave: Are you talking about emotionally?

Carkhuff: I'm talking to you, Dave. I'm not talking to anybody else.

Dave: Are you talking about me answering it emotionally, do you want me to answer it verbally?

Carkhuff: No, emotionally, right now.

Dave: If you hadn't hurt me I could do much better (Carkhuff breaks in.)

Carkhuff: Dave, don't play victim with me. You're a big boy now.

Dave: Okay, fine.

Carkhuff: Are my eyes better than yours? Answer that for yourself And if they are, is it worth the price? Answer that!

Dave: I think—I feel they are better than mine because I've incorporated (Carkhuff breaks in.)

Carkhuff: No, no, no, answer it in terms of what just went on between us, right now! Do I see into you better than you see into me?

Dave: Yeah, I think you're reading me.

Carkhuff: Sure! Then what's hanging you up, the price—that you can't get away with the smoothness and the clichés anymore? You can't get away with avoiding the responsibility when you get put on the spot anymore. Is that what's bothering you?

Dave: Maybe.

Carkhuff: I don't want to (Dave breaks in.)

Dave: Right. I would prefer not.

Carkhuff: You raised it: I've got to deal with it. You raised it out here on the stage; you've got to live with what you elicited now. Okay? That goes for you too, Ralph. Okay I'm not going to push it any further now. I don't know if you guys (demonstration group) want to sit down in front or if you want to just get out of here. I'll see you (Dave) later—maybe ride to Atlanta with us. I'd like you (demonstration group) to be available here. I'd like Bill and Brad and some of you who put something into it to comment on it. Carl, also. (End of demonstration)

Index

Group Counseling

A Developmental Approach

NEW ENGLAND INSTITUTE
OF TECHNOLOGY
LEARNING RESOURCES CENTER

DATE